Approaches to Teaching Puig's *Kiss of the Spider Woman*

Approaches to Teaching
World Literature

Joseph Gibaldi, series editor

Approaches to Teaching Puig's *Kiss of the Spider Woman*

Edited by
Daniel Balderston
and
Francine Masiello

The Modern Language Association of America
New York   2007

© 2007 by The Modern Language Association of America
All rights reserved. Printed in the United States of America

For information about obtaining permission to reprint material from MLA book publications, send your request by mail (see address below), e-mail (permissions@mla.org), or fax (646 458-0030).

Library of Congress Cataloging-in-Publication Data

Approaches to teaching Puig's Kiss of the Spider Woman /
edited by Daniel Balderston and Francine Masiello.
p. cm. — (Approaches to teaching world literature ; 97)
Includes bibliographical references and index.
ISBN-13: 978-0-87352-817-7   (hardcover : alk. paper)
ISBN-10: 0-87352-817-4
ISBN-13: 978-0-87352-818-4   (pbk. : alk. paper)
ISBN-10: 0-87352-818-2
1. Puig, Manuel. Beso de la mujer araña.   2. Puig, Manuel—Study and
Teaching.   I. Balderston, Daniel, 1952–   II. Masiello, Francine.
III. Series.
PQ7798.26.U4B4333 2007
863'.64—dc22   2007022803
ISSN 1059-1133

Cover illustration of the paperback edition: *Ecstasy*, by Maxfield Parrish.
Photo courtesy of the Archives of the American Illustrators Gallery, NYC.
© 2007 National Museum of American Illustration, Newport, RI.
www.americanillustration.org

Printed on recycled paper

Published by The Modern Language Association of America
26 Broadway, New York, New York 10004-1789
www.mla.org

CONTENTS

PREFACE TO THE SERIES

In *The Art of Teaching* Gilbert Highet wrote, "Bad teaching wastes a great deal of effort, and spoils many lives which might have been full of energy and happiness." All too many teachers have failed in their work, Highet argued, simply "because they have not thought about it." We hope that the Approaches to Teaching World Literature series, sponsored by the Modern Language Association's Publications Committee, will not only improve the craft—as well as the art—of teaching but also encourage serious and continuing discussion of the aims and methods of teaching literature.

The principal objective of the series is to collect within each volume different points of view on teaching a specific literary work, a literary tradition, or a writer widely taught at the undergraduate level. The preparation of each volume begins with a wide-ranging survey of instructors, thus enabling us to include in the volume the philosophies and approaches, thoughts and methods of scores of experienced teachers. The result is a sourcebook of material, information, and ideas on teaching the subject of the volume to undergraduates.

The series is intended to serve nonspecialists as well as specialists, inexperienced as well as experienced teachers, graduate students who wish to learn effective ways of teaching as well as senior professors who wish to compare their own approaches with the approaches of colleagues in other schools. Of course, no volume in the series can ever substitute for erudition, intelligence, creativity, and sensitivity in teaching. We hope merely that each book will point readers in useful directions; at most each will offer only a first step in the long journey to successful teaching.

Joseph Gibaldi
Series Editor

Part One

MATERIALS

Editions and Translations

The first edition of Manuel Puig's *El beso de la mujer araña* (*Kiss of the Spider Woman*) was published in Barcelona by Editorial Seix Barral in 1976. Prohibited in Argentina, the novel did not circulate freely there until after the end of the 1976–83 military dictatorship. A second edition was published in Spain in 1980, and other publishers have kept the novel in print. Seix Barral continues to publish dozens of printings of the novel. The first Argentine edition was not released until 1993 by Espasa-Calpe (a division of Editorial Planeta, a division of Bertelsmann). The 1976 edition had a cover illustration by Maxfield Parrish, *Ecstasy*, showing a woman on a mountain slope looking into the heavens; this image helped define the novel as the supreme example of a camp aesthetic in the Spanish-speaking world.

Puig's novel was widely translated almost immediately. The first translation appeared in Italy (Einaudi, 1978), followed by German, French, and English editions in 1979. A Portuguese-language version was published in 1980, followed by Danish, Swedish, Norwegian, Dutch, Greek, Japanese, Polish, Hebrew, Turkish, Chinese, and Czech translations (1981–94). Thomas Colchie translated the English version, published by Knopf in 1979 and subsequently reissued in several editions in the United States and Britain. This volume uses the Colchie translation as its standard for pagination: there are many printings of this translation, all with identical pagination.

In 2002 Colección Archivos, a UNESCO project in France, published an extraordinary critical edition of the novel. Edited by José Amícola and Jorge Panesi, with philological work on manuscript variants and the composition process supplemented by Julia Romero and Graciela Goldchluk, the volume includes a chronology of the author, interviews with the author, a dossier of early reviews and essays that map out the reception of the novel, and an extensive annotated primary and secondary bibliography. An accompanying CD-ROM contains Puig's entire manuscript archive (thousands of pages of outlines, draft materials, and typescripts), as well as the author's interviews with former political prisoners, his notes on film and music, and his research on theories of human sexuality.

See page 17 of this volume for an explanation of the system used for citing Puig's novel.

The Novel and the Author

Manuel Puig was born in General Villegas, a small, remote town in the southwestern part of the province of Buenos Aires, Argentina, in 1932. He spent much of an unhappy childhood there watching films with his mother (a pharmacist) at the Club Español. When he was fifteen, his father's wine distribution business failed, and the family moved to Buenos Aires, where Puig completed his secondary education. From 1950 to 1951 he briefly studied architecture at the University of Buenos Aires and began studying film. In 1956 he obtained a scholarship to study in Rome at the Centro Sperimentale di Cinematografia, where he learned the craft of film, but he rejected the neorealist model that was dominant in Italy in those years. He wrote film scripts in Rome, Buenos Aires, London, and Stockholm from 1958 to 1962. In this last year he began writing his first novel, completed in New York (where he was working for Air France) in 1966 and later published as *La traición de Rita Hayworth* (*Betrayed by Rita Hayworth*) in 1968; published in Argentina after much difficulty, it received only lukewarm reviews. Nevertheless, when the novel appeared in French in 1969, it was selected as one of the best novels of the year and became a best seller. His second novel, *Boquitas pintadas* (*Heartbreak Tango*) was published in 1969; like *Rita Hayworth*, it was set in Coronel Vallejos, a small town in the pampas closely based on Puig's birthplace. The profits from this second novel allowed him to quit his day job and devote himself to writing *The Buenos Aires Affair* (original title in English), published in 1973 and censored in Argentina for its explicit sexual violence. In 1972 and 1973 he visited Argentina to interview political prisoners for a new book project, but the chaotic and violent political situation forced him to seek exile in Mexico, where he remained until 1976. That year marks two significant events for our consideration: the 24 March coup in Argentina that installed a military junta that stayed in power until 1983 and the publication of Puig's novel *Kiss of the Spider Woman* in Spain, four months after the coup.

Later in his career Puig wrote four more novels: *Pubis angelical* (1979; *Pubis angelical: A Novel* [1986]), *Maldición eterna a quien lea estas páginas* (1980; *Eternal Curse on the Reader of These Pages* [1982]), *Sangre de amor correspondido* (1982; *Blood of Requited Love* [1984]), and *Cae la noche tropical* (1988; *Tropical Night Falling* [1991]). He also wrote plays, film scripts, short fiction, and chronicles, most of which have been published posthumously. He died in Cuernavaca, Mexico, in 1990.

As can be seen in *Kiss of the Spider Woman* and many of his other works, including his film scripts, Puig was fascinated by the world of the Hollywood divas in the 1940s. Before publishing his first novel, he wrote to Rita Hayworth explaining to her why he wanted to use her name in the title of the novel; Greta Garbo is also mentioned frequently. A walking encyclopedia of Hollywood movies, particularly film noir and musicals, and of Alfred Hitchcock, Puig collected clips of thousands of films retained on more than three thousand videotapes. The interrelation between film and prose fiction is a constant in his work.

Historical and Political Background

Kiss of the Spider Woman, as work on the manuscripts has shown, was begun in 1973; its action, dated precisely by the jail record that appears at the beginning of the eighth chapter, takes place in April and May 1975. This political moment in Argentina was exceedingly charged and complex, and it is useful to map out some of this history.

Argentina's modern history is indelibly marked by Juan Domingo Perón, a career military man. He remade himself in 1943–44 as minister of labor and then vice president in the wake of a military coup (one of several that stretched back to 1930). He won the presidential elections of 1946 and 1952 by the largest margin ever known in the history of the country. Perón achieved a unique and idiosyncratic synthesis of a populist nationalism somewhat inspired by Mussolini's Italy (which he had seen close-up during his years representing the Argentine military there). Overthrown in 1955 by an alliance of the Roman Catholic Church, the Radical Party opposition (the Unión Cívica Radical, a centrist democratic party), the United States embassy, and many from the business sector, Perón nevertheless dominated Argentine politics over the next two decades, returning from exile in 1973 and serving as president for the final months of his life; he died in June 1974. The period from 1955 to 1973 was marked by a series of military coups (1955, 1962, 1966) and by elected Radical Party presidents, none of whom was able to finish a term. The Peronist opposition to the military and Radical governments became increasingly strident, revealing a deep split between the Peronist Youth movement (allied with the Montoneros guerrilla group) and traditional Peronist trade unionists, both bureaucrats and workers. United mostly by a desire for the return of Perón, by now more an icon than an effective party leader, the two sides clashed violently over questions of ideology and political strategy. This division became apparent when Perón first returned from exile in December 1972; in a tragic massacre near Ezeiza airport, a Peronist Youth march was attacked by sharpshooters. Many leftist Peronists were swept up in the repression that followed; those jailed were the focus of a campaign for release of political prisoners in May 1973.

Many readers believe that *Kiss of the Spider Woman* refers to the military repression of the 1976–83 dictatorship, when over thirty thousand people would be "disappeared" and many more jailed and tortured. However, the novel actually refers to the earlier violent period just described and elides the release of political prisoners shortly after a Peronist politician came to power in March 1973. In May of that year, after huge street demonstrations, political prisoners were freed, initially from Villa Devoto prison in Buenos Aires and then from other prisons across the country. Villa Devoto is where Molina and Valentín in the novel share a jail cell from April to May 1975. Something worthy of classroom discussion is why Puig chose to situate the novel in a period when political prisoners had been freed from jail. After all, Valentín, the political prisoner, incarcerated in 1972, would have been released the following year. Did Puig have a reason for placing his characters in jail in 1975?

This dramatic period is marked by chaos, violence, and state terror, with a confusing array of factions on the left (Peronist and non-Peronist) committed to armed resistance. Perón had repudiated the Peronist Youth organizations shortly before his death. The strong-arm government of his widow, María Estela

Martínez de Perón, known as Isabelita, held power from 1974 to 1976, relying on such rightist Peronist groups as the Triple A, or Argentine Anticommunist Alliance, which was responsible for witch hunts against dissident leftists.

The novel turns partly on the character of Valentín, who embodies the revolutionary left; for many, he evokes members of the two major guerrilla groups active in the 1970s, the Montoneros and the Ejército Revolucionario del Pueblo (ERP). The Montoneros were devoted to the leftist Peronist cause; founded in 1969, they came to public attention in 1970 when they kidnapped and eventually killed an important military officer. The ERP, or People's Revolutionary Army, was founded in 1970 and was affiliated with Trotskyist and Maoist tendencies. The decade is marked by coalitions, dissent, and highly irrational military actions taken by these leftist groups, who suffered systematic repression by the junta of 1976 and were disintegrated by the end of the decade. Strikingly, in the novel Puig never clarifies whether Valentín is affiliated with the Montoneros, the ERP, or one of many smaller revolutionary factions.

Another strand in leftist organizing of the period emerged in Argentina in the early 1970s. A small group of activists founded the journal *Nuestro mundo* in 1970 and the Frente de Liberación Homosexual in 1971; the best-known figure to emerge was the poet and sociologist Néstor Perlongher. According to Juan José Sebreli, Osvaldo Bazán, and Flavio Rapisardi and Alejandro Modarelli, who have written histories of this period, Manuel Puig attended meetings of these groups, although he was not a public spokesperson for them in the way that Perlongher would be. Though Molina is not cast in the novel as a gay activist, he is imprisoned during the period of public emergence of a gay movement and of a significant gay subculture in Buenos Aires. Echoing many other international gay liberation movements that were taking off at the time, among them the groups that emerged in New York after the Stonewall riots of June 1969 and the French Front de Libération Homosexuel, the Argentine group (and similar groups in Mexico and Brazil) brought to public attention another way of doing politics. Equally significant was the emergence of feminism, which had a dramatic impact on liberationist theory and practice and theories of identity that would be important in Puig's novel. Feminist thought led to important self-critiques in many of the leftist groups; something of this concern is seen in Valentín's discomfort with his own positions regarding questions of gender and sexuality. The masculinist left, represented initially in the novel by Valentín, was often the subject of intense critique.

Reading the Novel

Kiss of the Spider Woman is surprisingly vague about precise dates, locations, and political affiliation or identification. We don't even know who the characters are in a conventional sense: we don't know what they look like, their ages, their places of birth, and, until chapter 8, we don't know their full names or even the country where the novel takes place. Instead, the reader initially encounters a fascinating and detailed evocation of a series of Hollywood B movies in the 1940s, most notably Jacques Tourneur's *Cat People* and *I Walked with a Zombie* and John Cromwell's *The Enchanted Cottage*. From Molina's retellings of these three films, and three others that are conflations by Puig of real films and those of his own invention, the reader gradually comes to learn about the two characters in the cell, their identities and feelings, their values and political visions.

Puig had already earned distinction in his first three novels for eliminating a unified narrator who would guide the reader through the text with descriptions of setting, place, time, and character. As early as *Rita Hayworth*, he constructs a novel out of interior monologues that are never situated: the novel is composed of voices, and characters are defined by their oral styles, their enthusiasms and preferences. Much of the novel *Boquitas pintadas* consists of dialogue, letters, song lyrics, the voices of radio soap operas, and a few brief third-person descriptions (almost like stage descriptions in a play). In *The Buenos Aires Affair*, Puig experiments with different styles of telling, from dramatic script to recorded telephone conversations to an unreliable third-person narrator; he also links state terror with sexual violence. *Kiss of the Spider Woman* grows out of these earlier narrative experiments. While the main text consists of a conversation between the two protagonists, other discourses (song texts, letters, footnotes, official documents, phone conversations) intrude on that dialogue as if to compete for authority in the novel. In particular, the eight footnotes on theories of sexuality (important in any discussion of the novel) form a counterpoint to the characters' dialogue; the notes, particularly the last one, in chapter 11, anticipate the romance between Valentín and Molina and explore the relation between sexual liberation and revolutionary politics.

Melodrama structures the characters' romance. Reading the details of the films lovingly re-created by Molina, we come to learn that the "boy meets girl" formula of Hollywood also directs the sentiments of the two characters. The characters reproduce the structures of the Hollywood films that have enthralled them, but, true to the Hollywood formula, a crisis interrupts their relationship. Melodrama requires intense passion that must submit to order; in this genre, we see the heroics of self-sacrifice when Molina finally recasts himself as the hero of a B movie of his own making. Sacrificing himself for the man he loves, Molina repeats the movie plots he has narrated all along.

Readings for Students

Materials that are worth making available to students are Frances Wyers Weber's early article "Manuel Puig at the Movies" in *Hispanic Review*, Santiago Colás's chapters on Puig in *Postmodernity in Latin America: The Argentine Paradigm*,

Carol D'Lugo's *"El beso de la mujer araña*: Norm and Deviance in the Fiction / as the Fiction," Paul Julian Smith's *"La Mujer Araña* and the Return of the Body," Francine Masiello's "The Spectacle of Difference," Lucille Kerr's "The Politics of Seduction," and Daniel Balderston's "Sexuality and Revolution: On the Footnotes to *El beso de la mujer araña*." For students who read Spanish, the most important collection of essays on *Kiss of the Spider Woman* is in José Amícola and Jorge Panesi's critical edition of the novel.

For those interested in Latin American film, basic bibliographies in English are in John King's *Magical Reels* and King and Nissa Torrents's *The Garden of Forking Paths* (on Argentine film).

Bibliographies on camp are in Susan Sontag's famous "Notes on Camp," Moe Meyer's *The Politics and Poetics of Camp*, Fabio Cleto's edited volume *Camp: Queer Aesthetics and the Performing Subject*, and Amícola's *Camp y posvanguardia*.

Background Readings on Puig

A useful introduction to Puig is Jonathan Tittler's book for the Twayne World Author Series; there is also a special issue of *World Literature Today, Manuel Puig*, dedicated to the author. The only biography of Puig is Suzanne Jill Levine's *Manuel Puig and the Spider Woman: His Life and Fictions* (also available in Spanish). Useful critical studies on Puig in English are Pamela Bacarisse's *Impossible Choices* and *The Necessary Dream* and Lucille Kerr's *Suspended Fictions*. Spanish-language readers should consult José Amícola's *Manuel Puig y la tela que atrapa al lector*, Alberto Giordano's *Manuel Puig: La conversación infinita*, Jorgelina Corbatta's *Mito personal y mitos colectivos en las novelas de Manuel Puig*, and Graciela Speranza's *Manuel Puig: Después del fin de la literatura*. A useful small book about *El beso de la mujer araña* is Juan Pablo Dabove's *La forma del Destino*. Good essays about Puig's relations with the cinema are collected in Sandra Lorenzano and Ana Rosa Domenella's *La literatura es una película*. An excellent volume of primary and secondary bibliographies on Puig is Guadalupe Martí-Peña's *Manuel Puig ante la crítica*.

Historical Context: Readings

Useful readings in English on this period include Luis Alberto Romero's *A History of Argentina in the Twentieth Century*, Donald Hodges's *Argentina, 1943–1976: The National Revolution and Resistance*, Robert Potash's *The Army and Politics in Argentina*, and Daniel James's *Resistance and Integration: Peronism and the Argentina Working Class* as well as the larger overarching study by Tulio Halperin Donghi, *Contemporary History of Latin America*, and David Rock's general history, *Argentina, 1516–1982*. On feminism in Argentina see Marifran Carlson's *Feminismo!*, Jo Fisher's *Mothers of the Disappeared* and *Out of the Shadows*, and Sarah Radcliffe and Sallie Westwood's *Remaking the Nation*. Useful works on the history of the gay movement are Juan José Sebreli's "Vida cotidiana: Historia secreta de los homosexuales en Buenos Aires," Flavio Rapisardi and Alejandro Modarelli's *Fiestas, baños y exilios*, and Osvaldo Bazán's *Historia de la homosexualidad en la Argentina*. Puig's articles "El error gay" and "Losing Readers in Argentina" also add significant background to contemporary readings of the novel.

Audiovisual Materials

Classroom discussions of *El beso de la mujer araña* benefit greatly from the use of the three films that are retold in the novel, Jacques Tourneur's *Cat People* and *I Walked with a Zombie* and John Cromwell's *The Enchanted Cottage*, all of which are available on video and DVD. The other three films narrated in the novel are conflations or inventions by Puig, based on the Nazi period films of Zarah Leander, the Mexican *carabetera* genre (such films as Arcady Boytler's *La mujer del puerto*), and films about Latin American playboys. A film adaptation of the novel is Héctor Babenco's *Kiss of the Spider Woman*, with William Hurt as Molina, Raúl Juliá as Valentín, and Sonia Braga as Leni the chanteuse and as the spider woman. Articles on Babenco's film include those by Bruce Williams, Kandace Holladay, Nadine Dejong, and Patricia Santoro; on Puig's use of cinema, there is Campos, "'I'm Ready for My Close-Up'" and "Los rostros de la ilusión." The Mexican genre film includes numerous references to the popular musical form bolero (Puig collected bolero lyrics while writing the novel, as seen in the Archivos critical edition [365–84]); audio recordings of boleros by such groups as Trío Los Panchos, Javier Solís, Luis Miguel, and Lucho Gatica are widely available (books on bolero include Rafael Castillo Zapata's *Fenomenología del bolero* and Iris Zavala's *El bolero: Historia de un amor*). A video interview with Puig (in Spanish) by Reina Roffé is available in the series Espejo de Escritores.

A Chronological List of Puig's Novels

La traición de Rita Hayworth, 1968 / *Betrayed by Rita Hayworth*, 1971.
Boquitas pintadas: Folletín, 1969 / *Heartbreak Tango: A Serial*, 1973.

The Buenos Aires Affair, 1973 / *The Buenos Aires Affair: A Detective Novel*, 1976.

El beso de la mujer araña, 1976 / *Kiss of the Spider Woman*, 1979.

Pubis angelical, 1979 / *Pubis angelical: A Novel*, 1986.

Maldición eterna a quien lea estas páginas, 1980 / *Eternal Curse on the Reader of These Pages*, 1982.

Sangre de amor correspondido, 1982 / *Blood of Requited Love*, 1984.

Cae la noche tropical, 1988 / *Tropical Night Falling*, 1991.

Part Two

APPROACHES

Introduction

Puig and the Boom

Since its publication in 1976, Manuel Puig's novel *El beso de la mujer araña* has stirred the hearts and minds of readers. The sensitive story of two prisoners, both seduced by the aura of cinema and by the chance of liberation offered by Hollywood romance, has captivated the imagination of a loyal and enthusiastic public. As a film, directed by Héctor Babenco and starring William Hurt and Raúl Juliá, *Kiss of the Spider Woman* received accolades for its daring experimentation with theme and structure; as a musical, its extravagant staging and song brought Broadway theater to new heights. But Puig's novel most notably entered the history of world culture as a text that expanded the idiom of the novel (mixing cinema, fiction, romance, and song) and challenged the third-person narration that was dominant in the Boom novels (thus going much further than most other Latin American writers of the period in questioning the idea of absolute truth). Puig complicated notions of character shaped by psychoanalysis and, using mass culture and politics, opened the doors to audacious forms of subjectivity and expressions of desire. A revolution of the word takes place in his texts.

Puig's novel is situated in the highly experimental narrative years of the 1970s. Following the international breakthrough of Latin American fiction the decade before—João Guimarães Rosa's *The Devil to Pay in the Backlands* (1956), Carlos Fuentes's *Death of Artemio Cruz* (1962), Julio Cortázar's *Hopscotch* (1963), Mario Vargas Llosa's *The Green House* (1966), and Gabriel García Márquez's *One Hundred Years of Solitude* (1967)—Latin American writers finally achieved cosmopolitan recognition for their literary endeavors. Their novels, associated with the so-called Boom of Latin American writing, were epic stories—large, overarching fictions that recounted the history of conquest and colonization of Latin America (García Márquez is exemplary in this respect) or narrated the conflicts between culture and barbarism that led to modernization. Cortázar's *Hopscotch*, whose intellectual heroes travel between Paris and Buenos Aires, takes in the whole of modern culture—from jazz to comics and modern art—to find an adequate place for the Latin American man of letters. Doubt, ambivalence, and internal quests unevenly pave the road for his protagonist's course of self-discovery and exploration. *Hopscotch* exemplified the modern urban novel in which nomadic characters struggled with past and present to find a home.

Boom novels gave us larger-than-life figures who fought to overcome their connections to backward traditions and secure a place in the lettered culture of the metropolis. At the same time, they expressed an existential angst that caused many of the writers to question the failings of history. In the light of the Cuban revolution and the projects of Che Guevara, which promised a socialist path for Latin America and the utopia of the *hombre nuevo*, many of Latin America's writers took up the cause of social change, hoping for revolution against the impoverished and alienated life determined by the capitalist market. The novels of the 1960s are enmeshed in these debates such that Cuba, the events in Paris in 1968, and postcolonial liberationist struggles come to occupy a keen place in Latin American fiction.

On this cultural backdrop of grand narratives and family sagas, Puig enters with a literary proposal of a highly different order. Starting with his first novel, *La traición de Rita Hayworth* (*Betrayed by Rita Hayworth*), Puig focuses on the petty dramas of the Argentine middle classes. Far from heroic, Puig's novels draw on scenes of small-town life to shape his melodrama of neighborly gossip, sexual betrayal, and not-so-well-behaved children. Soap operas, romances, and the plots of Hollywood film feed the story stuff of the minor figures who populate Puig's earliest novels, but the main protagonist is the voice. Variants of speech, clashes between educated parlance and the colloquial slang of the street, different memories of advertisement and song, various reproductions of cinematic detail, and sustained phone conversations among characters about the consumerist taste of an age remind us that Puig is immersed in the mass culture of his country (and, not coincidentally, in the work of James Joyce, whose pastiche of styles and voices caught the quick attention of Puig).

Puig's next novel, *Boquitas pintadas* (*Heartbreak Tango*), is another glimpse of small-town life and the failed middle-class actors who filled their time with steamy romance and often absurd betrayals. Each page of the novel offers a taste of mid-century Argentine life: greed, theft, family secrets, and convoluted schemes for petty deception, along with a movement of characters from small-town culture to the capital city. Puig paints a world on the verge of major change, using the colors of hilarious detail. His is a world in which nothing is original; all utterances are familiar echoes of something heard already; the desires, voices, longings, and thoughts are oddly prestamped and packaged. This wink toward some previous model, an excessive style of quoting an earlier genre (a film, a radio show, a blithe romance, even a phrase from advertising or the weekly serialized novel) pushes characters to the edge of excess. This approach, of course, is the definition of *camp*, an idiom and style linked with queer aesthetics that came into its own to poke fun at the pretensions of originality proclaimed by advocates of high culture. Clearly, Puig is not interested in the effects of the cold war on Latin American life, nor does he care to address the larger questions of resistance and survival that often entered the portraits of underdevelopment drawn by many Latin American thinkers of the previous generation. More precisely, if Cortázar and García Márquez assume the social conscience of Latin America with their obsessive concern about loss of independent identities under threat of United States expansion, Puig turns his attention to identities of another order.

With his third novel, *The Buenos Aires Affair*, Puig began to link identity with sexual repression and the terrorist state. Censored by the government, Puig's novel is an all-embracing look at 1960s art world culture, with its buy-sell rush on the global market and its cosmopolitan kingpins, while at home in Argentina, psychoanalysis and repression govern modern life. Some have seen this novel as a joke on the Lacanian brand of psychotherapy that dominated Argentine culture; others have viewed it as an ironic meditation on the values that left their mark on life in the 1960s. Both views may be right. In either case, Puig brings these problems to the surface through the popular genre of detective fiction, in which stories about abductions and murder are crossed with secrets and sex. National politics lurks in the dark background of this novel, prompting readers to draw connections between the fast-track scenes of global traffic and the violent behaviors of every stripe that emerge in the modern metropolis. Puig leads us to ask if the ultimate criminal is not the state.

In *Kiss of the Spider Woman*, a novel that embraces many of the formal and thematic concerns of Puig's earlier works, a radically new element appears: the world of cinema is represented in the novel through telling, listening, and reinvention. These modes of narration are shared by the two characters, who live out the dark world of their prison cell by repeating plots taken from Hollywood movies. While there is no original story in this novel, since even the relationship of Molina and Valentín seems patterned on some earlier script, the earlier plots also give way to invention. Hollywood glitter thus sets the path for self-knowledge and love. Even in citation, then, we can expect the eruption of something new. And, in this sense, *Kiss of the Spider Woman* is also a novel about the construction of identity, the invention of self and other, and the shaping of our affections in the world.

Teaching Kiss of the Spider Woman

Kiss of the Spider Woman is widely taught in a great variety of courses, in English and Spanish, in the United States and Canada, including courses on the modern novel, world literature, gender and sexuality, and the relation between literature and film. Puig is a canonical entry in courses on modern Latin American literature, both in English translation and in Spanish. Teaching this novel has always proven to be both a delight and a challenge. Students are quickly drawn to the conversational style of the novel and to the melodramatic seductions of the tale—almost copying the fascination of Molina for grand Hollywood films—and are sad when the novel comes to a close. Like Molina, students tend to identify with the heroes of fiction. But *Kiss of the Spider Woman* also presents pedagogical issues that need to be unfolded in the classroom. In courses on contemporary fiction in general, students need to understand the complex strategies of narration that are hidden behind the veil of innocent conversations between the two main characters. The concept of character and in particular the role of the brave protagonist—the heroic figure of the Western novel—help elucidate Puig's experiments in this important text. Another problem is how we read the novel and how Molina and Valentín read each other and interpret the cinematic world they describe. In this context, the strange emergence of unidentified narrative voices, the confusing styles in which Puig engages readers and forces them to identify with one character or the other, the ways in which the concept of realism is constructed and later dismantled, and the intrusion of the footnotes are all difficult topics for students.

Kiss of the Spider Woman is a demanding novel to teach because so much is unstated: who is speaking, where the protagonists are, what their political context is, whether the films they talk about are real or invented, what ideas they have about gay liberation and political change, how they really feel for each other. And for readers with limited preparation in theories of postmodernism, cinematic conventions, and the relations between elite and popular culture, the challenge of the novel is even greater.

Other problems emerge when the instructor attempts to contextualize the novel. Here, students rightfully inquire about the political and cultural history of Argentina: the role of the revolutionary left and its consideration of gender and the emergence of gay liberationist theory and feminist theories of desire as part of larger concerns in the 1970s. But students who are learning to read in the classroom also need to learn about the evolution of a text. Puig's many corrections and rewritings of the novel pose a problem to the stability of our reading. Delving into the history of *Kiss of the Spider Woman*, students inquire about authorial intention (many students repeatedly ask about the vague presentation of characters, the lack of physical description, the identities formed only by speech) and the planned transformation of the tale: Is the story of Molina and Valentín close to the Hollywood film plots that Molina describes? Who is the hero in the end? The prepared instructor wants to move toward Puig's understanding of gender politics and the politics of genre. Finally, because the novel draws on film examples and because it was adapted later as a successful script for theater and film—videos and DVDs supply easily available material for teachers and students—it is worth investigating the links among these different artistic forms.

The Essays in This Volume

Written by some of the most distinguished scholars in the field of Latin American literary criticism, the essays in this volume embrace many of the issues just described. Beginning with the novelist Ricardo Piglia's lecture on *Kiss of the Spider Woman*, delivered to an audience of students at the University of Buenos Aires, the critical odyssey presented in this volume is designed to help in the pedagogical challenge of teaching the novel. We have structured the volume by starting with close textual analysis and a study of voice (the essays by Lucille Kerr, Rosa Perelmuter, and Richard Young) and leading to the problem of reading—both reading within the text (Molina and Valentín are readers) and the external circulation of the novel (the essays by Juan Poblete, María Eugenia Mudrovcic, and José Amícola). Addressing the state politics and the sexual politics of the novel, the essays of Juan Pablo Dabove and José Maristany provide a platform from which to enter the world of *Kiss of the Spider Woman.* Graciela Speranza and David Oubiña pay detailed attention to the function and effects of the cinematic medium that is a central reference in the novel. Finally, Suzanne Jill Levine and Idelber Avelar discuss the relation between the novel and Babenco's film and (in Avelar's essay) offer suggestions for teaching both in the classroom.

Abbreviations Used in Page References for Kiss of the Spider Woman

Eng.   English translation by Thomas Colchie, 1978 and other successive editions

Span.   Seix Barral editions, almost all of which follow the pagination of the 1976 first edition

Archivos Archivos critical edition, 2002

The Puig Effect

Ricardo Piglia

There is a continuity between certain structures found in oral, primitive narration and the way genres and subgenres are used in mass culture: a capacity for constructing a story through a combination of certain types of fixed schemes. The use of stereotypes and formulas is an important tool for defining the contrast between different poetics. While Juan José Saer's poetics, for example, are based on the problematic of narrative innovation, Manuel Puig's tend to repeat certain plots and models of narration and content.

One of the problems that arise for someone working within a genre is how to incorporate into a fixed form elements that do not belong to it. Thus realist characters and situations, whose operational logic reproduces the logic of realist causality, should be set within those particular existing narrative stereotypes.[1] In *Kiss of the Spider Woman* the implausible situation that somehow needs to occur is the encounter between a homosexual man and a guerrilla fighter in the same prison cell. The novel, based on the stereotype of an impossible love, must explain why the two characters are locked up together. The explanation is the betrayal carried out by Molina, the gay man who is put in the cell to get information out of Arregui, the guerrilla.[2] We could say that the text is constructed on the basis of Molina's complicity with the state, which would justify a rather implausible narrative situation. We can analyze the elements of this explanation by looking at how the relation between the narrative formula and the realistic elements is constructed.

Puig is especially careful about the construction of the realistic explanation internal to the plot. Yet he makes a mistake: Puig disregards the 1973 amnesty. Arregui has been a prisoner since 1972; the amnesty declared in 1973 would have influenced events, yet this fact does not alter the narrative situation as constructed by Puig.

Puig juxtaposes the novel with social narration, especially cinematic narration. Divisions in the reading public are the driving force for transformation in the modern novel. In *Kiss of the Spider Woman*, it is clear that the public is divided or, better yet, that the text is about a divided public. Furthermore, there is an explicit debate in the novel between Molina and Arregui about the reception of the narration carried out between the two—that is, the stories from movies. In this state of imprisonment and throughout the novel, Molina recounts movie story lines to Arregui. We could say that Molina and Arregui each represent a different public. It is important to follow this debate in order to understand how Puig's preferred reception is constructed.

On the one hand, the novel discusses the political function of narration. Molina insists on the spellbinding character of the stories, whereas Arregui tends to see them in political terms (for example, he cannot accept that in one of the stories the protagonists are Nazis). For Molina, however, the stories are valuable for their own sake, and the narrative models employed are important because of how they are constructed and what kind of narrative heroes and systems are used.

On the other hand, in the confinement of prison, Molina gives narration another function, the function that Puig himself gives to it. The movies that Molina recounts to Arregui provide an escape from reality and construct an alternative world. We find the same idea in György Lukács: the novel deals with the division of the world, the opposition between the real world and an alternative world. The stories from the movies construct a counterreality in which a kind of ideal is clearly functioning that goes beyond Arregui's immediate political ideal.

This construction of a counterreality is a point of tension in the debate over the relation between novel and politics. Molina insists on a function that adds an educational element to the sacrifice, heroism, and glamour of the heroes that is much more important than the immediate, current, political content of the stories. Through the narration, Molina educates Arregui. The text recounts a seduction, but it also recounts a metamorphosis.

If we were to use the terminology of Gilles Deleuze, we would say that the novel talks about how to become a woman, in Arregui's case, and how to become a revolutionary, in Molina's case—that is, how someone is converted into the other (Deleuze and Guattari). Through the use of the narration, the text brings Arregui to a position contrary to his own sexuality and, in this impossible love between the two, puts Molina in the position of a conspirator, or at least as someone who attempts to conspire with the political group in which Arregui is enmeshed.

The text struggles against an immediate political reception of its contents and proposes a counterreality and an ideal value that goes beyond the immediacy of the real. In this ultimate function of the novel, we find a theory of politics. *Kiss of the Spider Woman* constructs a reality that escapes from the immediate here and now, a reality in which transformations, such as the transformation of the novel's hero, are possible. We witness the conversion of the hero, Arregui, as if the text revolved around the process of seduction.

The novel is established on the basis of a powerful narrative situation, similar to that of the *Arabian Nights*. As in the *Arabian Nights*, the receptor of the narration is there in front of the narrator. As it was for Scheherazade, the function of the narration for Molina is to affect the actual, real world. Yet since the stories take place in the time just before sleep, their interplay with dreams becomes very important. Puig uses the technique of dialogue in this novel, dialogue created from a confined situation in which there is nothing but narration. Furthermore, the movie stories recount, anticipate, and narrate, in a displaced way, everything we read later in the novel. They tell stories of metamorphoses in which bodies are transformed and stories of dual loyalties and betrayals. Therefore the movie stories serve as a displaced analysis of the significance and development of these themes.

As in the *Arabian Nights*, this text works with the story as a kind of quotation. Molina uses an already constructed narration that has the structure of a quotation. He functions as the narrator of the story, yet he is actually repeating someone else's discourse (here, from a nonliterary register), and, through a kind of appropriation, he converts it into a discourse in which his voice melds into that of the implicit narrator of the movies. Molina's narration of the movies reveals many of Puig's processes of narrative construction. There is a difference, although the division is blurry, between commenting on a narration while narrating it and embarking on a process of appropriation in which all distance is lost. In his narration, Molina recounts an already constructed story. That already constructed story can represent a certain genre or the formulas of a specific social register of narration. How Molina inserts himself into that preexisting narrative shows how Puig appropriates and crystallizes the stereotyped voices of popular narration and inserts his own voice into it. In this process, we can see how Puig uses tradition. If all implicit poetics are constructed from what one writes and its relation to existing texts, Puig's move is to bring to literature what does not belong there in order to produce a transformation and an innovation.

For Puig, the appropriate reception of a narration depends on the interests, projection, and identification of the person who receives the story, along with that extreme narrative world that plays out in the well-defined opposition between good and evil. The story fascinates us because all its elements conflict with those of the real context in which the story takes place. The narration of the movies both highlights the context—the two of them locked in a prison cell—and decontextualizes the narration, taking it to a plane of unreality.

The Puig effect, unique in Argentine narrative, consists of a kind of fragility: the story always seems to be on the verge of becoming lost between the light touch with which Puig guides it and the intensity and tension that he strives to attain.

Kiss of the Spider Woman marks a change in direction in Puig's poetics: in this novel he begins to work with stories from real life. Puig continued to transform his initial poetics that we saw in *Betrayed by Rita Hayworth*; from there he went on to reach the height of his popularity with *Heartbreak Tango* and then stepped back to reflect on the tension between the artistic world and the world of criticism and of mass culture in *The Buenos Aires Affair*. But with *Kiss of the Spider Woman, Pubis angelical*, and *Eternal Curse on the Reader of These Pages*, he began to work with recorded life stories, and, in this way, he incorporated a transformation that has occurred in the contemporary novel in all languages.

In this sense, it is interesting to note that Arregui was someone Puig knew and someone whose life story he recorded. Pozzi, the exile in *Pubis angelical*, was another character whom Puig knew in Mexico and whose story he also recorded. And the North American sociologist in *Eternal Curse on the Reader of These Pages* was someone with whom he originally made a financial agreement but later had problems with over the copyright. Puig records people's life stories and then counterposes a fictional voice that is always in a lesser position: it is the woman who dies of cancer in *Pubis angelical*; the semitraitor gay man in *Kiss of the Spider Woman*; the old Argentine, exiled and paralyzed, in *Eternal Curse on the Reader of These Pages*.

The way Puig uses the contrast between the documentary story and the fictional voice to create the structure involves an important technical innovation. That true voice, that documentary voice, has all the characteristics of the non-fictional element in the modern novel.

In Puig, this turn has to do with various issues. On the one hand, there is a drive toward textual realism. For Puig, reality is an array of voices. He has worked with a quotational structure as a central element in the relation between those who narrate and the social world. Thus the register of the social discourses cited is an important element.

On the other hand, Puig erases the narrator from the narrator's space, that is, the space of authority for the one who narrates. When we read *Don Quixote*, we know that the windmills are windmills and not giants because the narrator tells us so; the narrator is the one who can define the internal truth in a text. Puig's challenge to the authority of the narrator and the representations of that figure (running the gamut from point of view to interior monologue) allows us to understand an evolution of the novel. Puig is almost at the outer limit of this evolution because he uses collage, the superimposition of materials and empty space, in place of the narrator. The basic narrative procedures that Puig uses are direct dialogue, which creates the illusion that no one exists besides the two talking, and the superimposition of documents and materials—such as telephone conversations and police reports—that appear to come from the real world.

In the development of this form, it is natural that Puig began by incorporating recorded documents from real life as materials for his novels. This move, this tension between two narratives and materials, is connected to the structure of the quotation, textual realism, and the reproduction of voices and discourses and to the search for a new narrative structure in which everything is real material or is treated as if it were.

Puig manages to transform the direct, raw material into narrative structures with clearly constructed suspense, development, and enigma. For this reason, he usually works with extreme narrative situations. It wouldn't occur to anyone but Puig to lock up together in one room a guerrilla fighter exhibiting all the stereotypes of a macho, progressive, semirevolutionary culture and a gay man exhibiting all the stereotypes of the world of emotions. These two conflicting models are mediated by the world of movies, and they experience a process of transformation in the novel. In this play of different transformations in that stereotyped world, each character begins to occupy the place of the other, of his opposite. This reversal is never stated in the novel but is narrated through the movies that are recounted.

Puig places the problem of repression squarely in the middle of this metamorphosis; it is what unites and articulates these two stereotypes. In this sense, *Kiss of the Spider Woman* is a great political novel. The problem of repression— police repression, political repression, sexual repression—lies at the heart of the relation between hero and society (in a Freudian-Marxist line).

Kiss of the Spider Woman is developed through the opposition between "tell me all" and "don't tell me anything." Arregui asks Molina to keep recounting movies to him, and Molina tells Arregui not to tell him anything about his life, not to mention any names or anything about the things he is involved in. It is a way of explicitly establishing the distinction between the ideal world and the real world, in a novel that deals with everything in terms of narration. This play of "tell me what is not real" and "don't tell me anything that would connect me to any real knowledge, secret, or event" establishes a distance between the world of literature and fiction and the world of the state—that is, interrogation, torture, violence, and the obligation to tell all.

That which is left unsaid, that which begins to emerge in the novel, is the presence of the state, of the prison world, of the systems of control that revolve around the sort of laboratory experiment that is the relationship between the two men. And it is here that Puig's text joins that group of texts dealing with conspiracy, a common theme of the Argentine novel. Because, in one sense, *Kiss of the Spider Woman* is a conspiracy story: first the conspiracy of Molina and the state against Arregui, where Molina is a kind of double agent, and later the conspiracy of Molina and Arregui as they resist the situation of imprisonment and oppression to which they are subjected.

It is from this perspective that we should understand the use of the footnotes on psychoanalysis. Puig treats the world of psychoanalysis as if it were a great story of mass culture, a great creator of models of conduct, like a bourgeois soap opera, with sessions that are assimilated into the system of installments. This never-ending tale between two people, a tale that seeks some kind of secret and puts into play a melodramatic plot in episodic narration, is also psychoanalysis.

Puig once said, quite brilliantly, that the unconscious has the structure of a soap opera, that is, a structure of unspeakable desires, sexualized relationships, imagined crimes, and displaced perversions: characteristics of a powerful narrative. Making the connection between the world of mass culture and the world of psychoanalysis is one of Puig's greatest insights into how the real world functions, simply because it puts into play the relation between private life and the public sphere, between individual experience and social experience. Because, after all, what does it mean to experience something? One· can experience something the same way a Hollywood star does, with passions occurring in places filled with all the crystallized scenography of desire: luxurious locales, white telephones, long stairways down which descend women wrapped in silk.

In *The Buenos Aires Affair*, psychoanalysis functions as a support for a poetics of creation, sexualizing the role of the artist and establishing a relation between artistic production and the world of the unconscious. In *Kiss of the Spider Woman*, psychoanalysis appears as a voice of authority. Again we find the quotational structure—a voice that creates a truth describing how scientific history presents the problematic of sexuality. This use of psychoanalysis helps us see the point from which this novel is narrated. If we were to think in terms of a balanced structure, we would also have to imagine quotations and footnotes referring to the world of Marxism, that is, to another discourse. Puig, however, tries to establish a gaze that focuses on repression and transgression in terms of personal, private life. The social world acts on the personal life of the subject. Puig politicizes that very private space; he hypothesizes the relation between personal lives and the presence of society as a space of repressions and resistance.

In this way, Puig develops the discussion in the novel about the relation between individual and society. The heroes look at the world from a marginalized conscience and from that vantage point define the society that they resist as they try to create a kind of utopia, an alternative world. For that reason, it is interesting to analyze the way the novel ends: we find the classic model of the conversion of the hero but also the ambiguity of the final execution in which the hero dies.

The text is supremely utopian: in the place where the most repression is carried out, the main gesture of liberation occurs. It is in the prison cell where they are constrained, watched over, and repressed by the state that this micromodel of an alternative society is created, a society in which the other is no longer the enemy and no longer different. In this sense, the novel follows the genre. Lukács states that the hero wants to create an alternative world and that that world has the structure of a utopia. *Kiss of the Spider Woman* creates that utopia under what are possibly the most difficult of conditions. In this novel, to let go of the real world is to let go of the worst of what is real. But it is in prison that Molina and Arregui can use illusion and fiction to create an opening, the grand utopia that the novel has sought since Cervantes.

If we only read this novel as a story of the seduction of a heterosexual man by a homosexual man, we limit the text to an interplay among social and state control, political violence, the panopticon, and the function of the family. Puig tells of how a gay man refuses to stay in his place with respect to a guerrilla fighter. Yet at the same time this relationship of seduction and of overstepping one's bounds is developed in conjunction with utopia, with the relation between what one thinks and what one sees and with the way this petit bourgeois heterosexual in a sexually repressive structure recognizes this situation and transforms it. And the novel also examines the way this apolitical gay man, who is still tied to the apron strings and who has made a pact with the police, is transformed into someone capable of sacrificing his life for the sake of love.

Here we find ourselves at a point of indecision and ambiguity. We can view Molina's sacrifice in terms of the sacrifice of a Hollywood heroine but also in terms of a political statement. The relation between an impossible love and a political novel allows us to situate this novel together with José Mármol's *Amalia* (1855), in which an impossible love carries with it a decision to confront a political risk. The union of love and politics is a celebrated root of melodrama and has a great deal to do with the construction of a certain idea of the nation.[3]

We can best see this effect in the ending. In novels, the ending seems external to the plot and tends toward moralizing and abstraction. The moral is narrated, but often it functions as an element added on at the end. In *Kiss of the Spider Woman*, the plot is played out through the passage of each of the heroes into the place of the other, finishing with a double transformation. The ending then changes the narrative rhythm.

The genre tries to balance the ideal world and the real world. The novel brings the hero into the game and into the attempt to unite both worlds. In the end, the hero attempts to show that a resolution is possible, a resolution that does not actually exist in the real world—that is, a resolution where it is not necessary to sell out one's ideals in order to accept reality and make the real world bearable. That attempt, which underlies the construction of the narrative and the hero himself, uncovers in the end a compensation in the real world: the hero admits the power and weight of reality and, frequently, dies. The genre tends to follow this pattern, with some variations, because the problem the novel confronts has no solution.

Molina finds a way to unite the ideal and the real and to live out a love story that seems impossible, but that achievement costs him his life. Molina, like Bianco in Juan José Saer's *The Event* (1988) or Erdosain in Roberto Arlt's *The Seven Madmen* (1929), says that the world as it exists is unbearable and that we must find something greater to make it tolerable. The idea is that the world is senseless, and one cannot live in a senseless world. The answer can be revolution, like that of the Astrologer in *The Seven Madmen*, or it can develop from a fascination for the world of the others, those who remain separated from life in response to its general mediocrity, as occurs in *The Seven Madmen*. In *The Event* Bianco tries to dominate the material world with pure idea. Molina attempts to make bodies into sites of desire rather than socially established separations.

When he realizes this impossible love, which brings life closer to the model of the movies, he dies.

Thus in looking at the endings of novels, one must ask oneself what the relation is between the hero and the world and between the hero, who finds himself in a divided world, and the narrator. What kind of tension is established between the credulity of the hero and the cynicism or irony of the narrator? What happens when the one who narrates looks at the hero and recounts a story whose ending he or she already knows? Here Lukács brings in the concept of irony. The narrator, located in reality, looks at the movement of the hero as idealistic and somewhat poignant. There is a tension, then, between the two, a double consciousness that defines the site of the irony. The narrator casts an ironic gaze on the adventures of the hero.

The novelist must work with the trivial, melodramatic core. Thus art, form, elegance, and discretion are in constant tension with that space of the primary, melodramatic, excessive, trivial world. To resolve this issue, Macedonio Fernández establishes a sharp division between the two worlds by writing two distinct novels, *Adriana Buenos Aires: Última novela mala* (1974; "Adriana Buenos Aires: Final Bad Novel") and *Museo de la novela de la Eterna: Primera novela buena* (1975; "Museum of the Eternal Novel: First Good Novel"). Take out the bad, melodramatic novel, the serial story or soap opera that exists in all novels, and discover the museum, the site of artistic construction.

Confronted with the relation between art and life and examining the question of how the one affects the other, the first avant-garde movement maintained that instead of uniting these two spheres, we should separate them as much as possible. Gustave Flaubert's move is, in this sense, paradigmatic: his *Madame Bovary* believes in fiction and behaves according to the models fiction puts forth. The artist shuts himself away and creates his own style, which is his reaction to the general standardization. The difference between art and life is heightened by the artist because art is the site of resistance to society. And here, of course, we also find Saer. Puig is more complicated since he pays attention to popular reception, which mixes art and life and which produces an effect that often functions as a kind of utopia for artists.

Today's media construct stories that produce ways of living. Tom Disch stated that advertising is the fairy tale of modern society (Puig, "Thomas"). Thus we live in a society where the tension between art and life has been resolved— perhaps for the worse—by the way mass culture has dealt with this combination and has aestheticized daily life. Mass culture proposes a reception that tends to establish direct connections between the experiences of individual subjects and models of experience produced narratively.

The problem of the relation between art and life, present in Saer, Puig, and Rodolfo Walsh, can be interpreted, from a more technical perspective, as a debate about autonomy. What kind of autonomy does art have? How independent is art from society? What kinds of practice does it entail? Formalist and sociological criticisms participate in this discussion by talking about determination and the presence of the social element in artistic construction. I believe that

Walter Benjamin somehow resolves the autonomy problem, saying that it must be thought of in terms of reception and not production, that art is never autonomous from the perspective of production but it can be from the perspective of reception (221). Benjamin asks what role art plays in society, not the reverse, which is the issue raised by sociological criticism. Thus the point of the discussion is what type of relation can be established between works of art and the lives of subjects. The avant-garde position is to ask how artistic practice functions in society. For that reason, the avant-garde focuses on propaganda, intervention, and the rupture of places established for autonomous circulation (museums, theaters, books), trying to resolve the problem by first attacking the artistic institutions.

Puig picked up on how new social narratives have influenced the construction of the imaginary and the structures of behavior and experience of subjects. And he stated the issue in terms of what we could call popular reception, something completely different from specialized reception. Specialized reception, or academic reception, tends to establish a distance between different areas of inquiry. The liberal arts are a way of thinking about this distance—how to organize a history of literature, how to establish a relation between literature and history, whether we should divide literature by nationality or area, whether works should be studied in isolation or in relation to one another.

In contrast, there is the nonspecific, fundamentally popular reception, which tends to establish a connection and blur the lines between art and life, fiction and reality. It is the problem that we novelists have argued over since *Don Quixote*: how to make a fictitious tale real, how to make it believable, and, at the same time, how to make the characters appear to be confusing the world of fiction with the real world.

Saer maintains that art is a form whereas life is purely fluid; art has a structure and should not be confused with reality (85–86). Puig, in contrast, constantly narrates how to move from one level to the other and how to make people believe a fictional tale. *Kiss of the Spider Woman* is Molina's political education and Arregui's aesthetic education. Molina teaches Arregui to believe in a fiction. How one believes in a fiction is connected to the problem of the line between the imaginary sphere and the sphere of the real.

I believe this issue is of considerable importance. I don't know that it is necessarily important for writing a novel, but it is for understanding a function that goes beyond the space of literature—the function of the social plot. Those of us who write fiction can observe the question of belief and the tension between fiction and reality as they function over time. Literature is a minilaboratory studying a situation that has been continuously expanding and that today's world is always highlighting: how to make people believe, how to construct a fiction that functions socially.

Puig speaks of nothing else. That is, he speaks only of "bovarism," the sort of reader that Madame Bovary exemplifies, one concerned with how to believe and what models work to make people believe in fiction, how to make fiction produce an effect in the lives of those who believe in it. Puig narrates bovarism from *Betrayed by Rita Hayworth* to his last novel, *Tropical Night Falling*. He says that between private life and the public sphere there is a fictional space. The relation between private life and the public world is mediated—devised, we should say—by a series of stories that are a way to establish this relation—in moral, political, and formal terms.

NOTES

This essay, translated by Susan Benner, is adapted from a lecture given by the author in 1990 at the Facultad de Filosofía y Letras of the University of Buenos Aires as part of the class Las tres vanguardias (Saer, Puig, Walsh) ("Three Avant-Gardes: Saer, Puig, Walsh"). The lecture was transcribed from a tape recording by Darío Weiner and Patricia Somoza.

[1] A clear example of this problem is seen in the variations on the detective's psychology in North American detective novels. They show how a character was included in a preexisting formula, along with defined procedures and forms of progression in a story.

[2] Throughout the essay I refer to Valentín by his last name, Arregui.

[3] In this same vein, Antonio Gramsci said that Italian opera was a kind of melodrama in which extreme loves mixed with political situations to produce a conflict with no possible mediation.

Reading in the Dark:
Entangled Settings, Stories, and Secrets
in *Kiss of the Spider Woman*

Lucille Kerr

Regardless of what students know or don't know about Latin American literature, history, and culture and regardless of whether they have already read Puig
or seen the film version of *Kiss of the Spider Woman*, the question of reading,
and questions about reading, are critical for teaching this novel. My experience
teaching Puig's *Kiss of the Spider Woman* to undergraduates has been of two
varieties, serving different student populations. From a recent class about the
new Latin American narrative taught in English for nonmajors and nonminors
to classes on modern Latin American fiction and the Boom taught in Spanish
for advanced majors and for minors in their first upper-level literature class,
student preparation and interests have varied considerably. The classes had different groups, diverse backgrounds, and disparate expectations, to be sure. Yet
I have found that many of those differences virtually disappear when students
read *Kiss of the Spider Woman* for the first time. Indeed, having taught this
novel to different groups, I am often reminded how democratic first readings
can be.

Over the years a group of self-posed questions about reading have guided me
in preparing to teach this novel: How to teach students to read how Puig sets
us up to read? How to reveal the secrets of *Kiss of the Spider Woman* without
revealing too much, without denying students the pleasure of reading, if not also
the surprise of seeing, what the novel reveals? How to show first-time readers
the complex relation between the novel's narrative strategies and its thematic
concerns, between the story it tells in its "body" and the narrative it constructs

at its "feet," between the fictional dramas of its two protagonists and the textual performances of its author and reader? How to link reading *Kiss of the Spider Woman* to reading narrative fiction more generally?

Students do not, of course, come to the text as completely uninformed readers. At the beginning of the courses in which I have taught the novel, I usually assign secondary readings about the emergence of the new Latin American novel, especially about the Boom era and its authors, sometimes emphasizing essays from the period to demonstrate how critics initially responded to new narrative currents (e.g., Franco, "Narrador"; Fuentes; Oviedo; Rama, *Novela*; Rodríguez Monegal, "Latin American Novel," "Revolutionary Writing," *Boom*; Vargas Llosa "Novela," "Latin American Novel"). I assign essays about Argentine political history to provide relevant background for the novel and to underscore that, although the novel draws the reader into stories that pull both fictional characters and readers away from extraliterary reality, the historical context is critical for reading (e.g., Lewis; Snow). Drawing on these materials, I briefly introduce Puig's life and work, talk about his career in relation to other Latin American authors, and review some topics (such as high versus low culture, literary versus nonliterary forms, politics versus art) with which his name has become associated (see also Bacarisse, *Necessary Dream*; García Ramos; Kerr, *Suspended Fictions*; Levine, *Manuel*; Tittler).

In the first day's discussion, I aim to work with questions related to those I mention above. I start by asking how we literally begin to read, drawing directly on the novel's first chapter, which begins in a dark prison cell and in medias res. (Chapter 1 begins in the middle of Molina's nighttime narration of *Cat People* [dir. Tourneur, 1942] to Valentín, approximately five months after they become cell mates.) In a broad sense, I am directed by the question, How can one guide ignorant (in the etymological sense of "not knowing") readers to learn to read "in the dark"? That is, my goal is not only to guide students' reading of Puig's novel but also to help them learn to read on their own, even, or especially, when they find themselves in the dark.

I offer the locution "reading in the dark" both as a theoretical frame for reading and as a phrase one can use to organize discussion of the novel. Taken in its literal and figurative senses, this phrase makes connections among the verbs *to read, to see, to understand, to interpret,* and *to know.* As we talk about *Kiss of the Spider Woman*, we find ourselves shifting among these meanings as we read the novel and examine the process of reading itself. In practice as well as in theory, whether explicitly or implicitly posed to students, the question transforms itself into a set of related questions we consider throughout our discussions. How does Puig's novel position us to read? How do both his characters and readers learn how to read—in all senses of the term—throughout the novel? How might reading Puig change, or not, how we read beyond literature?

Whether teaching the novel in classes that meet twice a week for seventy-five minutes or three times a week for fifty minutes, I divide reading assignments to highlight the thematic and structural significance of the Spanish text's bipartite structure (its sixteen chapters are divided into two parts of eight chapters; the

English edition is not divided into parts). This plan highlights especially chapter 8, the final chapter of the first half, in which the text's revelations readjust the reader's vision and redefine the relationships between the protagonists, if not also those between reader and author. Furthermore, the space between chapters 8 and 9 emerges as a space between ways of seeing and reading. It creates a blind spot where the question of reading in the dark is posed for both the readers and the protagonists of the novel. Thus when the class meets twice a week for seventy-five minutes, I divide reading assignments into groups of four chapters; when the class meets for fifty minutes three times a week, I assign four groups of three chapters and two groups of two chapters (1–3, 4–6, 7–8, 9–11, 12–14, 15–16). Having most recently taught the novel in groups of four chapters, here I use that model to outline some of the possibilities for organizing discussion of *Kiss of the Spider Woman* and especially for exploring how we learn about reading in the dark.

First, to assist students with class preparation, I compose a reading guide for each set of chapters (the guide is posted on the course *Blackboard* site two or three days before the reading assignment is due). The guide comprises specific questions about the how and what of the novel to encourage students to integrate their thinking about narrative content and form, story and structure. Questions therefore address story information (who, what, where, when); focus on structure and technique (forms of narration, chapter divisions, the use of footnotes); deal with themes, concepts, and issues (power relations, high versus low culture, sexuality, cultural values); and draw attention to the reading experience (readers' point of view, author-reader relationship). These questions also give students a chance to consider aspects of the novel that we don't have time to discuss, then to connect those points to our dialogue in class and perhaps move to broader issues beyond the novel.

Chapters 1–4: Learning to See in the Dark

Arguably, the first four chapters establish most, if not all, of the novel's discursive, thematic, and structural parameters. Beginning at night in the middle of Molina's narration of *Cat People*, chapters 1 and 2 force first-time readers to be aware of what they don't know and to become conscious of how, when they begin reading, they are almost completely in the dark. While they begin to read for information (who the characters are and how to recognize them through their language, where and when the story takes place) and, unconsciously perhaps, adjust their reading to the text's internal rules (or, as it were, adjust their eyes to the dark), they are also being taught how the novel works and how reading is shaped by Puig.

Given that the opening chapters use direct dialogue and that the dialogue includes Molina's extended narration of a film that constitutes a second-level fiction, the novel provides an opportunity to recall basic concepts of narrative and narration and types of fiction (author, character, reader; narration in third person versus narration in first person; monologue, dialogue; realist versus reflexive fiction). Here, the syllabus also mentions reference materials about basic terminology and concepts that were discussed at the beginning of the course to prepare for reading our primary texts and to which some students return for review (e.g., Abrams; Cuddon; Harmon and Holman; Lentricchia and McLaughlin; Turco).

Referring to those concepts and terms, we talk about how we "see" through the characters' language, how visual effects are created by verbal material, and how the reader is inserted into the scene as a virtual spectator and eavesdropper on both the prison story in which Molina and Valentín "star" and the film stories Molina presents for Valentín to "see" (see also Masiello, "Jailhouse Flicks"). These opening chapters therefore may be used to cultivate students' abilities to read—and see—simultaneously from the unself-conscious position of a naive reader absorbed into the novel's fictions and from the critically conscious perspective of an experienced reader aware of how to read from outside the text. Furthermore, one can make students aware of yet another, more informed, reading position, from which we grasp the novel's heuristic value and see how it teaches us about narrative fiction and reading.

In the first pages of chapter 1, the reader must adapt to the sounds and sights inside the cell without the aid of an omniscient narrator. By the time we reach the end of chapter 4 we have adjusted to the setting sufficiently to be able to understand what is going on in the story and have become accustomed to the novel's narrative techniques. In the initial chapters the dialogue between Molina and Valentín establishes their cordial and yet conflictive relationship and situates them as marginal figures locked away on the periphery of society (see Débax, Ezquerro, and Ramond). The conversation presents them as distinctive, if not opposing, figures who can be recognized through the language they speak. They are identified with different needs and desires, aligned with discrete interests and ideologies, and associated with different activities and spaces. Valentín, the heterosexual leftist, reads political philosophy by the light of day; Molina, the homosexual window dresser, narrates romantic films in the dark of night. While underscoring the differences between them, class discussion might also suggest how these chapters begin to identify, as much as contrast, the two figures with each other. In particular, attention can be drawn to the parallels between Molina's films (*Cat People* in chapters 1 and 2 and the Nazi film in chapters 3 and 4), the story of his relationship with the waiter Gabriel in chapter 3, and Valentín's story of his comrade-girlfriend in chapter 2: they are all sentimental and romantic tales about desire, love, and loss.

The introduction of footnotes in chapter 3 creates a natural framework for discussing the author-reader relationship and literary versus nonliterary conventions, as well as the novel's commentary on contemporary society and culture. Moreover, Molina's and Valentín's shared methods of narration converge with Puig's narrative techniques at the end of chapters 1 and 2 and provide corroborating material for analyzing the author-reader dialogue. Discussion of that convergence can lead to observations about structure and theme that prepare students for analysis of the novel's ending.

I begin discussion by focusing on footnotes generally: what sort of texts use footnotes and what kind of information notes usually provide; how footnotes can be read as both marginal to and essential for the main text, as unimportant supplements to and critical components of the textual body above them. This general discussion allows students to think about the notes as both narrative devices and conveyors of information. It also allows them to conceive of the space dedicated to the notes on the written page as the space in which the author reveals himself, speaking more directly to the reader albeit through the voices of other authors. Because the first footnote is presented as a response to Valentín's confessed ignorance about homosexuality, that is, as a reply to his request for information about "people with your [Molina's] type of inclination" (Eng. 59, Span. 66, Archivos 53), it brings up issues of reading. Chapter 3 sets up an identification between the novel's reader, to whom the notes are directed by Puig, and Valentín, who asks a question that some of Puig's uninformed readers might also ask. The footnotes have a didactic character: they aim to teach the (Latin American) reader about homosexuality in eight installments inserted into chapters 3, 5, 6, 7, 8, 9, 10, and 11 (see also Amícola, *Manuel* 85–97; Balderston, "Progresos"; Kerr, *Suspended Fictions* 220–26; Macchi; Christ, "Interview" 27–28; Coddou 12). I also point out to the class that, whenever we read the footnotes, we are seeing what the characters themselves cannot see. The notes are situated outside the space of the fiction, at the foot of the text's pages, where the reader-author dialogue is exposed. The notes also create for the text a privileged place "above" and "outside" for the reader and for discussion of reading more generally. At the same time, the notes leave the characters—especially Valentín—in the dark, "below."

I propose at least two ways of looking at the development of the reader's relationship to Valentín as the footnotes' story about homosexuality progresses. On the one hand, the novel's reader is cast as a surrogate for Valentín, but as the reader becomes more informed and less ignorant, the gap between what the reader knows and sees and what Valentín sees and knows increases. On the other hand, it is not only the degree but also the kind of knowledge acquired by Valentín and by the reader that matters. Without revealing how the prisoners' story unfolds, we can speculate about how we might eventually consider whether Valentín actually learns as much, if not more, from his experience with Molina than the reader learns from reading. These suggestions also push the class to remain attentive to the reading process itself and to become aware of how Puig positions, and also contends with, his reader.

Discussion can shift from comments about the footnotes as narrative devices and authorial signposts to comments about the narrative techniques at the end of chapters 1 and 2. Developing further the references to the author-reader dialogue in discussion of the first footnote, one can present these chapter endings as examples of the novel's reflexive, or metafictional, features. At the end of chapter 1, when Molina interrupts the narration of *Cat People* to leave Valentín hanging, and at the end of chapter 2, when Valentín reciprocates by cutting off his narration about his comrade-girlfriend, the characters also talk about their narrative strategies. When each interrupts his narration to the other (a conventional technique of serial fiction, Molina explains), the interruption is designed either to keep the listener interested (e.g., Valentín in chapter 1 [Eng. 25–26, Span. 31–32, Archivos 21–22]) or to repay the other narrator for withholding information (e.g., Molina in chapter 2 [Eng. 46–47, Span. 52–53, Archivos 41–42). The point to make here is essentially that the characters' manipulation of each other in the fiction mirrors Puig's manipulation of the reader in the text. One can show how the novel both thematizes and performs these manipulations, how Puig acknowledges what he is doing with his reader underneath the characters' conversation.

One might then borrow the novel's technique to create suspense for the next class discussion, which deals with chapters 5–8. At the close of chapter 4, the narration of the Nazi film and the story of its star Leni ends, but the story of Molina and Valentín remains open, and the episode of Molina's illness is unresolved. In the subsequent class, one can answer questions about what happens next. One can link the movement between the fictions in the cell and the fictions of the whole novel and consider how these different but related fictions are a distraction, if not an escape, from what is going on around the prisoners, the story, and the text. Arguably, the film narration distracts Molina from his pain, if not also Valentín from Molina's plight; likewise, the reader is distracted from both the story of the cell mates and the world outside the prison. When the movie ends, both the characters and the reader return to the conditions of the prison cell, Argentine history, and the realities of Latin American society and culture. These are all part of the novel's texture and structure, although they are, in a way, covered up in the sentimental and melodramatic film stories that fill a major portion of the initial chapters. Here, as when discussing the shift to frames outside the cell and the prison in chapters 8, 14, and 15, I take the opportunity to remind the class about Latin American history during the 1970s, the real-world setting to which the fates of Puig's characters are connected. I also suggest that, as the students read the rest of the novel, they think about whether they see *Kiss of the Spider Woman* as an artfully escapist or committed text and whether or not they see Puig as a political writer (see also Amícola, *Manuel Puig* 139–56; Corbatta, *Mito personal*).

Chapters 5–8: Reading Surprises

Given the significant revelations about Molina's pact with the warden (and also students' surprise at seeing what has been hidden from them as well as from Valentín), I use chapter 8 to both start and end discussion of the group of chapters. This chapter concludes with Molina still in the warden's office dictating items that will help him to hide from Valentín the truth of the conversation outside the cell. That is, he needs to create the illusion that he has seen his mother, who has brought him a package of food. The fiction he creates aims to hide his agreement to act as the warden's informant about his cell mate and, therefore, his betrayal of Valentín. We take up this scene by talking about how it dramatizes the structures of power in which both Molina and the warden are situated, if not trapped; how it develops parallels between the conversation of prisoner and warden and the footnote about repression inserted underneath their conversation; how it enacts an economic exchange of goods and services between the food from Molina's "mother" and the freedom promised as payment for Molina's work as a secret agent.

Staged in the warden's office, the chapter takes us outside the prisoners' cell. We not only discover Molina's pact with the warden and his betrayal of Valentín. We also become aware that, like Valentín, we have been kept in the dark throughout the first seven chapters. The revelation of Molina's, and Puig's, secrets is critical. There is a realignment of knowledge and vision that changes the distance between the reader and the characters. Let in on the novel's treacherous secrets, the reader leaves Valentín behind and seems to move closer to Molina, whose strategies of deception, along with those of the novel's author, are now clear. Yet as the discussion of the novel's ending later suggests, it is questionable that the reader is no longer reading in the dark. Indeed, the shift in the reader's perspective from reading in the dark to reading in the light and, by implication, from an identification with the blind figure (Valentín) to a position identified with the figure of vision (Molina), becomes a topic for discussion.

We move back to chapters 5, 6, and 7 to look at how the text prepares for these revelations while the story advances beyond the first chapters. Chapters 5 and 6—the only chapters in the group that include films—provide an opportunity to make comparative observations about the stories and endings characteristic of Molina's films and the narrative techniques deployed by Puig. Significantly, chapter 5 takes place not in the dark but during the day, when it is light and Valentín is reading. Molina, still feeling unwell from the poisoned food he has eaten and abandoned by Valentín, who rejects Molina's idea of telling another film because he wants to read and study, must resort to entertaining himself. Virtually left in the dark, Molina decides to think about a romantic film with a happy ending (Cromwell's *The Enchanted Cottage* [1945]). The film in the next chapter, however, returns to the tragic and formulaic endings of the first two films. (The film in chapter 6 is a romance-tragedy about a wealthy young man's conversion into a revolutionary; it implicitly parodies Valentín's own story, as revealed in chapter 10.) This film's images are incorporated into Valentín's nightmarish dream in this chapter, after he becomes ill, like Molina before him (Eng. 124–29, Span. 128–33, Archivos 107–11).

Here I comment on the narrative techniques introduced in these chapters (direct interior monologue, stream of consciousness, dreams, prison documents), emphasizing the novel's heterogeneous, rather than homogeneous, quality. I suggest that the text displays a deceptively uniform appearance and that, later, we might think in similar terms as we reconsider the characters' sexual identification. We talk about the opposition between Molina's and Valentín's interests ("low" culture films, melodrama and romance, and emotional involvements versus "high" culture texts, political theory and intellectual debate, and unsentimental relationships) as thematized in their conversations in the first half of the novel. At the same time, I lead students to consider the erosion of that opposition in the familial relationship that develops over the next few days, when Molina cares for Valentín and helps him recover from being poisoned. We recall that Valentín becomes sick and soils himself and that, as he cleans and feeds Valentín, Molina plays the role of a mother caring for her child. Valentín regresses to an infantile state in which he is totally dependent on Molina for both food and comfort and also for entertainment or playtime, which Valentín-as-infant also desires, if not needs. (Here I typically refer briefly to Freud's theory of sexuality and to psychoanalysis more generally, suggesting supplementary readings for interested students; see also Laplanche 8–24.) Without revealing too much about later chapters, I suggest that in these scenes Molina plays the role of mother-savior, who, by rescuing Valentín from pain and by pampering him, virtually reprograms his cell mate, perhaps so that he may later "grow up" to have different needs, if not desires.

Chapters 9–12: Embracing the Dark

Here, too, I organize discussion around a key chapter, in this group chapter 11. The chapter includes Molina's second conversation with the warden, in which the possibility of Molina's release is introduced and Molina succeeds in getting another package of food from his "mother"; the conclusion of the novel's fifth film, Jacques Tourneur's *I Walked with a Zombie* (1943), a melodrama about treachery, trust, and familial relations that resonates with the prisoners' own stories (the protagonist betrayed by trusted family figures, the zombie as a figure of the prisoners' "living-dead" existence); the letter Valentín dictates to Molina for his middle-class girlfriend Marta, the ideologically inappropriate object of a desire that is beyond ideological control; the novel's final footnote, presenting a theory of homosexuality as a revolutionary practice; and the first sexual encounter between Molina and Valentín.

We can read the virtual reprogramming of Valentín by Molina in chapters 9–11 as an artful redirection of energy from reading to listening and talking, from the realm of the textual to that of the oral, from theory to practice. Literally unable to read in the dark, Valentín depends on Molina for light (the candle belongs to Molina, as he reminds Valentín in chapter 10 [Eng. 192, Span. 196, Archivos 173]) as well as for the film entertainment. Valentín surrenders his books and his role as reader to the fantasies and films—that is the pleasures—

preferred by Molina. Thus Molina will appear to teach Valentín how to see (differently) in the dark and, later, to embrace its possibilities.

Students invariably notice that the final footnote in chapter 11 precedes Molina's and Valentín's sexual encounter, and they often wonder about how the two events might be related. I reveal the identity of Dr. Anneli Taube—she is in fact Puig, who produces a happy ending for the story about homosexuality beneath the prison scenes. We look back at the series of notes, talking about the logical progression from one theory to the next (we also note the extraneous nature of note 2, in chapter 4, which advances the fictional story of Leni, the star of the Nazi film, as if she were a real person) and the parallel techniques deployed in the stories above and below. I find it helpful to provide a visual aid so that students can see how we read between these textual sequences. Drawing parallel horizontal lines to represent the two story levels and vertical lines between the horizontals to show where the footnotes are inserted in each chapter, I produce a diagram that visualizes how the horizontal movement forward from chapter to chapter is interrupted—held in suspense—by the vertical movement from chapters above to notes below. We see more literally how the process of reading becomes an up-and-down and back-and-forth movement between body and feet. The discussion focuses on the notes' teleology and the relation between these separate but interconnected narrative sequences and endings; it also returns us to figures of reading.

I ask students to describe what happens when the footnotes end and to consider whether the fiction in the text's body might enact what is theorized at its feet. First, I point out that, when the footnote sequence is ending, Molina also begins to speak for himself instead of being spoken for by outside authorities. He begins to communicate his experiences directly and authoritatively to both Valentín and the novel's reader. (Here one can anticipate discussion of the last four chapters by asking students to pay attention to how Molina's voice becomes more authoritative later on.) Second, we see another parallel between Valentín and the novel's reader. When the reader, who has been reading the footnotes for Valentín, no longer has any footnotes to read, Valentín's texts of political theory also seem to disappear—he virtually stops reading. Furthermore, Molina is cast by Valentín as a political, if not revolutionary, figure, first in their conversation (following the final scenes of the zombie film, they talk about the possibility of Molina contacting Valentín's revolutionary comrades [Eng. 251–52, Span. 255–56, Archivos 230–31]) and then, finally, in their physical embrace. The scene of sexual intimacy therefore seems to enact a natural ending of the footnote story about homosexuality below and to show Taube's theory transformed into a revolutionary practice above.

The characters' embrace produces a complex, and somewhat unreadable, conflation of figures and voices. In the final lines of chapter 11, Molina says that he felt "As if now, somehow . . . I . . . were you" ("Que ahora yo . . . eras vos") while Valentín remains silent (Eng. 219, Span. 222, Archivos 196). Students find this combination of figures and identities, and Molina's formulation itself, difficult to sort out, and we talk about that difficulty. We consider how questions of identity are bound up with ideas of difference and that to identify is also to differentiate; we suggest different ways to understand what Molina tries to describe. We propose to read this statement as figuring Valentín's virtual disappearance into the figure of Molina or as Molina's virtual transformation into Valentín and so on (see also Echavarren 71–74). We follow these reading possibilities into the next chapter, which presents Valentín's last attempt to suppress practice and promote theory. The day after they have been intimate, Valentín briefly tries to read and study, aiming to find a "remedy" so as to "save" himself and recover his former identity (Eng. 221, Span. 224, Archivos 204). But reading is again replaced by speaking and listening; scientific and theoretical discourse, seen directly (footnotes) or indirectly (Valentín's texts), is silenced by the discourse of popular culture (the Mexican cabaret film that Molina begins to narrate in chapter 12). Students often comment that this turn in events is not unexpected; they (like Valentín) have learned to expect, if not also desire, another film story.

Chapters 13–16: Shedding Some Light on Things

Inevitably, discussion of chapters 13–16 combines analysis of the entire novel with comments about the final chapters. Like the novel as a whole, these chapters are not difficult to read. That is, events are presented chronologically and only one new narrative technique is introduced (at the beginning of chapter 14 hidden dialogue is added to direct dialogue, interior monologue, and written document [Eng. 245–46, Span. 249–50, Archivos 226–27]). The story takes us from inside the prison on the day preceding Molina's release (chs. 13–14) to his activities over the next two weeks and then to his death (ch. 15). In chapter 16 we go back inside the prison where, after Molina has been killed, we see Valentín in the prison infirmary in the final scene.

Following the (reading) path from inside to outside and back again, I use the written document in chapter 15 to draw attention to how we see things and to focus on how the reader's vision is shaped by the text—or by Puig. We talk about how the novel draws attention to the repressive systems and structures in which Molina and Valentín are caught when the text reproduces those mechanisms (see also Borinsky; Green). We use the prison report chronicling the surveillance of Molina after his release as a means to consider the larger story of repression, violence, and imprisonment that surrounds the text (I have students recall the secondary reading about Argentine history and recapitulate events of the 1970s). And we explore how the novel distracts us from the larger frame as it confines the characters within the space of the cell, limiting the reader's vision as well.

I try to show how the surveillance document brings the outside within the scope of our vision, which coincides with that of the panoptic eye of government surveillance (see also Foucault, *Discipline*). We also consider the fallibility of this apparent omniscience and the incomplete reading produced by the document that is supposed to see and tell all. As an all-seeing document, the report seems to place the reader even above the reading position offered in chapter 8 and, therefore, in a better position to read the novel as a whole. We also understand, however, that the surveillance report sees only surfaces, what is physically visible and audible. It cannot see what it aspires and is supposed to be able to see. Molina is supposed to be the warden's eyes and ears inside the cell, but Molina's betrayal of the warden blinds the prison eye, which cannot, in the end, penetrate and control what happens inside the prisoners' cell or determine what develops between them. Still, seeing as we do from above everyone else inside the novel, our vision is, arguably, omniscient—imperfectly omniscient, I suggest, because that vision is controlled by the author (see also Borinsky 57–58). Drawing on the reference to the self-enclosed space of the cell, I remind the class that in chapter 11 the characters themselves have explicitly theorized, if not dramatized, their freedom from the prison system's mechanisms of control, which the surveillance report would otherwise document. Valentín describes their cell as a desert island protected from structures of oppression (Eng. 202, Span. 206, Archivos 185). This vision is the paradisiacal island image to which the novel returns in the final chapter and from which the figure of the spider woman emerges.

To end discussion, I draw students' attention first to chapter 14, where the characters' dialogue offers two key phrases for reading the novel's ending, and then to chapter 16, where we attempt to see how these phrases end the text. We recall that Molina offers the phrase "enigmatic ending" (Eng. 259, Span. 263, Archivos 235) to describe the ending of the Mexican cabaret film he has just finished telling Valentín (ch. 14). Valentín then offers his interpretation of the phrase and tells Molina that he is "the spider woman, that traps men in her web" (Eng. 260, Span. 265, Archivos 237). Molina is delighted by his cell mate's interpretation. Despite the explicit identification of Molina as the spider woman and the apparent validity of Valentín's interpretation, the aim is to have students consider how this phrase resists, rather than surrenders to, interpretation and how questions of reading remain.

These two phrases become entangled in the novel's final scenes, where the question of who is the spider woman converges with the question of how to read an enigmatic ending. In Valentín's morphine-induced delirium dream, the reader virtually hears Valentín hearing Molina's voice in the voice of Marta; we see Marta/Molina materialize to comfort Valentín. Students attempt but fail to differentiate definitively among these voices. They are unable to fix one identity or the other; they read the voices as the voices of one figure or two or more that, together, call up the image of the confounding figure created by Molina's identification with Valentín at the end of chapter 11.

The figure of the spider woman emerges from this delirium of voices, appearing in the enigmatic ending of a film similar to the last film narrated by Molina to Valentín (Eng. 280, Span. 285, Archivos 257). Here it is not difficult to see the explicit reference to an enigmatic ending as a reflexive characterization of the novel's final pages. Emphasizing the idea of endings, we turn to the figure of the spider woman to complete our discussion—on an enigmatic note, of course. Seeing how both Molina and Valentín ensnare each other in their own webs (the web of the homosexual who tells film tales, the web of the heterosexual who talks about political struggle) and how the reader is at the same time ensnared by Puig—they are all spider women—we see this figure suggest but then resist a uniform reading. We step back from this figure and from the text to talk self-consciously about the different ways we might read the spider woman and Puig's novel. The final part of our discussion of *Kiss of the Spider Woman* therefore attempts to shed some light on the experience of reading in both practical and theoretical terms. We conclude our conversation by discussing—and sometimes debating—what this reading experience has taught us about reading novels more generally and what we have learned about reading in the dark.

Narrative Voices in
Kiss of the Spider Woman

Rosa Perelmuter

Tout est séduction, tout n'est que séduction.
—Jean Baudrillard, *De la séduction*

Whenever I teach *Kiss of the Spider Woman*—and I do so sometimes yearly, sometimes every other year—my students (undergraduate majors if they are reading the novel in Spanish, nonmajors taking an elective or looking to fulfill the aesthetic perspective requirement if they are reading in English), unaccustomed to finding footnotes in a literary text, frequently ask whether they are required to read them. I realized early on that the connection between the various parts of the novel—the dialogue between the prisoners, the films narrated in the novel, and the footnotes surrounding the text—is not always understood by readers. I therefore decided to discuss the different voices that narrate the novel (and within the novel) and serve as stand-ins for the traditional, omniscient narrator. Here I focus on the two most prevalent narrative voices: Molina's and the voice of the anonymous narrator of the footnotes that my students are indeed required to read. While I use a narratological approach, I largely dispense with the terminology associated with this method, not because I don't regard it as valuable, but because it adds a level of complexity not usually welcomed by students.

The topic of repression is easy to perceive in *Kiss of the Spider Woman*. Not only does the novel take place toward the beginning of Argentina's most politically oppressive and violent periods, but its setting is limited almost exclusively to a Buenos Aires jail, home of the cell mates Valentín Arregui Paz and Luis Alberto Molina. The first, Valentín, jailed two years before Molina for "promoting disturbances," remains in prison, still awaiting trial. The second, Molina, is sentenced in 1974 to eight years in prison for what is ambiguously termed "corruption of minors" (Eng. 148, Span. 151, Archivos 131). Such severe punishment for the different activities of the protagonists brings to the fore both the oppressive policies and wide reach of the Argentine government in the 1970s, persecuting both an apolitical gay man and a heterosexual political activist. Manuel Puig's denunciation of repression, which is central to the novel, is reprised in the tales interpolated throughout the novel, where we find a succession of characters who represent or encounter different inflections of the repressive impulse. When we think of the movies narrated by Molina—with characters such as Irena, Leni, the "ugly little maid," the wounded flyer, the young race car driver, the newlywed young woman, or the ex-actress and singer—it becomes clear that their stories in one way or another evoke the theme of repression. Even in the footnotes—especially from the fourth to the seventh—repression as a psychological concept applies to politics as well as to sexual behavior.

Something entirely different occurs when we consider the structure of the novel, which can hardly be characterized as strict or repressive. If anything, the novel flows freely, without the tight control of an omniscient narrator.[1] The absence of such a narrator has become a characteristic feature of Puig's novels and has been interpreted variously. Some critics insist that the narrator disappears altogether, without a trace. "The narrator not only does not intervene," observes Pere Gimferrer, "but doesn't even seem to propose any interpretation of this content" (25). Others maintain that the apparent absence of the omniscient narrator is just that, an apparent absence. Alicia Borinsky's assessment is representative: "A rigorous application of the notion of omniscient narrator on the novel would show *Kiss of the Spider Woman* to be a perfect example of the ubiquity of such a narrator" (57).

These positions, though divergent, are not incompatible. The novel clearly lacks a distinct narrator who intervenes directly and offers opinions in his or her own voice, someone who speaks from what Gérard Genette would call an extradiegetic level. But even though there are no specific references to the enunciation, to the overall narrating instance, there are many narrating acts within the text.

First, we have Molina, the obliging narrator of the films recounted in the novel (he would be considered by Genette an intradiegetic-heterodiegetic narrator); second, we have the voice of the anonymous narrator of the footnotes (an extradiegetic-heterodiegetic narrator); and last, we have Valentín, who prefers to tell real stories, in which he acts as a homodiegetic narrator (Eng. 130, Span. 135, Archivos 112), but who recounts, at least in the form of interior monologues, his own version of the fourth movie (Eng. 124–29, Span. 128–33, Archivos 104–07; Eng. 145–47, Span. 148–50, Archivos 126–27) and the final "film" of the novel, in which he mimics Molina's role as an intradiegetic-heterodiegetic narrator (Eng. 276–81, Span. 282–87, Archivos 255–58).[2] These narrative voices govern the text so often and so skillfully that they have been used to challenge the notion that the novel lacks an omniscient narrator. For Juan Manuel García Ramos, Molina is "the clearest example" (334) of the presence of a traditional narrator in Puig's works.

Molina is clearly the prevalent narrative voice and plays the part with uncharacteristic firmness and resolve. In all other respects, he seems to be anything but self-assured: he is an effeminate homosexual who describes himself and his friends as "silly girlfriends" ("amigas locas") (Eng. 215, Span. 218, Archivos 193), "so easy to scare, so wishy-washy" ("muy . . . miedosos, flojos") (Eng. 203, Span. 207, Archivos 185) and who is proud to enjoy the passive role where sexual relations are concerned (Eng. 243, Span. 246, Archivos 222). As he explains to Valentín, "if a man is . . . my husband, he has to give the orders, so he will feel right. That's the natural thing, because that makes him the . . . the man of the house" ("si un hombre . . . es mi marido, él tiene que mandar, para que se sienta bien. Eso es lo normal, porque él entonces . . . es el hombre de la casa") (Eng. 243–44, Span. 246, Archivos 222). Molina's passivity is also manifested in his behavior outside the jail cell, when he appears before the warden. The reader gathers from the transcription of one of these conversations that Molina trembles (Eng. 149, Span. 152, Archivos 132), cries (Eng. 150, Span. 152–53, Archivos 132), and appears diminished, a fact that is borne out by the long footnote on repression and domination that crosses this section of the text (Eng. 151–54, Span. 154–55, Archivos 133–34). But when Molina recounts films to Valentín, he is neither passive nor faltering but rather takes charge of the situation. His behavior could even be characterized as manly, according to his own definition of the word. "—And what's masculine in your terms?" ("¿—Qué es ser hombre, para vos?"), Valentín asks early in the novel, to which Molina replies:

> —It's lots of things, but for me . . . well, the nicest thing about a man is just that, to be marvelous-looking, and strong, but without making any fuss about it, and also walking very tall. Walking absolutely straight, like my waiter, who's not afraid to say anything. And it's knowing what you want, where you're going.   (61)

> —Es muchas cosas, pero para mí . . . bueno, lo más lindo del hombre es eso, ser lindo, fuerte, pero sin hacer alharaca de fuerza, y que va avanzando seguro. Que camine seguro, como mi mozo, que hable sin miedo, que sepa lo que quiere, adonde va, sin miedo de nada.
>
>   (69, Archivos 55)

As a narrator Molina is able to walk tall, straight, without fear, and with full knowledge of what he wants and where he is headed. It is he who makes most of the decisions when it comes to story time: he chooses the movies, tells them his own way, and generally decides how and when to end them.[3] On the first evening, for example, Molina interrupts the film about the panther woman at a key point, claiming that he is too sleepy to continue (Eng. 8, Span. 14, Archivos 10). Anxious to hear what happens next, Valentín begs him to go on, but Molina holds firm and gets his way. The excuse about being too sleepy is revealed as just that, nothing but an excuse; a couple of days later, Molina reveals his hand when he assures his cell mate that "there's not much more to go now, for tonight I mean" ("ya falta poco, por esta noche quiero decir") (Eng. 25, Span. 31, Archivos 21). We realize then that Molina knows in advance just how much of the story he will reveal at a given time. Throughout the novel, Molina stops his narration at key moments, casually remarking with studied indifference, "But I'll tell you the rest next time" ("y otra vez te la sigo") (Eng. 191, Span. 195, Archivos 172). He thus provokes the impatience—and at times the anger—of his helpless listener.

We might even say that with this behavior we see a reversal of roles, since Molina behaves not like the subordinate of the man of the house but rather like the stronger member of the couple, the one who gets to call the shots, or in this case tell the story. Storytelling in effect allows Molina to seduce or manipulate

Valentín.[4] What's more, Molina treats the act of narration as if it were a sexual act where he plays the active manly role. The connection between seduction and narration has been amply studied (see, e.g., Barthes, *Plaisir*; Baudrillard; Chambers), but what interests me here is that Molina's words betray his understanding of the erotic dimension of language or, to put it differently, the erotic power of narration. Two examples come to mind. The first takes place at the beginning of the novel, when Molina, explaining why he stops the movie at particular moments, tells Valentín pointedly, "I like to leave you hanging, that way you enjoy the film more" ("Me gusta sacarte el dulce en lo mejor, así te gusta más la película") (Eng. 25, Span. 32, Archivos 22). The words in Spanish reveal the relation between sex and language much more explicitly than in the English translation, but both versions still manage to convey the connection between pleasure and narration. The second example occurs while Molina is telling himself the third movie and remembers that the servant girl, with just a few words, is able to impress the flyer. Following that, he wonders nostalgically, *"how does it happen that sometimes someone says something and wins someone else over forever?"* ("¿qué pasa que a veces alguien dice algo y conquista para siempre a otra persona?") (Eng. 107, Span. 111, Archivos 92).[5] Thus we see that Molina understands the relation between discourse and power, between saying and wooing, and that he knows how to take advantage of the seductive power of words. Only when he narrates his films, does—can—Molina flirt with (earlier I called it "manipulate") Valentín; only through narration is he able to seduce and conquer. Although in order to have sexual relations Molina needs to be subjected and insists on playing the passive role ("I don't enjoy it any other way" ["no gozo más que así"] [Eng. 243, Span. 246, Archivos 222]), in his role as narrator he shows that he can subject, seduce, or "give the orders," to return to his own definition of what it means to be a man.

Even when engaged in conversation with Valentín, Molina cannot separate himself from the influence of the world of films, and often both levels—the diegetic (the "real" events relating to the two prisoners described in the novel) and the metadiegetic (the events described in the movies that are recounted in the novel)—show a certain degree of contamination. So Molina describes Gabriel, the waiter with whom he is in love, as "[a] movie star" ("un galán de película") (Eng. 61, Span. 69, Archivos 54); he suggests that Valentín use the name of Jane Randolph, the actress who plays the part of the architect in the first movie (Eng. 44, Span. 50, Archivos 40), to name his girlfriend; and he dubs Valentín's discussion of that relationship *The Mystery of Cellblock Seven* ("El misterio de la celda siete") (Eng. 43, Span. 49, Archivos 39), as if it were a film. Valentín handles the narration of his real-life love in a similar fashion, even pausing his story with phrases that resemble those of Molina: "—I'll go on tomorrow, Molina" ("—Mañana te la sigo, Molina") (Eng. 46, Span. 52, Archivos 41).

Reality and fiction are thus commingled, acquiring a similar rhythm and sharing the same narrative conventions. When Molina decides to resume the narration of a film, he often depends on his listener to remember the exact place where he left off (Eng. 9, Span. 15, Archivos 11, and many subsequent examples);[6] he does the same when he gets ready to continue with his story of Gabriel. Molina thus asks Valentín to recall the point of the story where they had left off, to which Valentín replies, much as he would regarding a movie, that they were talking about the matter of a salad (Eng. 64, Span. 71, Archivos 56). In fact, Valentín is so caught up in the story of Molina and Gabriel that when Molina pauses, Valentín pleads impatiently, "—Don't leave me hanging" ("—No te calles, no me dejes en suspenso") (Eng. 69, Span. 76, Archivos 60), just as he often does when he listens to Molina's films.

The stories, be they real or fictional, slowly manage to seduce Valentín, and his spiritual need for them soon becomes physical as well: *in my cell I can't sleep anymore because he got me used to listening to him tell films every night, like lullabies* ("*no puedo dormir porque él me acostumbró a contarme todas las noches películas, como un arrorró*") (Eng. 279, Span. 285, Archivos 256), Valentín confesses close to the end of the novel. When one evening Valentín, recovering from his ailments, remarks that there is still a gratification he seeks (Eng. 157, Span. 163, Archivos 142), it turns out to be not—as Molina maliciously suggests—sexual but rather textual. What Valentín wants is a film, to surrender to Molina's voice, to be satisfied by his cell mate—and not the other way around—through the power of his words.

The erotic dimension of the act of storytelling is nowhere as clear as in the last chapter of the novel. Even though Molina has left the cell and we know that he has been killed in the streets, the narrative situation remains the same: Valentín is still engaged in conversation with someone whose voice, effeminate before, now appears to be feminine. Semiconscious because of the morphine he has received from a caring nurse, Valentín imagines (or dreams) that his former girlfriend Marta is with him, although, interestingly enough, he is not the one who possesses her but rather it is she who penetrates him: *"Marta, darling, I hear you speaking inside of me"* ("*Marta querida, te oigo hablar adentro mío*") (Eng. 276, Span. 282, Archivos 255). The act of speaking or narrating, which earlier we saw as a vehicle or form of conquest, here appears as a sexual act. Valentín marks the moment of climax with these words:

> but to you, Marta, I'll tell everything, since I feel the same as I felt with you, because you're with me, and soon this jet will spurt out of me, white and warm from my insides and I'm going to flood her, oh, Marta, such joy, yes I will tell you everything so that you won't go away then, so that you'll be with me every minute, especially now, in this instant, don't think of leaving me, this precise instant! the most beautiful of all, now, yes, don't move, it's better quiet, now, now   (278)

> pero a vos Marta yo te cuento todo, que siento lo mismo que sentía con vos, porque estás conmigo, y que ya pronto me sale un chorro blanco y caliente de adentro, la voy a inundar, ay, Marta, qué felicidad, yo te cuento todo

*así no te vas, para que estés conmigo en todo momento, sobre todo ahora,
en este instante, ¡que no se te ocurra irte en este preciso instante! El más
lindo de todos, ya sí, no te muevas, callada es mejor, ya, ya*

(284, Archivos 256)

"It's better quiet," Valentín says to Marta, just as not much earlier he whis-
pered to Molina when they were making love (Eng. 218, Span. 221, Archivos 196). Hence it becomes clear that Marta—whose name is repeated often
throughout this last sequence—is a mere stand-in for Molina, who, conversely,
is not mentioned by name even once. Just as earlier Valentín needed Molina
to speak to Marta (in chapter 9 he dictates a letter to her, asking Molina to
write down the words that uncharacteristically pour out of him), he now needs
Marta in order to speak to Molina, to tell him everything, perhaps even what
he tells "her" at the very end—that he was afraid of losing her (Eng. 281, Span.
286–87, Archivos 258).

At the same time, in this last chapter of the novel, Valentín behaves more
than ever like Molina. If before he was reserved and taciturn and claimed to
be unable to recount any movies (e.g., Eng. 97, Span. 102, Archivos 87), by the
end, not only does he tell all but, in the style of Molina, he also seeks to win
over his listener. As Francine Masiello observes, "The dream clearly borrows
from the cinematic tales he and Molina had absorbed so thoroughly in order to
displace anxieties" ("Jailhouse Flicks" 19). The visions (what Valentín describes
seeing on a screen [Eng. 280, Span. 285, Archivos 257]) that he describes in
this interior dialogue may be considered a pastiche of the words previously
exchanged between the prisoners, about both real and fictional topics. Not surprisingly, the film to which Valentín alludes most often is the second, the one
about Leni, which Molina had called his very favorite (Eng. 56, Span. 63, Archivos 51). Even though Valentín had objected to the movie's pro-Nazi content, he
remembered it well (Eng. 87, Span. 97, Archivos 79), as Molina observes. He
brings it back at this point in the form of a dream as a likely response to Molina's
desire to see that movie all over again. Thus even though Molina is no longer
alive, even though his name is not mentioned at all, his voice still predominates
in this sequence as Valentín repeats his words and appropriates his customary
function as narrator. Lucille Kerr points out something similar when she notes
that "[Valentín's] discourse appears as the merging of their two voices in his
final appearance" (*Suspended Fictions* 191). Marta, as we noted earlier, may be
Molina, but Valentín turns out to be Molina as well.

In the final sequence, then, Valentín blends into or becomes one with Molina
or, in this instance, one with Molina's voice. The first time the two of them made
love, Molina felt a similar bonding experience, a coming together of sorts, as if
he had turned into the other: "—It seemed as if I wasn't here at all . . . like it
was you all alone. . . . —Or like I wasn't me anymore. As if now, somehow . . .
I . . . were you" ("—Me pareció que yo no estaba . . . que estabas vos sólo. . . .
—O que yo no era yo. Que ahora yo . . . eras vos") (Eng. 219, Span. 222, Archivos

196). That same expression of unity is found in the lyrics of several of the songs featured in the movie narrated by Molina in chapters 12 through 14. Puig clearly designed the invented film around six well-known romantic songs—mostly boleros, or what Molina calls sad, slow, tropical songs (Eng. 227, Span. 229, Archivos 205)[7]—to emphasize themes of loss and recuperation, submission and domination, love and sacrifice. As such, it bears comparison with the struggle and feelings of the two prisoners. The first line quoted from "Flores negras," the first bolero featured in the movie—"Even though you're . . . a prisoner" ("Aunque vivas prisionera") (Eng. 227, Span. 229, Archivos 207)—easily recalls the situation of the men. Other lyrics reinforce the sentiments expressed by Molina regarding his feelings of unity with Valentín. Such is the case with "Estoy enamorado" (" . . . I live in you . . . you live in me" [" . . . estás en mí, . . . estoy en ti"] [Eng. 240, Span. 243, Archivos 220]) and "Me acuerdo de ti," where the sentiment is reprised: "I carry you within me, deep inside of me . . . I carry you in my heart, you are a part of me . . . " ("Te llevo muy dentro, muy dentro de mí . . . Te llevo en el alma, me acuerdo de ti . . . ") (Eng. 257, Span. 261, Archivos 235). Throughout the novel, and especially in these last chapters, a series of role reversals undermine the dialectical configuration, the series of distinctions established at the beginning of the novel, when the two prisoners not only were well differentiated but also seemed opposites in every way: narrator-listener, female-male, apolitical homosexual–politically committed heterosexual, Molina-Valentín. In the end passage, in that monologue that is also a dialogue, we are left with what could be called a synthesis: a narrator who is also a listener, an entity who is male but also female,[8] a politically committed heterosexual who speaks like an apolitical homosexual; someone who, while not Molina, is also not Valentín.

Even though Molina's is indisputably the prevalent narrative voice in the novel, there is another, much less obvious, but also significant voice that is found in the frequent footnotes. We can describe the narrator of the footnotes, except for the second, as an anonymous voice, without a clear origin or direction, that utters a series of observations parceled out throughout the novel (the last one ends in chapter 11, shortly before the prisoners make love for the first time) and connected through the theme of homosexuality and by references that occasionally speak back to earlier footnotes (e.g., phrases making reference to the research of D. J. West [Eng. 97, Span. 102, Archivos 86]). The footnotes, according to Puig, were meant to educate his reader about subjects such as homosexuality and sexual determinants (Coddou 12). They have a distinct guiding hand, a narrator who collates, summarizes, and never provides direct quotations, thus breaking one of the standard conventions of this type of discourse.[9] Additionally, when paraphrasing the scientific studies discussed in the footnotes, this narrator does not shy away from giving an opinion or a personal judgment:

> If in fact the data prove to be of interest, the theory thereby formulated by Lang is marred by a failure to account for the normal physical characteristics of a large majority—99 percent—of homosexuals.   (63)

Si bien el dato resulta interesante, la teoría formulada por Lang se debilita fatalmente al no lograr explicar las características físicas normales de la gran mayoría, 99 por ciento, de los homosexuales.   (68, Archivos 55)

Words such as "prove to be of interest" or "is marred" betray the subjectivity of the narrator,[10] who, in establishing a sort of dialogue between the researchers, places himself among them. Consequently we find that the narrator of the footnotes expresses himself in a manner not unlike that of the narrator of the films: firmly, with authority even—or perhaps especially—when he invents his sources.[11] His control, moreover, is apparent not only in what and how he expresses himself but also in how he interrupts the novel to do so.

The interruptions produced by the footnotes fundamentally respond to two motivations. The first, which provides another point of contact between the two narrators, seems to be the result of a desire to create suspense. This would apply, for example, to the first footnote, where the asterisk interrupts the narrative before Molina can satisfy Valentín's desire to know more about Gabriel, the young waiter whom Molina loves from afar (Eng. 59, Span. 66, Archivos 53), and to the third footnote, since the reader must stop just short of finding out whether Valentín, who claims that he doesn't remember any films, will indulge the indisposed Molina by recounting one for him (Eng. 97, Span. 102, Archivos 86). The second motivating factor is a need or desire to fill a void or a lack in the text;[12] that is, some footnotes appear at moments when something needs to be added or clarified and neither of the interlocutors seems fit to provide an answer. Both motivations are present in the first footnote. Thanks to the interruption, on the one hand, there is a delay in the action, since the reader must wait to hear the rest of the story about Gabriel. On the other hand, the footnote explains something that had remained unexplained or unexpressed in the text, since the asterisk appears when Valentín, at once intrigued and uncomfortable by the references to Molina's love interest, confesses to Molina that he hardly knows anything about homosexuals: "I know very little about people with your type of inclination" ("yo de gente de tus inclinaciones sé muy poco") (Eng. 59, Span. 66, Archivos 53). The footnote begins to fill this void as it furnishes information about the subject, though the receiver of the information is presumably the reader, not Valentín.

The fourth and fifth notes occur—as does the first—as a result of a reference in the text to tendencies or behaviors typical of homosexuals. The fourth interrupts the dialogue at a moment when Molina, who likes to think of himself as a woman, refers to himself in the feminine, asking Valentín (and this gendered language is only obvious in the original Spanish), "you think I'm some kind of nitwit?" ("¿te creés que soy tan tonta?") (Eng. 129, Span. 133, Archivos 111). The fifth also comes about when Molina uses another "cliché of femininity," as Puig has called these expressions ("cliché de la feminidad"; qtd. in Chamorro), describing a bolero to Valentín as divine (Eng. 137, Span. 141, Archivos 121).[13] These references seem to promote footnotes that return to the topic of homosexuality, and what is described in them can be understood as an official or scientific explanation of Molina's behavior. In the fifth footnote we find a discussion of the fixation of the male homosexual with the maternal figure, while in the text, especially in the pages that follow or run along with the footnote (Eng. 137–43, Span. 144–48, Archivos 122–24), Molina appears to be putting into practice the theories expressed in the margins. He—like the protagonist of his fourth movie, who has a special weakness for the mother (Eng. 116, Span. 120, Archivos 101)—here behaves in a clearly motherly fashion as he cares for Valentín during his illness.

All the footnotes are in some way or another related to the text. Alicia Borinsky notes this connection, but considers it a hostile one:

> The dialogues between both [Valentín and Molina] are an open challenge—because of their discursive makeup—to the narration launched by the footnotes. The figure that suggests most aptly what this encounter reproduces is that of war. (49)

While there are features that distinguish the footnotes from the main text (their language and tone, the absence of dialogue, their distribution on the page, etc.), the similarities outweigh the differences. I turn now to these points of contact. The sixth footnote, whose theme is sexual repression, is motivated by an allusion to the repressive tactics employed by prison authorities. Molina, who is engaged in conversation with the warden and whose words reach the reader through a transcription of that conversation, suggests that they stop poisoning the seriously debilitated Valentín. The warden's answer is categorical: "Molina, you underestimate the proficiency of our personnel here. They know exactly how to proceed in these matters. Weigh your words, my friend" ("Molina, usted está subestimando la capacidad de nuestros técnicos. Ellos sabrán cuándo parar y cuándo seguir. Tenga más tino, compañero") (Eng. 151, Span. 154, Archivos 133). The answer highlights the degree to which the prisoners are at the mercy of the police, and the patronizing words of the warden, who ironically calls Molina "compañero," only point to the warden's contempt. At that exact point, the prompt appears, leading us to a footnote that clearly deals with repression. It is positioned as if to comment on the aggressive exchanges occurring in the text. The note begins:

> In *Three Essays on the Theory of Sexuality*, Freud points out that repression, in general terms, can be traced back to the imposition of domination of one individual over others, this first individual having been none other than the father. (151)

> En *Tres ensayos sobre la teoría de la sexualidad*, Freud señala que la represión, en términos generales, proviene de la imposición de dominación de un individuo sobre otros, siendo ese primer individuo no otro que el padre. (154, Archivos 133)

These words bring together the themes of political and sexual repression. From the absolute domination and false paternalism of the warden in the text, we jump to an analogous situation described in the footnote—the domination and repression of sexuality imposed by the paternal figure of authority.

The seventh footnote interrupts another dialogue, this time between Molina and Valentín. Because Valentín is ill and cannot concentrate on the movie his cell mate is recounting, Molina suggests that he rest, offering the advice, "—Then try not to think about it. That only makes it worse" ("—No pensés, que te hace peor") (Eng. 163, Span. 168, Archivos 146). These words give way to a footnote that, appropriately, deals with the theme of sublimation, a concept that describes the ways the subconscious expresses what has been repressed. The final two footnotes do not interrupt dialogue but instead are generated by moments of silence. The ninth one, the last, seems to take advantage of a pause in the dialogue (Molina puts off his narration of the movie about the zombies because Valentín wants to rest for a while [Eng. 205, Span. 209, Archivos 187]) to wrap up the running commentary on homosexuality. The asterisk that signals the eighth footnote appears next to an ellipsis, Puig's way of representing silence in the novel. Here the footnote breaks with convention insofar as it is not attached to a word and serves as a conclusion to the chapter. There is no return to the text in this instance because the footnote takes over and fills in for Molina, who feels rejected and hurt and refuses to speak any further to Valentín (Eng. 193–95, Span. 197–99, Archivos 173–75). The note fittingly addresses the instances of rejection experienced by homosexuals, again seeming to comment on what has just transpired in the text.

The second footnote, which I have left for the end because of the difference in its content, originates in a similar way to the ones just discussed. It takes place as a result of a pause in the narrative, this time when Molina decides to end his narration of the second movie because a sleepy Valentín does not seem to like it. Molina, clearly bothered by Valentín's lack of interest, warns him that he does not plan to continue recounting the movie, not even to say how it ends. Valentín is quick to accept his decision and ends the discussion with a curt dismissal (Eng. 81, Span. 88, Archivos 72). Following a brief "good night," the cell mates cease to speak, and it is then that the footnote appears. As with the first footnote, this one seems to fill a void. What Molina's pride keeps him from expressing is provided in the lower margin of the text, though in a different guise and directed to a different audience. Unlike the rest of the footnotes, this one is introduced by a heading that purports to explain its content. It claims to be not a continuation of Molina's narration of the movie but the center pages of a "press-book" from Tobis-Berlin Studios supposedly destined for its international distributors. After the first paragraph, however, it becomes evident that this fragment is not from a typical press release. The studio text presupposes a reader who knows the story of Leni (that is, of the movie featuring Leni) up to the exact moment where Molina left off his narration. The prisoner's last words refer to Leni's preparations to leave for Berlin (Eng. 81, Span. 88,

Archivos 72), and the first words of the footnote address Leni's arrival in the German capital.

Now released from the constraints of Molina's spotty memory and Valentín's dislike of superfluous details and the movie's pro-Nazi content, the footnote flows freely, with lengthy descriptions and quotations of political speeches that in no way resemble what would be expected of Molina or of the pages of a press release.[14] The account, moreover, is not about the actress who plays the role of Leni but about the character of Leni, who is readying herself for a movie that is to bear the title of "Destino" ("Her Real Glory" in the English translation). Thus the so-called press-book about this "superproduction," far from taking the reader to a real text, advances further into the fictitious world created by Molina.[15]

While the rest of the footnotes, as I have indicated, have a connection or a correspondence with the text, this one goes beyond that, since it becomes a continuation of the text. And I use the word *continuation* not only because the information communicated in the footnote forwards the plot of the movie recounted by Molina but also because the footnote, which ends with a promise to continue (Eng. 95, Span. 94, Archivos 77), actually returns later in the main narrative once Molina decides to go on with the film (Eng. 87, Span. 97, Archivos 79). One might even argue that both narrations, although separated by their layout on the page, become confounded. Hence in the second part of the story recounted by Molina, Valentín seems to know a detail—that Leni saw "the film about the two criminals . . . back in Berlin" ("la película de aquellos criminales que le mostraron en Berlín") (Eng. 91, Span. 99, Archivos 80)—that had been explained only in the footnote (Eng. 91, Span. 91, Archivos 74). We thus find that at this point Molina takes for granted that Valentín knows something that has only been uttered in the subordinated text. And Valentín, who calls Molina on the slightest oversight, here allows Molina, without so much as a question, to refer to a detail about which he could not possibly have known. Thus it becomes clear that, just as the footnote presupposes and requires information in the main text to be understood fully, the main text also presupposes and requires the information in the footnote.

This example allows us to see the connection between the three principal narrative levels of the novel: the diegetic (the events that occur within the world of the narrative), the intra- or metadiegetic (the events described in the films that Molina narrates), and the extradiegetic (found in the "scientific" or pseudo-scientific information introduced and mediated in the footnotes). This relation could be explained neatly by using the term "collaboration" and distinguishing between two types—narrative and thematic. We can speak of narrative collaboration because the film about Leni continues in the second footnote, while the second footnote also continues in Molina's subsequent narration of the film. In all three narrative levels (text, film, footnote), there is a thematic collaboration as well. We find it in the story of the two prisoners when Molina agrees to collaborate with the prison authorities (Eng. 82, Span. 91–92, Archivos 74–75); it is also present as a theme in the footnote where we hear about Leni's work as a spy (Eng. 95, Span. 94, Archivos 77); and it reappears in the movie narrated in two parts in the text, where the heroine, who bears a German name and a French surname, must decide whether to side with the Nazis or the maquis. It is interesting to note, also, that these narratives are to be understood as simultaneous activities, since Molina agrees to collaborate with prison authorities while Leni does the same with the Germans. While Molina is away from the cell, speaking to the warden and agreeing to spy on Valentín in exchange for his freedom, the hiatus between the first and second part of the movie takes place; at that very spot, the second footnote—detailing Leni's "conversion" as a German spy—appears.

This example brings to light the variety and importance of the narrative voices in the novel. The anonymous narrator of the second footnote, who "collaborates" with Molina to recount the story of Leni, is—like Molina—a traditional narrator, one who handles adroitly the third-person narration and the *dicendi*, who is both subjective and omniscient, quotes extensively, and maneuvers long descriptions. In the remaining footnotes, similarly, the narrative voice is as subjective and adept, since the periodic interventions are much less arbitrary and marginal or unrelated to the plot than might have been imagined. Not unlike the narrator of the footnotes, Molina has firm opinions and is able to speak deliberately about the information he conveys. As a whole, the narrative voices in the novel, though well differentiated both by position and purpose, manipulate and shape the main story that unfolds before us. Through them Puig is able to tell his masterful tale with all the advantages and privileges of the most consummate of omniscient narrators.

NOTES

[1] The back cover of the Spanish edition states, "The outline of *Kiss of the Spider Woman* at first glance appears to be extremely simple. Without the external intervention of the author, the book is shaped as a succession of dialogued scenes between two interlocutors. . . ." ("El esquema de *El beso de la mujer araña* es, en su apariencia superficial, de una extremada simplicidad. Sin intervención externa del autor, el libro se configura como una sucesión de escenas dialogadas entre dos interlocutores. . . . ").

[2] For definitions of the narrative levels identified by Genette, see *Figures II* (202) and *Narrative Discourse* (227–31). As mentioned in my introduction, while Genette's theory of narratology is helpful in unpacking thickly layered texts, his terminology can be daunting; I therefore prefer to use it minimally in most of my classes, especially in those for undergraduates. I have also found that Shlomith Rimmon-Kenan's narratological synthesis makes Genette much more accessible.

[3] I don't mean to imply that Valentín has no say in any of the decisions regarding the narration of the films. In fact, he objects several times because he wants to have a more active role (see, e.g., Eng. 15, Span. 21, Archivos 15). In addition, it is he who sets the schedule for the narration of the films, limiting them to the evenings (Eng. 9, Span. 15,

Archivos 11) and halting the narration when he is distracted (e.g., Eng. 37, Span. 43, Archivos 35) or when he prefers to study (Eng. 96, Span. 101, Archivos 85). Nevertheless, except for Valentín's mandate to avoid erotic descriptions and discussions of food, Molina determines what and how much is to be narrated.

[4] I concur with Alicia Borinsky's assessment that the movies are for Molina an instrument of seduction (65 and elsewhere). See also how Ross Chambers, no doubt inspired by Baudrillard, puts it: "Puig's novel . . . illustrates the power of narrative to change relationships" (9), and "seduction, producing authority where there is no power, is a means of converting (historical) weakness into (discursive) strength" (212). By contrast, Maurice Molho characterizes Molina as a calculating and manipulative homosexual who sets out to trap or seduce Valentín with his bedtime stories. My understanding of Molina's "seduction" and "manipulation" differs fundamentally from Molho's.

[5] The quotation is in italics, following the style of the novel. Here and elsewhere, Puig sets the characters' thoughts or interior monologues in italics. These are instances of what Dorrit Cohn calls a "quoted monologue," when a character's mental discourse is provided, thus creating "the illusion of a fiction that 'tells itself' without the ministrations of a narrator" (14, 169).

[6] On the rare occasion that Valentín does not remember where they left off (as Molina gets ready to wrap up the Mexican movie, which they know will be their last together), his lack of recollection becomes a clear indication of his change in mood. While he grudgingly agrees to hear the rest of the movie, he is despondent and perhaps even angry (although he denies it), probably because Molina has refused to take a message to his fellow activists (Eng. 260, Span. 256, Archivos 231).

[7] The six songs whose lyrics are quoted in the movie are "Flores negras," written by Sergio de Carlo (Eng. 227, Span. 229–30, Archivos 207); "De un mundo raro," by José Alfredo Jiménez (Eng. 231–32, Span. 234, Archivos 210); "Ausencia," by María Grever (Eng. 237, Span. 240, Archivos 218); "Estoy enamorado," by M. Ruiz Armengol and J. A. Zorrilla (Eng. 240, Span. 243, Archivos 220); "Noche de ronda," by Agustín Lara (Eng. 241–42, Span. 244, Archivos 221); and "Me acuerdo de ti," by Gonzalo Curiel (Eng. 257–58, Span. 261–62, Archivos 235). See Leal and Orovio for the lyrics of all but "De un mundo raro."

[8] After having sex with Valentín, Molina also felt transformed, as if he were neither male nor female (Eng. 235, Span. 238, Archivos 217).

[9] Traditionally, footnotes contain the quotations that corroborate the corresponding observations in a text (see Benstock; Balderston, "Sexuality"). In Kiss of the Spider Woman the only footnote that contains quotations is, ironically, the second one, the most "fictitious" or least scientific of all.

[10] Regarding the footnotes Pamela Bacarisse similarly observes, "Their quasi-scientific nature gives them an impersonal, even objective air, but they are not, of course, either impersonal or objective" (Necessary Dream 114).

[11] For Suspended Fictions, Lucille Kerr verified the authenticity of the names, titles, and references mentioned in the footnotes and concluded that the mention in the final note of Anneli Taube and the eloquent elaboration of her theories are the product of Manuel Puig's imagination (230n6; 224–26; 235n40). In an interview with Ronald Christ in 1979, Puig acknowledged that he invented one of the excerpts: "All the notes are quotations . . . except for one" (qtd. in Bacarisse, Necessary Dream 250n66). See also Balderston, "Sexuality."

[12] I use the word "text" not with the formal meaning that Genette gives it but simply to designate that part of the novel that excludes the footnotes.

[13] See Chamorro. The word "divino" appears often in the novel and is always uttered by Molina.

[14] In an interview with Marcelo Coddou Puig describes how he came to fashion the press release: "I wrote it in a style copied from Nazi documents: I spent two weeks in New York Public Library, the one on 42nd Street, reading Nazi propaganda. That's how come, for example, the 'citations' taken from speeches by the Füehrer and Goebbels are genuine" (12; my trans.).

[15] There is yet another intertext to the footnote. The Nazi propaganda, which Puig carefully researched to create this second film, doubtless included the work of another Leni—Leni Riefenstahl, the director of *Triumph of the Will*, the official record of the Nazi Party Congress held in Nuremberg in 1934 (acknowledged by some as the greatest documentary film ever made), and *Olympia*, about the 1936 Olympic Games in Berlin. It is this second film that leaves its greatest imprint on *Kiss of the Spider Woman*, especially in the "continuation" of the second movie found in the second footnote of the novel. There are many points of contact, such as Leni's "gymnast's arms" ("brazos de gimnasta") (Eng. 84, Span. 89, Archivos 72), and the description of the German youth: "These are the young gymnasts of both sexes, dressed in black and white for their gymnastic exhibition. And then Werner says, as if to comment upon this truly olympic vision at which Leni cannot help but stare in awe . . . " ("Son jóvenes atletas de ambos sexos, vestidos de negro y de blanco en sus exhibiciones gimnásticas, y entonces Werner dice, como comentario a la visión olímpica de la que Leni no puede quitar los ojos . . . ") (Eng. 88, Span. 90, Archivos 73).

Building a Web:
The Construction of Meaning
in *Kiss of the Spider Woman*

Richard Young

Structure and Meaning

Works of literature are artifacts assembled to represent or reproduce aspects of social life through the medium of a rhetoric that locates them within given literary traditions and against a set of formal characteristics. The structure of a novel, how it is organized and how its various elements are interconnected, is therefore a function of how the world it represents is viewed. This structure, far from serving merely as a container into which content and meaning are placed, also produces meaning. Who tells the story and how it is told, what manner of discourses are employed and how these are textualized are consequently relevant to how the reader approaches and understands the represented world. Such considerations are especially pertinent to *Kiss of the Spider Woman*, a novel that confronts the reader with an unconventional narrative structure. Accordingly, in this essay I identify the novel's principal structural elements and comment on how these require an active reader to be drawn into the text and be an accomplice to the generation of meaning.

Narrative Discourse and the Reader

Although novels are usually thought of as narrative texts containing a story told by a narrator, *Kiss of the Spider Woman* has no overall or primary narrator. It contains the following autonomous documents or discourses, none of which tells a story in ways that novels conventionally do: fragments of an ongoing conversation, occupying most of the book, between Molina and Valentín, two men confined to the same prison cell; fragments of interior discourse of these two characters; conversations between Molina and the prison warden, one of which includes a list of provisions to be bought for Molina and written by him; the warden's side of a telephone conversation with his superior; two written reports, one a summary of the record of the two men prepared for the warden, the other a report on Molina's movements after his release from prison; a one-sided exchange between Valentín and a member of the staff of the prison infirmary, followed by Valentín's interior delirium; and, finally, a series of long footnotes. Although these elements are autonomous, lacking a narrator to introduce them, contextualize them, or relate them to one another, they have a certain order determined by the kinds of discourse they are as well as by their content and how they contribute to the novel.

With the exception of the footnotes, these texts, mainly spoken, may all be attributed to characters in the fictional world of Molina and Valentín, and all of them contribute to how we know and understand their world. The footnotes, by contrast, do not originate with any of the characters and stand outside their fictional realm. Among the texts that do derive from the world of the two men, there are the prison cell conversations between Molina and Valentín, in which Molina's narration of the stories of several films is embedded, the interior discourses found throughout the novel, as well as the exchange in the infirmary and Valentín's hallucination, which have formal characteristics comparable with those of the prison cell conversations. The other texts that belong to the fictional world of Molina and Valentín are produced outside the context of their cell. They are formally different from the prisoners' conversations not only because they include written texts but also because the passages of spoken language are codified in ways that distinguish them from the oral discourses of Molina and Valentín in the prison cell. I return to these differences, but first I take up the general status of the reader.

As a literary narrative, *Kiss of the Spider Woman* is a liminal text that does not fit conventional taxonomies easily (see Martin 130–51), although it does belong to a range of varying experimental narratives that had become increasingly numerous by the time Puig published *Kiss of the Spider Woman* in 1976. His novel contains no single point of view to which the different elements of discourse enumerated above are subordinated, neither an omniscient third person located outside the world of the text who narrates what is going on within it nor an internal narrator who appears within the narrative as one of its characters or as a contemporary witness. Nevertheless, standing behind the work is the figure to whom Wayne Booth referred as the "implied author" (70–71), the figure whom the reader has in mind as the one responsible for the creation of the novel, regardless of its narrator, and who is often identified with the real author. For *Kiss of the Spider Woman*, there are reasons to identify this figure with Puig. It was his fourth novel, and by then he had established an inclination for narratives configured as a collage of texts, as well as a predilection for reference to the phenomena of popular culture. He had also become recognized as an author whose engagement with fiction was extraordinarily personal, as Suzanne Jill Levine's biography has shown. For the reader of his novels, however, the author's presence is implied rather than overtly stated. It is the reader who brings the author to the work but must also engage the novel in a way that goes beyond the identification of its autobiographical sources. Citing Julio Cortázar's felicitous reference to the figure of the accomplice reader, Jonathan Tittler argues that "the reader must be seen as more than routinely engaged in a collaborative act" (61). In effect, *Kiss of the Spider Woman* is a kind of do-it-yourself novel that involves the reader in its construction. In the absence of a primary narrator, the reader must supply the missing overarching perspective, perhaps attributing it to Puig as implied author, and must decide how the various texts that constitute the novel are related to one another and what kind of meaning they convey collectively. This responsibility makes the reader a

willing participant in a process of entrapment, seduced by what the novel initially holds out and then caught in the web represented by the continuous
process of reading.

Conversations in a Prison Cell

There are several reasons for giving the prison cell conversations between
Molina and Valentín primacy and taking them up first in a consideration of
how the different discourses figure in the organization of the novel. The conversation that opens the novel provides the point of departure from which
the reader begins to construct the fictional world. As the novel proceeds, the
conversations dominate the text, filling the first seven chapters of the eight in
part 1 and, with the exception of chapters 15 and 16 at the end of the novel,
occupying most of part 2. They offer a basic story to which the reader always
returns, and their presence is felt even when other kinds of discourse com-
mand attention.

The formal structure of the prison cell conversations places demands on the
reader quite different from those customarily made in works of fiction. The dialogue appears on the page as a screenplay or a dramatic text from which the
names of the dramatis personae have been stripped, and no authorial commen-
taries are provided to contextualize the dialogue in the way that stage directions
do. From the first page, the reader confronts a conversation without knowing
any of its contexts: who the speakers are, where they are located, or why the
topics they are discussing are of any concern to them. As the pages are turned,
the reader must track the alternating voices of the two speakers and develop
the structure of the conversation entirely from their speech. The comparison
with a dramatic text is valid, but not exact, since the conversations are conveyed
in a more radical form than either drama or the novel conventionally allows.
Because Puig presents them without the mediation of either narratorial or
authorial comment, greater emphasis falls on language, and greater immediacy
is given to the construction through language of the real and imagined worlds
of Molina and Valentín.

The intelligence of the implied author stands behind it all, of course, but this
form of unmediated presentation creates an illusion of independence, allowing
the points of view of the two characters to dominate so that they appear to control the directions taken by their conversation. All these twists and turns create
an illusion of spontaneity, of a conversation apparently unfolding as a natural flow
of language punctuated by the silences of one or both of the speakers marked in
the text by suspension points. The organization of the conversations, however,
is anything but arbitrary. Their microstructure is based on a variety of discursive forms, such as extended commentary or narrative, question and answer,
and impromptu or calculated observation, that determine the sequence of each
conversation as a logical series of individual utterances alternating between the

two speakers. A principle of alternation also underlies the larger structures of the conversations: the content of the dialogues, and therefore also some of the more salient aspects of their form, swings between the narration of film stories and the discussion by Molina and Valentín of their personal situations.

This alternation between reference to the real and the imagined worlds of Molina and Valentín also provides the basic rhythm of the novel. Though some of the films were invented by Puig (see Kerr, *Suspended Fictions* 192–93; Campos, "Rostros"), they are real enough to the two characters, and Molina has seen them. The stories he tells from them belong, however, to the world of the imagination, distinguishable from the reality of the prison cell and the lives of the two prisoners before they were incarcerated. Yet the stories dominate their conversations, anchoring them in the same way that the conversations anchor the novel as a whole.

The novel begins not only in the middle of a conversation but in the middle of the first film narrative, *Cat People*. Thereafter, with the exception of chapter 7, each chapter in which the prison cell conversations figure includes a film narrative. (They occur in twelve of the sixteen chapters of the novel.) Moreover, the pattern first established in the telling of *Cat People*, a story in five fragments spread over two chapters, is more or less sustained by the narrations that follow. The pattern is such that the reader establishes Molina's film stories as the mainstay of the prison conversations. Indeed, the novel obtains much of its forward momentum from expectations either of the next segments of a film already begun or the beginning of a new one after another has ended.

Between the segments of film narrative Molina and Valentín talk about their real world. Their conversations range over a number of topics, of which the most significant are their affective relationships outside the prison. Their conversation also makes it possible to discern what is happening to them in the cell and to trace, in particular, their growing intimacy. Yet, although we might readily separate references to the real lives of the characters from references to the world of their imagination, the two subjects of their conversations are thoroughly intermingled.

The stories of the six films narrated in *Kiss of the Spider Woman* may also be thought of as framed narratives contained within the main story of the lives of Molina and Valentín. The basic structure underlying the inclusion of a story within a story, often referred to as "metanarration" (see Martin 135), has precedents in the *Thousand and One Nights*, Chaucer in England, Bocaccio in Italy, María de Zayas and Cervantes in Golden Age Spain, and, closer to home for Puig, the embedded narratives in Ricardo Güiraldes's *Don Segundo Sombra* (1926). Yet, as with much else in Puig's novel, there is little in the author's use of the structure that is strictly traditional. Since *Kiss of the Spider Woman* has no narrator, there is no formal passage from one narrator to another. Instead, the metanarrations are fully integrated into the conversations between Molina and Valentín as utterances spoken by the former. At the same time, Valentín asks questions and offers comments not just about the content of the stories but also about how Molina is telling them, and Molina himself repeatedly alludes to aspects of his narration. The film stories are consequently self-reflecting. They contain references to their own narration and composition and might be termed what Linda Hutcheon has called "narcissistic narratives" (17–35), narratives that reveal the process of their own creation. This structure is so central to Puig's novel that to examine it further would lead us to the heart of his work, to an understanding of the presence of the film narratives and how, through the roles of Molina as storyteller and Valentín as an active, questioning listener, the novel acquires the character of a commentary on storytelling. It would also lead us to explore the relation between imagined and real worlds and to understand, in particular, how the imagined, in this case popular film and its narratives, may become a source for the modeling of real behavior and sentiments.

Thickening the Plot from Other Sources

Although the preceding comments address some of the elements in the organization of the prison cell conversations, they do not clarify their bearing on the plot of the novel and their relation to the other texts it contains. The conversations are not merely a mechanism for conveying stories and talking about them; they are an integral element of a plot. For the first seven chapters, however, it is difficult to see how what takes place in the prison cell might be constructed as a plot, if a plot, albeit in simple terms, is construed as a series of events surrounding a conflict that may be sequentially organized by chronology or causality. Molina and Valentín argue repeatedly, but there is no significant issue that sets them against each other or unites them in a common struggle. They have differences of opinion, a consequence of differences in outlook, personality, history, and identity, but there is no central conflict around which to organize the disparate elements of their conversation. The dramatic interest of these chapters lies more in the drama of the film narratives and in the tension that arises between the two characters in the light of their reactions to the film stories and the general differences between them.

The principal organizing feature of the first seven chapters is a chronology developed through variations on a pattern established in chapter 1. This chapter contains three segments of *Cat People*. As each of them ends, Molina and Valentín bid each other goodnight (e.g., Eng. 9, Span. 15, Archivos 11) and anticipate the continuation of the story on the following day. Each segment of film story and conversation about the film and other topics is also separated typographically from the next by three lines of suspension points running across the page (or by extra space in the English translation). With some variation, this pattern is maintained for most of the chapters consisting of prison cell conversations. The underlying rhythm of the novel is thus set by a chronology formed by the passage from one day to the next and by the passage of two or three days in most chapters, although, strictly speaking, the movement, most often, is from one night to the next. The film narratives, like bedtime stories, are told at night after the rituals of the evening meal and the extinguishing of lights in the cell. As in the *Thousand and One Nights* or Chaucer's *Canterbury Tales* and similar anthologies, storytelling becomes a nightly routine, not just a way of passing time, but a way of constructing it. The first seven chapters of the novel are thus organized principally as an iterative chronological sequence. What elements of causality are contained in it are a function of the ordering of the segments of film narratives—the end of one entails the promise of the beginning of the next—or of the incidents in the daily life of the prisoners in their cell. As yet, however, none of these elements can be configured as a plot. All this changes with chapter 8, the last chapter of part 1 in the Spanish text, in which several new elements are introduced.

The change in the format of the text is the most immediately perceptible difference. There is still no primary narrator, but the implied author's presence is felt more strongly, and the sources of written and spoken texts are identified. The chapter begins with a brief report (Eng. 148–49, Span. 151–52, Archivos 131) prepared, as indicated in its heading, by a secretary for the warden of sector 3 of the Buenos Aires Penitentiary where Molina and Valentín are detained. It contains a paragraph each on Molina and Valentín with details of their legal and prison histories, including mention of their having shared the same cell since 4 April 1975. In the text of the dialogue following this report, principally between Molina and the warden, the identity of the speakers is given according to the conventions of a drama or film script. Subsequent interviews, in chapters 11 (Eng. 197–99, Span. 201–04, Archivos 181–83) and 14 (Eng. 245–50, Span. 249–54, Archivos 267–29), are similarly formatted, and the sources of other later texts (the warden's side of a telephone conversation with his superior, a list of provisions prepared by Molina, and a surveillance report on Molina in chapter 15) are all clearly stated. Of the texts derived from outside the prison cell only Valentín's delirium in chapter 16 follows the format of the prison cell conversations.

The change in format emphasizes the official nature of the discourses involved. The speakers are identified not by names but by their rank or station, which establishes them in the roles they play in relation to one another. Molina's interventions in the interviews in the warden's office are designated by the term *procesado*, the same term used to identify him after his release in the surveillance report. The change in perspective is also signaled in the warden's reference to Valentín by his last name, Arregui, instead of the first name familiar to the reader from the prison cell conversations, where Molina and Valentín are able to speak as themselves in a freer, more natural discourse. In addition to their formality in format and language, the interviews with the warden also reveal information about the two prisoners that could not have been derived from their conversations in the prison cell. In particular, the discovery that Molina has agreed to obtain information from Valentín in exchange for his own release makes it necessary to reconstruct the significance of the prison cell conversations and to recognize the plot underlying a narrative sequence that had hitherto appeared to depend principally on its chronology. The confinement of the two men in the same cell, Molina's movie narratives, the symptoms of food poisoning suffered by them both after eating prison food, and Molina's care for Valentín were clearly all part of Molina's attempt to ingratiate himself with Valentín in a carefully calculated plan of seduction designed to extract information. Once this motivation is discovered, the second part of the novel cannot be read in the same way as the first, even if Molina's eventual intentions are unclear and the open ending of the novel leaves several questions unanswered about the two prisoners (see Kerr, *Suspended Fictions* 191–92, 202–04; Tittler 55–57). From the reader's perspective, the relationship between the two men now hinges on a dramatic conflict in which lives are at stake.

A View from the Footnotes

The texts discussed in the preceding paragraphs are clearly part of the fictional world of Molina and Valentín. They are derived from characters who also belong to this world, and they contribute to our understanding of it by broadening the context of the prison cell conversations. The footnotes that punctuate the novel, however, function differently. An asterisk draws attention to the notes, attributed not to a source located within the prisoners' world but to an implied author situated outside it. Language reinforces the separation of the world of the author of the footnotes from the fictional world of the characters in the novel, both in the way the footnotes are written and the content they convey. The footnotes have the formal structure of standard written Spanish, in contrast to the direct speech of the two inmates, most of which is eminently colloquial Argentine Spanish and has an order typical of impromptu conversation. Moreover, the notes are not used in the same way as footnotes in other works of literature or in formal or scientific discourse, where they are conventionally introduced as a kind of parenthetic commentary intended to elaborate on a point of language or content. After the first two footnotes, the justification for the footnotes is slender, not to say arbitrary.

The first note occurs in chapter 3, prompted, apparently, by an exchange between Molina and Valentín:

> —Just a minute, Molina, you're really wrong. If I ask about him it's because I feel somehow . . . how can I explain it?
> —Curiosity, that's all you feel.
> —That's not true. I think I have to know more about you, that's what, in order to understand you better. If we're going to be in this cell together like this, we ought to understand one another better, and I know very little about people with your type of inclination.*   (58–59)

—Un momento, Molina, estás equivocado, si yo te pregunto es porque tengo un . . . ¿cómo te puedo explicar?
—Una curiosidad eso es lo que tendrás.
—No es verdad. Creo que para comprenderte necesito saber qué es lo que te pasa. Si estamos en esta celda juntos mejor es que nos comprendamos, y yo de gente de tus inclinaciones sé muy poco.*

(66–67, Archivos 53)

The asterisk at the end draws attention to the note that begins halfway down the page and consists of a commentary on D. J. West's discussion of theories of the biological origins of homosexuality. The note appears to address questions raised by Valentín but answers them for the benefit of the reader in a style quite different from the one in which they were raised. The pretext for the second footnote seems even slimmer. About halfway through chapter 4, after Molina's narration of a second segment of a film made in Nazi Germany, he and Valentín bid each other goodnight (Eng. 82, Span. 88, Archivos 82). An asterisk then draws attention to a footnote that consists of a publicity release issued by a film studio reporting on the visit of the French actress Leni Lamaison to wartime Berlin and the production of a film titled *Destino* (*Her Real Glory* in the English translation [82]). There is an implied connection between the content of the footnote and the story of the film told by Molina, but his narrative provides no direct pretext for the introduction of the note, whose author offers no comment allowing the reader to contextualize it further. These are also the conditions under which the remaining seven footnotes in the novel are introduced. Since they are all concerned with a discussion of homosexuality, they may be taken as a commentary on Molina's identity and conduct and are generally relevant to topics that figure in the continuing conversation between him and Valentín, but they are inserted at apparently arbitrary moments. In chapter 5, for example, an asterisk takes the reader to a footnote when the prisoners are talking about choosing their next film narrative (Eng. 97, Span. 102, Archivos 86), but the content of the note continues the theorizing of homosexuality begun in the note in chapter 3. Similarly, a footnote in chapter 11, on theories attributed to a certain Danish doctor, Anneli Taube, is signaled to the reader without any apparent pretext, just as the two main characters are about to take a break from their conversation (Eng. 205, Span. 209, Archivos 187).

Although the footnotes seem to appear arbitrarily, their presence overall is entirely systematic. The notes are clustered in chapters 3 through 11, one note per chapter. The notes are long, by any standards, each continuing across the bottom half of an average of three pages. The longest, in chapter 4, stretches over most of seven pages. Without entering into precise details of content, which have been addressed by others (see Colás, "Latin American Modernity" 90–93; Kerr, *Suspended Fictions* 219–26; Tittler 49–51), I concern myself principally with aspects of their general impact and implications for the organization of the meaning of the novel. It is evident, for example, that the reader can hardly ignore the footnotes. They are not the kind that can be taken in through a momentary glance to the bottom of the page. They absorb the reader, displacing the story of Molina and Valentín for pages at a time and reducing the space it occupies to just a few lines on some pages so that the footnotes do not so much complement the main text as run parallel to it, amounting to a counterdiscourse that the reader must integrate somehow into the novel. Integration, however, is likely to be obtained less by reconciling differences than by recognizing contrasts.

The footnotes offer a perspective on homosexuality derived from a review of theories and concepts presented in scientific writings, including those by West alluded to above, Sigmund Freud, Otto Fenichel (Eng. 137, Span. 141, Archivos 121), Wilhelm Reich (Eng. 153, Span. 155, Archivos 133), and several others. By contrast, the view on the subject that emerges from the story of the two prisoners arises from their conversation surrounding narratives from popular cinema, the lived experiences of a gay man (Molina), his identity, and the relationship developed between the two men in their cell. The story's view imposes itself more strongly than the footnotes' view. Not only do the texts that represent the experiences of Molina and Valentín dominate the novel; Molina's homosexual identity is already established on its own terms (see, e.g., Eng. 29, Span. 35, Archivos 29) before the explanations provided in the footnotes begin to appear. The footnotes, if only because of their length, endeavor to usurp the reader's attention, but they lack the life of the dominant text and are by nature a subordinate discourse from which the reader eventually turns.

The connection between the narrative and discussion of the German film in the main text and the publicity release presented in a footnote is similarly structured. The footnote is subordinate to the main text, appearing after Molina has already narrated two segments of the German film. The film enters the conversation between Molina and Valentín in the light of Molina's lived experience of it, and their discussion of it is personalized, derived from subjective reactions to it. The footnote deals with the production of the film, not unlike the way in which footnotes about homosexuality are concerned with its production, and it uses the codified discourse of the publicity statement and political propaganda embodying all the intentionality that such discourses imply. The difference between the text and its footnotes is thus akin to the difference between the subjective experience of a phenomenon and an attempted objective description of it. In the end, the reader is faced with two juxtaposed views that must be somehow reconciled or understood as a consequence of the contrast struck between them.

Building a Web and Constructing Meaning

It requires an active reader to bring together the footnotes and the main text, just as it requires an active reader to combine all the components of *Kiss of the*

Spider Woman and decide on its meaning overall, however relative the value of that meaning is. The world from the perspective of the footnotes is hardly that of the prison cell conversations, any more than these conversations remain untouched when set against the texts from outside the cell. Above all, meanings are unstable, both because perspectives shift and because the texts themselves are not entirely reliable. The footnotes draw mainly on historically authentic figures and their writing, but two of them are fabrications (see Colás, "Latin American Modernity" 90). The news release concerning the German film is a fiction, as is Anneli Taube, whose writings on homosexuality, discussed in the final footnote, are a hoax. Readers may or may not recognize the difference. Those that miss it will be caught in the deception, while those who see it are left to wonder about other transgressions of fact and other deceptions practiced in the novel: Molina's deception of Valentín and the warden's deception of Molina; the film narratives as a false model of reality and the origin of the narratives themselves, not all of which, like the footnotes, are authentic. All is potentially deceptive, and there is a sense that the novel's characters and its reader are its willing victims.

Molina and Valentín willingly surrender to the film stories, just as the reader of the novel willingly surrenders to them and to the novel as a whole. The reader, of course, is conscious of how fictions deceive and how both Molina and Valentín have been trapped. In fact, Valentín has an intuitive sense of entrapment and expresses it through the metaphor of the spiderweb. Explaining his reticence to kiss Molina, Valentín remarks: "You're the spider woman, that traps men in her web" ("Vos sos la mujer araña, que atrapa a los hombres en su tela") (Eng. 260, Span. 265, Archivos 237). Two pages later the prisoners exchange a kiss, and Molina agrees to carry information to Valentín's comrades once he is released. The trap set by the prison warden has been sprung, and Valentín is caught. Or does he walk knowingly into it, as his identification of Molina as a spider woman seems to suggest? The second reference figures in Valentín's morphine-induced epiphanic vision of himself in the final chapter. In this hallucination resonant with Molina's film stories, Valentín sees a woman, as on a movie screen, who is described by Valentín's unconscious voice in a style that is pure Molina:

> *with a long dress on, that's shining, "Silver lamé, that fits her like a glove?"*
> *yes, "and her face?" she's wearing a mask, it's also silver, but . . . poor*
> *creature . . . she can't move, there in the deepest part of the jungle she's*
> *trapped in a spider's web, or no, the spiderweb is growing out of her own*
> *body, the threads are coming out of her waist and her hips, they're part of*
> *her body, so many threads that look hairy like ropes and disgust me, even*
> *though if I were to touch them they might feel as smooth as who knows*
> *what.*   (280)

> *con un vestido largo que brilla, "¿de lamé plateado, que le ajusta la figura*
> *como una vaina?", sí, "¿y la cara?", tiene una máscara, también plateada,*
> *pero . . . pobrecita . . . no puede moverse, ahí en lo más espeso de la selva*

está atrapada en una tela de araña, o no, la telaraña le crece del cuerpo de
ella misma, de la cintura y las caderas le salen los hilos, es parte del cuerpo
de ella, unos hilos peludos como sogas que me dan mucho asco, aunque tal
vez acariciándolas sean tan suaves como quien sabe qué.

(285, Archivos 257)

The image of a spider woman is more graphically elaborated here than in chapter 14, although the sensation of entrapment it conveys, with the accompanying feelings of attraction and repulsion, desire and danger, is the same in both cases. The location of the images at the end of the prison cell conversations and at the end of the novel places them at strategic points of culmination. The location of the second image in a context that recapitulates particular details of Molina's stories affirms that the earlier narrative has indeed brought us to this point. Each of his stories, viewed retrospectively, is a variant of the same basic theme of the dangers of attraction and desire, an exemplification, in other words, of the archetypal fate of the male spider, who is attracted to the female and killed by her after mating. The same theme is exemplified in the story of Molina and Valentín, whose encounter in prison is a story of attraction, desire, separation, and death in a world where, as in the world of the romantic hero or heroine of popular cinema, they are doomed from the start. Thus the reader who constructs these relationships perceives a frame story that reflects and is reflected by the stories it contains, a structure conventionally referred to as *mise en abyme*, or the mirror in the text (see Colás, "Latin American Modernity" 79–81). Such a reader, however, is not solely a distant observer, for the processes that engage Molina and Valentín in the stories of which they are characters, narrators, or active listeners are those that engage the author and reader of *Kiss of the Spider Woman*. It is the reader, after all, who, through the act of reading, not only constructs the web in which the characters are ensnared but is ensnared by the web woven by the author.

The High Stakes Adventure of Reading
(in) *Kiss of the Spider Woman*
Juan Poblete

> When I close a book
> I open life . . .
> I love adventurous books,
> books of forest or snow,
> depth or sky
> but hate
> the spider book
> in which thought
> has laid poisonous wires
> to trap the juvenile
> and circling fly.
> Book, let me go.
> > —Pablo Neruda, "Ode to the Book"

This essay on *Kiss of the Spider Woman* concentrates on reading *in* the novel. I start with a close reading of the first two chapters, where different aspects of reading and reading positions are enacted. The reading positions are those of the implied reader, the critical reader, and the pleasure-driven reader defined by subjective identification. I then move to the ways in which this novel complicates these distinctions and demands their simultaneous use and cross understanding. I end by deconstructing the exclusionary opposition of a popular reading mode and a so-called elite reading mode.[1]

The Reading Lesson

"Something a little strange, that's what you notice, that she's not a woman like all the others" ("A ella se le ve que algo raro tiene, que no es una mujer como todas") (Eng. 3, Span. 9, Archivos 7). Those are the first words of Puig's novel, and they are read here as a crucial metafictional warning. They are metafictional because they refer from within the text to the construction of the text itself. In this case, they allude to a (recommended) way of reading. They are crucial because they both structure and enable our relation with the text. They warn us to pay attention, to notice, to try to understand what seems otherwise strange and different in the text and in the characters. That these lines appear to be part of a dialogue whose participants have not yet been identified should also indicate how efficiently and effortlessly this novel will ensnare us, dragging us immediately into its plot. Unknowingly, we have become actors in something called *Kiss of the Spider Woman*. This nameless voice is also talking to us. We have been placed in the textually constructed subject position of the implied reader. We have been rendered a discursive effect. It is the voice of Molina, who is telling a story to Valentín, his cell mate. The story is communicated verbally, but it often insists on the multiplicity of codes and processes involved in an adequate understanding of its meanings. From this moment on, the text counts on our implicit presence and active effort to decode and recode the articulations between those different types of codes and texts. The absence of a third-person narrator, who traditionally ties the different textual voices and strands into a single textual fabric, makes our labor as readers even more crucial. An important part of the literary success of *Kiss of the Spider Woman* depends on this ability to make the reader simultaneously an effect of its discourse and an active part of a conversation where two subjects try to use and change the other only to discover that the meaning of their relationship depended less on its results than on the activity of engaging with each other and the other's discourses (not unlike the manner in which a book belonging to a reading formation is an open-ended yet socially located conversation between an author and his or her readers). Thus *Kiss of the Spider Woman* begins allowing us some insight into how literature as a social discourse works in our lives.

If we now go back to Molina and Valentín's conversation, we see how the first two chapters carefully develop a theory of reading and of reading subjects and thus a theory of literature.

> [Molina] . . . A little further off, near the giraffe cage, there's some boys with their schoolteacher, but they go away quickly, the cold's too much for them.
> [Valentín]—And she's not cold?
> [Molina]—No, she's not thinking about the cold, it's as if she's in some other world, all wrapped up in herself drawing the panther.

[Valentín]—If she's wrapped up inside herself, she's not in some other world. That's a contradiction.

[Molina]—Yes, that's right, she's all wrapped up in herself, lost in that world she carries inside her, that she's just beginning to discover.   (4)

. . . Un poco más lejos, cerca de las jaulas de las jirafas hay unos chicos con la maestra, pero se van rápido, no aguantan el frío.

—¿Y ella no tiene frío?

—No, no se acuerda del frío, está como en otro mundo. Ensimismada, dibujando a la pantera.

—Si está ensimismada no está en otro mundo. Esa es una contradicción.

—Sí, es cierto, ella está ensimismada, metida en el mundo que tiene adentro de ella misma, y que apenas si lo está empezando a descubrir.

(10, Archivos 7–8)

Although the schoolchildren and the teacher are quickly brushed aside, their presence—their implicit witnessing—reminds us of our own reading position as we observe how this story unfolds. Irena is sketching the panther, that is, she is representing it through particular artistic conventions and using a specific code; Molina is retelling a story he once saw as a movie; Valentín is trying to reconstitute the whole scene in his mind using his imagination (and so are we, the readers who read the writing). The subjects using the codes, the languages that allow the representations, and the surfaces where they take place vary. What remains the same is a structure of Chinese boxes, a *mise en abyme* that emphasizes the possibility of a world that is simultaneously out there and in the subject, a world where it's possible to be at once wrapped up in oneself and in another world. This world that so effortlessly combines the internal and the external is shared by the subject and the world of literature. Both are constituted by this dynamics of expression and repression that connects what is directly present with an other side at once absent and active. The two classic mechanisms of signification, metonymy (the organization of elements used in a certain discursive order) and metaphor (the evocation of what is absent by the discursive effect of what is present), come together to offer a picture of how the subject and literary meaning occur.

Valentín, like the reader, begins to inhabit vicariously this other world: "I picture her dark-looking, not too tall, really nice figure, and she moves like a cat. A real piece." ("Yo me la imagino morocha, no muy alta, redondita, y que se mueve como una gata. Lo más rico que hay.") To which Molina replies, "Who didn't want to get aroused?" ("¿No era que no te querías alborotar?") (Eng. 5, Span. 11, Archivos 8), reminding Valentín of his earlier counsel against erotic narrations. ("Look, remember what I told you, no erotic descriptions. This isn't the place for it." ["Perdón, pero acordate de lo que te dije, no hagas descripciones eróticas. Sabés que no conviene"] [Eng. 4, Span. 10, Archivos 8].) Molina also reminds his cell mate that he has a second side, an other side where his rationality gives way to his not-so-repressed desires. Not unlike classic cartoons of the little white angel and the red devil on Tom or Jerry's shoulders or, to give a more contemporary example, the two sides of the computer-generated Gollum/ Smeagol character in the *Lord of the Rings* films, Valentín and Molina come to represent two aspects of a split subject, perennially in need of dialogue and connection. Molina has repressed his political side but highly values his right to a gendered difference, whereas Valentín cannot acknowledge his desires because they go against his political convictions in the struggle for equality. Molina thinks he lives in the world of the movies; Valentín loves the "wrong" woman. One is the repressed other of the other (see Colás, *Postmodernity*). From this viewpoint, *Kiss of the Spider Woman* is one of the best practical introductions to our contemporary understanding of subjectivity. The subject here is a position in or an effect of other voices, ideas, and social discourses (movies; books; educational, child-rearing, legal, and political texts). In his or her interrelations with these multiple and evolving discourses, the subject learns to make sense of the self and to engage in a social performance of that subjectivity.

To unpack this subjectivity fully we need to understand a central metaphor in *Kiss of the Spider Woman*, namely, the cell, protected by bars and located in a socially oppressive context. Inside the cell, the two characters imagine that they have the power to know others, a power they display as they retell movie plots; their inner conflicts and desires actively produce new meanings. Thus the cell comes to represent both the limits and the possibilities of their agency as subjects and of the textual literary space. Max Weber once described capitalist modernity as an "iron cage" where the modern individual was subjected to the imperatives of bureaucratization and rationality and separated from the values of noninstrumental reason (181). In *Kiss of the Spider Woman*, the Marxist revolutionary and the gay subject, two historical agents who have embodied attempts at changing or refusing the alienating modern conditions of the individual (inequality and heteronormativity), first collide and then transform themselves in the spatial limits of the cell. Thus the cell functions as a semantic space structured by binaries such as inside/outside, visible/invisible, present/absent and replicates as a microcosm both the structure of the subject and the functioning of literature.

Sigmund Freud envisioned the constitution of the modern psyche as if it were a hydraulic structure where a dam acting as a barrier (originating in the Oedipus conflict) keeps some desires repressed and under pressure, thus constituting the unconscious. The unconscious surfaces through cracks in the barrier that he called symptoms (dreams, slips of the tongue, jokes; see Meltzer). Jacques Lacan debiologized (and debourgeoisified) Freud's understanding of the unconscious and the oedipal complex by reconceptualizing it in linguistic terms. The Lacanian unconscious is structured like a language (constantly and endlessly producing meaning by the mechanisms of metaphor and metonymy or deferral and displacement). The subject is the always partial result of this process of signification, a moment, an effect or a position of stasis in a constant discursive flow (see Meltzer).

The cell in *Kiss of the Spider Woman* is thus a textual spatial surface for the representation of the subject-formation drama. As in the Oedipus myth, Molina and Valentín come to discover the other inside. To do this, they share a series of movies whose signification they have to elucidate in an extended deployment of close reading.[2]

The Reading Lesson 2

Kiss of the Spider Woman is a story told through the retelling of remembered movies, as well as through boleros, official transcripts, dreams and hallucinations, and psychoanalytic footnotes referring to real and invented authors. In this sense *Kiss of the Spider Woman* is less a traditional novel than a discursive patchwork, an amalgam of multiple threads that can be connected in heterogeneous ways. To that extent one could say that *Kiss of the Spider Woman* offers unprecedented access to the discursive production of meaning in and through literature. In the first two chapters of the novel and through the retelling of the Jacques Tourneur film *Cat People* (1942), Valentín and Molina develop at least two different ways of reading the same text.

> [Valentín]—Who do you identify with? Irena or the other one?
> [Molina]—With Irena, what do you think? She's the heroine, dummy. Always with the heroine.
> . . . .
> [Molina]—And you Valentín, with who? . . .
> [Valentín]—Go ahead and laugh. With the psychiatrist. But no making jokes now, I respected your choice, with no remarks. Go on.
> [Molina]—We can discuss it later if you want, or tomorrow.
> [Valentín]—Okay, but go on a little more.
> [Molina]—A little bit, no more, I like to leave you hanging, that way you enjoy the film more. You have to do it that way with the public, otherwise they are not satisfied. On the radio they always used to do that to you. And now on the TV soaps.
> [Valentín]—Come on.   (25–26)

> —¿Con quién te identificás?, ¿con Irena o la arquitecta?
> —Con Irena, que te creés. Es la protagonista, pedazo de pavo. Yo siempre con la heroína.
> . . . .
> —Y vos Valentín, ¿con quién? . . .
> —Reíte. Con el sicoanalista. Pero nada de burlas, yo te respeté tu elección sin comentarios. Seguí.

—Después lo comentamos si querés. O mañana.

—Sí, pero seguí un poco más.

—Un poquito no más, me gusta sacarte el dulce en lo mejor, así te gusta más la película. Al público hay que hacerlo así, si no no está contento. En la radio antes te hacían siempre eso. Y ahora en las telenovelas.

—Dale.   (31–32, Archivos 21–22)

The crucial term here is *identification*. It refers to the effect of narratives (cinematic, literary, etc.) on the spectator or reader. Valentín fancies himself in the position of the critical spectator capable of untangling the discursive web in a professional, noninvested way. Molina fancies himself as the heroine whose larger-than-life beauty and feelings advance the action. For both men reading has been turned into a technology for the formation of subjects. The difference is one of emphasis. While reading psychoanalytically or in a Marxist fashion seems to analytically emphasize the rational-scientific uncovering of the truth of social reality, reading for pleasure seems to place a premium on the forms of libidinal investment the reading subject develops with the text or in connection with the text. The difference is that the psychoanalytic or Marxist approach is closer to the Enlightenment view of reading as a formative tool for accessing information, whereas the pleasure-seeking approach, in a more romantic, expressive vein, highlights the internal processes generated by reading in the subject.[3] There is a long and complex line of thinking about this distinction that cannot be examined here. Suffice it to say that it has been crucially used to distinguish between the fundamental mechanisms of high culture and popular culture. While the benefits of high culture are said to be based on critical thinking and distancing, the pleasures of popular culture are said to depend on a more sensual and direct identification with the feelings and passions being represented. Unsurprisingly these two poles have also been gendered: the active, rational pole is described as masculine and characteristic of high culture, and the uncritical, feeling-based one is seen as feminine and dominant in popular culture. In 1963 the Argentine writer Julio Cortázar (in)famously described these two types of readers as the "lector hembra" ("female passive reader") and "lector cómplice" ("active, participatory reader").[4] Some ten years later the Caribbean critic Stuart Hall talked about three possible ways of decoding a text encoded in a particular ideological situation: the hegemonic position, operating inside the dominant code and coinciding with it; the negotiated position, which accepts the macroterms of hegemonic ideology while it understands the message as situated in micro or local conditions; and the oppositional position, which detotalizes the message from its preferred code to retotalize it in an alternative critical frame. Valentín and Molina frequently play with these positions and their possible combinations throughout the novel.

If we now consider the death of Irena's male psychiatrist, who crossed the line between the analytic-detached and the participatory-engaged positions, and the death of Irena, unable to control her inner feelings and killed by her other self, we begin to see how the dichotomy high/low, masculine/feminine starts to unravel. As the novel progresses, neither position is seen as satisfactory. *Kiss of the Spider Woman* then proposes two fundamental postulates: first, that the binaries masculine/feminine, reason/feeling, high culture / popular culture, critical distance / emotional investment must be undone if the true location of the subject and of literature in mass mediated times is to be understood and, second, that the masculine/feminine, resistant/passive binaries mistakenly presuppose an always already constituted and stable subject whose essence, preexisting one's engagement with social discourses, determines a fixed and unilateral reading position.

Irena's tragic destiny is the first in the series of movies told in *Kiss of the Spider Woman* and reveals the particular, sophisticated narrative mechanism of the novel. The film plots collectively advance the action of the central story of Valentín and Molina by anticipating their respective complex destinies.[5] That is to say, the intertextuality offered by mass and popular culture pushes forward the elements of the central story. Thus the popular culture elements used by high culture end up taking over and occupying all the narrative conventions of high culture. Their supposedly separate semantic procedures (suspense, clear and exaggerated stories, and direct identification, on the one hand; intricate cross-referencing, formal complexity, and active demands on the reader, on the other) become indistinguishable or confused. Looking at the long quotation above, we can see the supposedly uncritical Molina recommending a critical conversation on the issue of spectator identification while controlling the means of narrative production; at the same time, the allegedly critical distance of Valentín turns into an all-consuming passion for the story, an anxious urge for more narrative. If the psychiatrist's reading mode was based on depth (everything has to be read, symptomatically, as a sign of something else, a deeper meaning that demands uncovering), Molina's direct identification with the numerous heroines is based on breadth (an experience that is lived multiple times). Contemporary lives and discourses, *Kiss of the Spider Woman* pragmatically shows us, require a sustained use of both depth and breadth because "if you study something, you transcend any cell you're inside of" ("si estás estudiando algo, ya trascendés la celda") (Valentín, Eng. 78, Span. 85, Archivos 70), but "there are reasons of the heart that reason doesn't encompass" ("hay razones del corazón que la razón no entiende") (Molina, Eng. 259, Span. 263, Archivos 236). So when in the episode of poisoning, the tables are turned and a strong, maternal Molina has to care for a weak, infantilized Valentín, both of them are reborn, this time carrying inside a more recognizable and operative aspect of the other. By the end of the panther story, this transformation is already becoming evident:

> [Valentín]—I'm sorry it's over.
> [Molina]—So what, I'll tell you another one.
> . . . .
>
> [Valentín]—I'm sorry because I've become attached to the characters. And now it's all over, and it's just like they died.   (41)

—Me da lástima que se terminó.
—Y bueno, te cuento otra.
. . . .

—Me da lástima porque me encariñé con los personajes. Y ahora se terminó, y es como si estuvieran muertos.   (47, Archivos 37–38)

Reading Revolutions

According to Guglielmo Cavallo and Roger Chartier, there have been three revolutions in the history of reading in the West. The first two are classic and have structured the field in ways that it now seems appropriate to complicate. The first reading revolution was the predominance of silent reading when the printing press made the book the dominant format for reading. The second revolution was the transition from intensive to extensive reading when the printing press became mass-market and industrialized toward the end of the Euro-American eighteenth century. Intensive reading was characteristically exemplified by religious reading and especially by the reading of the Bible: a few texts read over and over in a deep hermeneutical exercise. Extensive reading was a less rigorous, faster reading of many texts circulating widely in the new industrialized market. Intensive readers were supposed to be focused on quality, whereas extensive ones settled for quantity. The last reading revolution has been brought on by the advent of computers. Electronic reading (and writing) has come to question many of the defining aspects of our modern reading formation: juridical notions such as copyright and authorship and aesthetic categories such as integrity, stability, and originality.

Kiss of the Spider Woman seems to tackle all three revolutions. While in 1976 computers had not yet produced the form of electronic reading now familiar to us, Kiss of the Spider Woman seems to anticipate the logic of the hypertext (which itself combines two older forms such as the volume or roll and the codex), where multiple links take the reader from one narration or form of discourse into a different one while their semantic connections or hierarchical organization are left for the reader to ascertain. More interesting are, perhaps, the other two reading revolutions that take place in Kiss of the Spider Woman. Valentín's concentrated silent reading of his political texts interrupts at first the many movies playfully narrated by Molina. That is to say, every time his Marxist intensive reading begins, our pleasure of the extended film stories is interrupted. Serious writing and film start then in this oppositional relation: you can have one or the other but not both. Critical distance and direct identification are in this context polar opposites; they are contrasting mechanisms that belong to two separate spheres of engagement. In fact, Kiss of the Spider Woman, like recent studies on the history of reading, works toward a full hybridization of both modes, deconstructing their antinomic presentation. Intensive readings fully coexist with extensive ones. Genre readers' devouring their extended list of favorite books in a summer is as intense as Molina's experience of multiple films. This undoing of cultural hierarchies is not an accident but a reflection of the historical location of the novel's genesis and publication.

Before this extraordinary meditation on our investments in narratives of all kinds, Puig had published three partly autobiographical novels. *Betrayed by Rita Hayworth* (1968) dwells on homosexuality and identification with the movies. *Heartbreak Tango* (1969) focuses on pulp fiction, serialized radio soaps, popular music, and small town love life. *The Buenos Aires Affair* (1973) has as one of its central characters a man who kills a homosexual in a sexual encounter gone violent and subsequently joins the Communist Party. When conceiving *Kiss of the Spider Woman* in the 1970s Puig—who in the 1950s had lived under what he described as the authoritarian and homophobic regime of Juan Domingo Perón—lived outside Argentina. By 1976, the year of the book's publication, the country was under the brutality of a new military dictatorship. Hence, by the time of his writing *Kiss of the Spider Woman*, the connections between the formation of the subject, narratives, and the violence and possibilities of politics (sexual and otherwise) had been sufficiently developed in Puig's life. These questions received their masterful summa in the form of a novel.

Around 1976 Latin American fiction was undergoing a crucial transformation. The classic novels of early capitalist development in the first third of the twentieth century had pitted man (seen here as a civilizing masculine agent) against nature (seen here as a feminine force in need of reining in and proper exploitation), whereas the 1940s and 1950s had seen the emergence of social narratives that dwelled on the issues brought about by the rapid so-called modernization of life in the continent: issues ranging from indigenous questions and displacements or migrations to cosmopolitanisms and urban vernacularisms. The 1960s and early 1970s had been the time of the Boom novels, which, in attempting to tell some of the central macrostories of a continent (from civil wars to transnational companies, from revolutions to political corruption, from aristocratic to bourgeois/proletarian times), became the first truly Latin American novels and joined a modern hemispheric publishing market (created, paradoxically, by Spanish international companies). To this history of the Latin American literary imaginary, Puig, and others such as Luis Zapata and Severo Sarduy, added not only a queer perspective but also a central engagement with a different modernizing force. Along with the state, the city, and the national bourgeoisie came the national and international mass media, which, in no less forceful a way, had been shaping the sensibilities of twentieth-century Latin Americans. From this viewpoint, the Boom itself could be seen as the result of a market development that turned literature into a mass-market international Latin American commodity and generated a reading public of hemispheric potential. Literature became Latin American at the same time it became a mass-mediated discourse.

Puig's early oeuvre made this dynamic between literature and mass media a central component of his novels. Puig understood that cultural transformations in modernity have also often sparked gendered cultural debates. The history of mass popular culture has been accompanied, in different contexts, by a remarkably consistent pitting of the dominant high culture—conceived as masculine and difficult and as labor intensive both at the moment of production and reception by a select few—against an always emergent popular culture, conceived as feminine, fast, easily produced, and easily consumed by the amorphous many. In writing a novel without a narrator, with a number of juxtaposed, contiguous, and imbricated discourses of different cultural provenance, Puig mixed the logics of conventional literary reading (intense analytic close reading) with those of mass-mediated culture (extensive subjective identification through, for example, cinema's star system, which provides us with imaginary alter egos onto which our desires and anxieties can be projected). By placing Molina and Valentín in a cell, having a one-on-one extended conversation, Puig created a highly concentrated version of the interactions of individuals and society in the discursive constitution of modern subjectivities. By having oral narration (both as production and as reception) as the central mechanism fueling the plot and by combining written and visual (if narrated) discourse, he forced us to view literary narration as only one of narration's relevant current forms and the literary variety of subjectification as only one of many present in the daily life of contemporary Latin American subjects.[6] Finally, by having the two protagonists exchange their destinies and die at the end of the novel as victims of state violence—one dreaming his impossible escape in a filmlike manner, the other killed in a war he hardly understood—Puig reminded us of the political economy surrounding this utopian encounter in a prison cell. All close readings of the novel must also come to terms with this, its final reading lesson.

The Chilean sociologist José Joaquín Brunner has wondered about the future of sociology in an era of failed metanarratives and suspicion toward macrovisions, when both the novel and the World Bank seem to describe the complexity of contemporary life more compellingly ("Sobre el crepúsculo" 28). Margaret Somers and Gloria Gibson have also talked of narrative as the other of sociology: from its own disciplinary viewpoint sociology generates explanational theories, whereas narrative offers space for descriptive discourses. Somers and Gibson propose that narrative is constitutive of our social being, that our identities and social actions are constituted by what they call emplotted stories, which have not simply representational but also ontological value (41).

In late modernity, Puig discovered, individual originality at the level of both authorship and readership was always the result of a retelling of social discourses, the subject was always work in progress, and literature could help us understand the whole process. Like Scheherazade, whose predicament Molina and Valentín enact so powerfully, *Kiss of the Spider Woman* teaches us a crucial reading lesson: we live because we tell stories whose meanings are, to a point, up for grabs and in need of constant interpretation in a field of complex power struggles. The stories are about ourselves, the world, and others. When the stories end, so does life.

In the end, what Pablo Neruda was referring to in his written poetic "Ode to the Book" is a tension or a dynamic between literature and the subject in the world. Books trap us in their spiderwebs of textuality and connections, moving us seemingly away from the world, but in so doing they open up new vistas of our world and of ourselves. Or, to put it in more precise terms that Puig perhaps would have approved, books allow us to see the fabrics of our lives in the world and their multiple investments and dependence on forms of narrative, literary and otherwise.

NOTES

[1] This essay is based in part on my experience teaching *Kiss of the Spider Woman.* Literature 1 is a big, writing-intensive lecture class; it fulfills general education requirements and is one of the literature majors' two mandatory classes at the University of California, Santa Cruz, where I teach. It is taught in English and is supposed to introduce students to the close reading of literature in different genres and across different epochs. My version of it is a Latin(o/a) America–based syllabus that jumps from short fiction to drama, from Sor Juana to Neruda, from Carolina Maria de Jesus to Richard Rodriguez. At the very core of this class, I have placed *Kiss of the Spider Woman.* My goals in this class are many. First, I want to decenter a particular understanding of the universality and atemporality of literature and literary values. Second, I want to teach a refined understanding of close reading and to make evident some of the limitations of a conventional use of this critical tool. Here is where *Kiss of the Spider Woman* becomes the centerpiece of my effort. I devote two of the class's ten weeks to a detailed reading of the novel. I mention this pedagogical context partly because it suits the nature of the Approaches series but also because it allows a full understanding of the ways in which this particular use of the semiotic possibilities of *Kiss of the Spider Woman* determines here a concrete activation of some of its (many) potential meanings. The classroom setting, as Tony Bennett has reminded us, uses the texts in particular ways to produce particular effects on specifically conceived subjects in the university, or, more generally, the school system, one of the most structured contemporary reading formations. He defines a reading formation as "a set of discursive and intertextual determinations that organize and animate the practice of reading, connecting texts and readers in specific relations to one another in constituting readers as readings subjects of particular types and texts as objects-to-be-read in particular ways" (70). Thus the signification of *Kiss of the Spider Woman* is as much in the text as it is in the reading conventions and practices that are used in a particular context for the elucidation of its meanings.

[2] Although the bibliography on Puig is extensive, I have found Colás, Levine, and Speranza particularly useful for my reading.

[3] I have elsewhere shown how, at least in Latin America, the modern national literature class was created in different contexts toward the end of the so-called long nineteenth century, in a pedagogical effort to constitute a nationalized written space for the expression and control of the (national) self. During the first third of the twentieth century literature (and writing) at this specific school level played a very important role in the state-sponsored constitution of a national hegemonic identity (see Poblete). Later the new mass media would add the out-of-school time to the processes of national formation

in the two paradigmatic cases of Argentina and Mexico, where strong national culture industries such as radio and film were complemented by the work of international mass media such as Hollywood films. Puig himself grew up in Argentina in the midst of a particularly intense version of these processes.

⁴ Cortázar later apologized for the unfortunate patriarchal names of his categories.

⁵ Think, for example, of how Leni's conflict between love and politics is solved by bullets, the zombie is sacrificed for the sake of others, or love conquers seemingly insurmountable differences in the *Enchanted Cottage* story. (This last film can be read as our moment of access to some of the most important generative procedures of the novel.)

⁶ It is thus no accident that *Kiss of the Spider Woman* has generated a film and a Broadway show. Its spectacular dialogic nature does not simply lend itself nicely to adaptations of this kind, it is itself constituted in dialogue with these other forms of contemporary popular culture.

Breaking Away from the Readership Cult: The Reception History of *Kiss of the Spider Woman*

María Eugenia Mudrovcic

The challenge of *Kiss of the Spider Woman*—to readers in general but especially to teachers of undergraduates in the United States—is how and how not to read the novel. I confront this challenge, since these students tend to deal with "Third World stuff" by distancing themselves from what they see as predictably happening in faraway places like Latin America. An in-class screening of Héctor Babenco's 1985 film version of Puig's novel will only intensify this feeling. Shot in English with American actors and based on a script written by Leonard Schrader, the film *Kiss of the Spider Woman* ultimately ends up being, despite its Latin American director, a Hollywood film about Latin America. Yet the impact that the movie had on Puig's literary reputation cannot be underestimated (Kerr, "Manuel" 330; Speranza 122). After it was shown at Cannes and nominated for four Academy Awards, the novel became his best-known work and defined Puig as a spider woman–type of writer. For many, *Kiss of the Spider Woman*—a fictional text that talks about movies, desires to be a movie, and seems to fulfill its own desire through Babenco's commercially successful film—has become, almost by default, Puig's most "lucky text" (Norris 179).

But this somehow happy ending must not erase the less glamorous beginnings, when the novel was banned in Argentina back in the 1970s. Manuel Puig traces in detail the uneasy fate of his first books in "Losing Readers in Argentina," a literary and political memoir he read at the 1984 Index of Censorship Conference. The story is relatively well known now: following the almost unnoticed publication of *Betrayed by Rita Hayworth*, his second book, *Heartbreak Tango*, became an instant best seller, but Puig's honeymoon with his national readership, though sweet, was too short-lived. It only lasted until 1973, when his third novel, *The Buenos Aires Affair*, was seized during Héctor José Cámpora's term on grounds of "pornography," and Puig, out of his country at the time, decided "never to go back" ("Losing" 56). By 1976 no Argentine publishing house dared to undertake the publication of *Kiss of the Spider Woman*—a novel that "irritated the [ruling] junta [military] very much" by presenting a homosexual and a political activist in a Buenos Aires prison, "each seeking to change reality in his own way" (56). The book ended up being published in post-Franco Spain by Seix Barral, then the most prestigious literary press in the Hispanic world, but (there is always a "but" in Puig's troublesome route to literary consecration) "the reviews were lukewarm, and the novel did not arouse any great interest" (56). Years later Juan Goytisolo talked about the "distrust, scorn and rejection" produced by Puig's *Kiss* during a "moralizing and sectarian" period in which anything coming from Latin America was expected to assume an outspoken and unequivocal position in favor of the revolution. Certainly Puig's portrait of a left-wing activist seduced by the cinematic arts of his "apolitical and homosexual cell mate" was far from complying with the clichéd image of what a Latin American Marxist-Leninist was intended to do and to be for the European intelligentsia (Goytisolo 121).

In France, *Kiss* was submitted to Gallimard, but the publishing house rejected it (even though Puig, "according to the contract, owed them a book" [Letter to Cabrera Infante, 26 Feb. 1977]) because the reader's report signed by Héctor Bianciotti was "horrendous," claiming, among other charges, that it "wasn't well written" (Levine, *Manuel* 302). Thanks to Severo Sarduy's mediations, the novel was finally published by Seuil in 1979, became a best seller soon after, and in 1981 was included in university curricula nationwide. The successful reception of *Kiss* (which did not appear in France until some scenes with sexual content were censored [Levine, *Manuel* 305]) was nonetheless quite atypical.

In Brazil, where the novel was printed without the footnotes, its fate followed the path of distrust described by Goytisolo, but this time militant gay groups were offended by Puig's portrait of Molina as a lightweight and banal queen instead of a heroic character. In the yearly lists of books produced by Brazilian media for 1982, *Kiss* was completely ignored with only these two infamous exceptions: *Leia livros*, after consulting five renowned literary critics, only mentioned Puig's novel once to discredit it as a "commercial adventure," while *Istoé* listed *Kiss of the Spider Woman* under its insidious column "Mistakes of the Year" (Puig, letter to Rodríguez Monegal, 3 Jan. 1983).

In the United States, the resistance generated by *Kiss* was also discouraging for Puig. According to Thomas Colchie, *Kiss*'s translator and later Puig's literary agent, an unwritten policy that prevented books with homosexual content from being highlighted in major newspapers was regularly followed until the publication of John Cheever's *Falconer* broke the ice in 1977, and novels like *Kiss* started to find a place in the catalogs of highly respected publishing houses such as Knopf. After a difficult translation process ("[the English translation] is giving me the willies. . . . I thought it would be easy, but the kitsch voice of Molina doesn't come through in direct translation, and you have to re-create it entirely," Puig complained in a 1977 letter to Cabrera Infante), the first reception of the novel by mainstream New York media was, to say the least, rather tepid. The *New Yorker* (key for New York audiences as well as for Puig) decided not to back its former intention of publishing an excerpt of the novel, replacing *Kiss* by Guillermo Cabrera Infante's *Three Trapped Tigers* at the last moment. In the *New York Times*, Christopher Lehmann-Haupt spent a good half of the one-third-page coverage devoted to Puig's novel questioning both the "clumsy academic style" of the footnotes and the translation that "makes Molina and Valentin sound unnaturally stilted and indistinguishable from each other." Lehmann-Haupt's final remarks about the book were far from laudatory:

> Still, Molina's richly melodramatic movie plots lend the dialogue an entertaining, if artificial, narrative drive. And the combined effect of the

footnotes and the dialogue keeps you thinking so hard, you barely realize you are not being moved.

In the *New York Times Book Review,* Robert Coover not only seemed reluctant to back Colchie's "stiff and hasty" translation ("[i]t fails to capture Mr. Puig's easy colloquial flow, and the voices of the two very different protagonists are not distinguished" [31]), he was also more openly critical or skeptical about the novel itself, panning *Kiss* as "a rather frail little love story that Mr. Puig's fans will perhaps find thin and disappointing" (15). Months after *Kiss's* release in the United States, it was clear that among the New York media *Christopher Street* stood alone in championing the book. Ronald Christ's cover-story interview in the April 1979 issue spotlighted Puig "as a hot celebrity in gay New York" (Levine, *Manuel* 319) and acted as a counterdiscourse for the criticisms that the novel had raised elsewhere. Yet regardless of the obvious efforts made by *Christopher Street,* at this point any attempt seemed useless in refuting disparaging remarks about the novel or about Puig (years later Jaime Manrique would recall how New York mainstream "could not forgive a major author of 'the boom' for coming out with a gay novel" [17]). As a result of *Kiss's* failure, Puig could not find a United States publisher for his next novel, *Pubis angelical,* and it took him four years—an unprecedented amount of time for a Latin American Boom writer—to get *Kiss of the Spider Woman* published in a paperback edition.

Puig was convinced that there are two types of books, those that die and those that live on. And if at first *Kiss* was a flop with intellectuals and critics everywhere, it turned out to be one of those books that live on (Manrique 18). The troublesome route *Kiss* transited at its beginnings changed course when the movie version opened a sudden and unexpected path to commercial success and critical acclaim for Puig. Jaime Manrique would later recall this turning point as a type of Aladdin's genie lamp effect:

> [A]t age 52, Puig was "hot" again. In fact, he was more famous than he had ever been. All his books were reprinted again. For the first time in a long career, he was financially secure. He was finally receiving the accolades he craved. . . . [W]hatever the quality of Babenco's version of *Kiss,* Puig should have been delighted with it since it restored his international reputation. (18–19)

Manuel Puig needed to wait almost ten years after the book was first published in Spain—the time it took for Babenco's film version to be released—to be able to say about the novel:

> [E]lsewhere it was to become my best-known work—I am now known as the author of *Kiss of the Spider Woman* . . . now I am published in Japan, Israel, Cuba (at last), Sweden, Poland (at last)—but I'm of no interest to my fellow-countrymen . . . I'm read in translation. ("Losing" 85)

Is there a price to be paid—as Puig seems to suggest—for being of interest to readerships other than his local Argentine audience? What are the losses sustained when one becomes a writer in translation? Or, to address the most notorious "translation" of *Kiss of Spider Woman*, is Babenco's film the kind of movie Puig's story sought to be? A quick answer to this last question can be found in a letter Puig also wrote in 1985:

> The movie. A bomb, without the slightest nuance, Babenco was a nightmare; as soon as I had given up the rights he disappeared, and to avoid me he fell into the clutches of a United States scriptwriter (Paul Schrader's brother, equally a drag) and then into the clutches of William Hurt, who totally brainwashed the idiot Babenco and turned everything into a typical Scharade, slow and lugubrious, while Miss Hurt played a tortured neurotic New York queen, just as pathetic as she is in real life. Anyway, they cut away the most important part of the story, which was the queen's joie de vivre, and all the humor. [Raúl] Juliá was better, even though they killed the part. They also killed off the motivations that made the story believable. The way it ended up, Valentín might be bisexual or God knows what. Anyway, whatever little remained seems to have reached the audience, which at least helped sell more books.
>
> (Letter to Rodríguez Monegal, 30 May 1985)[1]

It is clear that Babenco's movie is not the kind of movie Puig desired his story to be. In the process of film retelling, some of the changes implemented by Babenco could be considered subtle, but others were not, like those Puig regrets in his letter, and produced a radical change of color, humor, and meaning in the story. Obviously Puig was hoping to find a Pedro Almodóvar, but he met Babenco instead. Feeling uncomfortable with the gay topic, "which Babenco thought might be too much for mainstream audiences" (Levine, *Manuel* 333), he limited the number of sex scenes to one (although in the novel they take place over the course of several nights), making it unclear if Valentín is acting out of compassion or something else. Also, Molina's film repertoire is reduced to only the Nazi propaganda movie, shifting the novel's stress from the equating of sexual desire with death to the topic of a woman's betrayal of a man and a country she loves. Needless to say, the multiplicity of roles played by Sonia Braga (Leni, Valentín's girlfriend, and the fantasy spider woman at the end of the movie) not only displaces the gay focus of the novel but also helps project a generic idea of Braga as a campy incarnation of the ideal woman. And last, Molina's looks and behavior experience a gradual change: Hurt ceases to act as the drag queen with dangling earrings and a barrette in his hair, as he appears in the first scene, and ends up, following his appearances in gray cell clothes (not gender marked), dressed in conventional male attire among a street crowd after his final release from prison. At this point, it is easy to agree with Robert Sklar's conclusion: "Through both performance and costuming, the film seems to be saying that Valentín's reciprocating his love (as well as their discussions about what a 'man' is and does) [has] made a man out of Molina" (39).

Clearly, the movie leaves the viewer with the impression that the force of love is able to wash away any queer behavior or revolutionary ideas, making Molina act as less of a queen and Valentín as less of a revolutionary. Shifted from the 1970s in Argentina to an indeterminate Brazilian present, Babenco's setting probably benefits from the easy presumption of an existing generic state of repression in contemporary Latin America. In Puig's novel, Valentín had been arrested for "promoting disturbances" among strikers at an automobile assembly plant. In the movie, Valentín is only a revolutionary by (if such a thing is possible) contiguity: he is a journalist whose only crime consisted in giving away his passport to an old revolutionary leader. The rationale behind Valentín's association with an armed cadre remains unclear, as do Molina's motives for contacting the armed group at the end of the movie, unless (following Sklar's speculations) one reads Molina's desire to join the guerillas as another step toward reinforcing his newly discovered "manliness" (39).

Undoubtedly the movie cleansed away both the joy and darkness that Puig's tour de force gave to political and sexual roles. But this reading does not erase the fact that, as Puig puts it, "whatever little remained [from the novel in the movie] seems to have reached the audience." During the first eight weeks in the United States, the $1.8 million production of *Kiss of the Spider Woman* generated $4.6 million, big box-office dollars that well surpassed any expectation for a small, foreign-made movie (Trachtenberg 134). How then can it be explained that while the book was banned in Argentina during the dirty war, the movie became a great success at precisely the moment when Ronald Reagan was launching assaults on the Sandinista revolutionary government in Nicaragua? One thing, however, seems clear: Babenco's movie refuses to back up the efficiency of revolution as a political or gender-based way to change. And here the film version of Puig's novel starts a trend that would be regularly followed during the 1990s by many Latin American films made for North American consumption, among them *Like Water for Chocolate*, *Amores perros*, and *Y tu mamá también*. But to cast Babenco's *Kiss* as a force for political appeasement can only miss what becomes the movie's major source of displacement. In Babenco's linear, redemptive, and sacrificial romance, love ends up playing the major role in the story, almost leading us to erase the role that politics (politics of cinema, gender, and an oppressive Argentine regime) plays in Puig's novel. What the movie ultimately tells its viewers is that love is, as Michael Boccia wrote, "the only way to conquer the oppression of a society and for people to achieve freedom and dignity" (424). The absolute trust that builds up in the transformative power of love is tied to the faith in the individual in a capitalist society, especially one eager to find a sentimental alternative to revolution. This reading supplied by the film also works against the novel's ideology, which refuses to melt into any equivocal humanism and repeatedly exposes an economy of seduction based on contamination and barter. Perhaps Babenco's movie is trying to satisfy politically correct expectations. If it is, Puig's *Kiss*, for sure, is not. By reducing everything to its essence, *Kiss*'s cinematic translation betrays that part of the novel that wants more than what is strictly essential or correct; Puig finds a partial solution in the campy delirium of excess. Obviously Babenco is aiming at something tragic but nevertheless aggressively moral; something, as Pauline Kael wrote in the *New Yorker*, that "makes a show of [the picture's] commitment to the highest human values. Puig's novel is saying that queens may be useless, silly window dressing, on the order of movie romances, but that can be lovely fun, can't it?" (61).

Kael is also right when she concludes that Babenco's drama is "as phony as the forties screen romances that Molina is infatuated with" (61). But I do not propose that we scorn Babenco's film in class. My main goal is not to work on what the film could not translate well from the novel but to work on what the novel gains from this bad translation. Reconstructing *Kiss*'s reception helped my students expose a final paradox: Puig's novel started to be read the way it was supposed to be read only because the movie failed in its translation. As Abraham Moles says about the educational uses of kitsch, "the simplest way to acquire 'good taste' is to submit 'bad taste' to a process of ongoing revision" (78). Thus if kitsch defines an "aesthetic lie" (Eco 84), it can, as such, be of definite didactic value: following Moles's optimistic approach, one can argue that an aesthetic truth is attainable through its aesthetic lie. In other words, Puig's *Kiss* can be accessed through Babenco's movie, as indeed happened when the film's release led to a Nobel Prize nomination for Puig, several homages to the author, and countless acknowledgments of his importance as a finally consecrated Latin American writer.

NOTES

All Spanish quotations are translated by Francine Masiello, unless otherwise indicated.

[1] The Spanish original of this passage reads: "La película. Un bodrio, sin la menor sutileza, Babenco fue una pesadilla, ni bien cedí los derechos desapareció y por evitar mi influencia cayó en las garras del guionista US (hermano de Paul Schrader, pesado como él) y finalmente de W. Hurt que lo colonizaron totalmente al zopenco de Babenco y así salió una schraderada típica, lentísima y lúgubre, la Hurt hace una queen neoyorkina torturada y neurótica, triste como es él en la vida real. En fin, le quitaron lo principal a la historia, que era la alegría de vivir de la loca, y el humor. Juliá está mejor, pese a que el personaje no existe más. Tampoco quedaron en pie las motivaciones que hacen creíble la historia. Así como quedó, Valentín puede ser un bisexual o vaya a saber qué. De todos modos lo poco que quedó parece que a la gente la toca, que sirve por lo menos para hacer vender más libros."

Puig's Poetics of Fusion

José Amícola

Kiss of the Spider Woman is Manuel Puig's great moment of narrative experimentation. Puig uses the compulsive dialogue sustained between two protagonists to allow the characters to unfold in their search for vicarious experience. The tension between the two forms the basis of a contrapuntal poetics that is maximized as the novel advances.

In the closed space of the cell (an analogue for the closed space of the novel?), Molina assumes the narrator's function, telling stories drawn from six Hollywood-style films of the 1940s. As a postmodern Scheherazade, Molina addresses, instead of a merciless sultan, an incredulous and resistant listener, one who refuses to suspend disbelief in the stories he hears. Valentín, the political activist who listens to Molina's tales, thus claims purity in a Cartesian way and, within the logic of the text, steers clear of the passive listener's role that is usually cast as feminine. In the tiny space of the cell that serves as an arena of discursive struggle, Molina becomes an almost anachronistic defender of oral tradition, typically identified with women (and linked to the style of telling fairy tales to children to capture their imagination), whereas Valentín finds himself filling the role of a modern and objective person, belonging to the late twentieth century and aiming to transmit information and leave personal experience aside. Yet rational individual that he is, Valentín—who wants to suppress his emotions and feelings—becomes anxious when he feels compelled to take on the part of the aggressive male and destroy those myths that his cell mate has forged. The gradual transformation of the characters becomes obvious as the novel progresses and leads to a fusion of identities that is central to Puig's project for his book.

Encounter, seduction, and fusion are the terms at play in *Kiss of the Spider Woman*. Let us advance slowly. The first important point to observe in Puig's narrative world is that the act of telling hides a complexity of meanings. As more or less careless readers, we bury ourselves in the first lines of the text, drawn in by the cadence of a voice that purports to tell us a story. Reading page after page, we slowly realize that the story in question is the plot of a Hollywood movie; at the same time, we learn that the narrator drags his attentive listener into his story as well, fused as one with us, the readers of the novel. We all are seduced by the tale.

The first story that Molina tells is a recycled version of Jacques Tourneur's film *Cat People*. The narrative shows a series of strange and secret messages that initially defy reader comprehension. At first, the reader believes, at least in principle, that the framed tale is frivolous and has nothing to do with the reality of the reader or with the lives of the characters in an Argentine penitentiary cell in the early 1970s. We find ourselves reading with the same pejorative slant that Valentín takes when he first hears the tale; we assume it is a mere secondary text that doesn't really deserve our attention. Yet by choosing *Cat People*,

Molina proves that he is not entirely banal or hopelessly condemned to bad taste. After all, critics now consider this movie a significant challenge to the formulaic horror films that we know.

Jacques Tourneur, the director, was able to build, despite the producer's demands, a work based on the visual ambiguity of the message (Friedrich 202). Tourneur's capacity for abstraction certainly attracts Molina. When he recounts the film to Valentín, Molina relates the feelings and emotions he experienced when he first watched the film. *Cat People* thus appears filtered through the consciousness of this second narrator, whose untrained eye has approached the film with a certain ingenuousness even though the multiple levels of meaning in the film have not been lost on him. We see these ambiguities of meaning at play in the famous scene of the movie in which the protagonist (Irena) is approached in a New York restaurant by an unknown woman with catlike features. The stranger acknowledges Irena in a foreign language as if to signal recognition among equals, but Molina is unable to decipher the greeting. Nevertheless, he understands that Irena's uneasiness has to do with a stigma that has now been exposed and that touches her most intimate fears: she belongs to an almost extinct and cursed race of people who turn into ferocious beasts, destroying those they love when the moment of sexual intimacy draws near. Looking for what the text does not say, we now know that the unknown woman of Tourneur's film utters a phrase in Russian—"moia sestra, moia sestra!" ("my sister, my sister!")—which leads Irena to panic. Today one thinks of this phrase as a subliminal sign of lesbian recognition, which could only have been articulated in the Hollywood of 1942 in a foreign tongue (Newman 31).[1] Beyond the implications of a sexual taboo, the scene also draws attention to Molina's performance as he tries to attract the interest of his listener and force him to accept a winking acknowledgement of a desire that cannot be spoken.

Molina leads his listener and readers to a strange moment in the film in which we are obliged to reconstruct some missing information. Neither Hollywood nor Puig supplies us with a translation of the unknown woman's greeting in the film, and Molina is incapable of perceiving that the sentence in Russian refers as much to a secret brotherhood as to a sisterhood that would exclude men. He can only intuit a strong power of exclusion; the ominous gothic tones that inscribe the phrase contribute to the mystery of the exchange. But this chain of associations that links Molina with Irena and Irena with the Russian speaker also extends to include the reader and Valentín. The multiple levels of listeners and speakers exemplify the complexity of what is being told. By referring to a Hollywood film language that is already doubly codified, Molina acknowledges an imminent danger, a sign of the gravity that later plays out in the erotic realm of the novel. Slowly, this level of reading becomes qualitatively more political (at least for the readers, insofar as we come to know much more than the characters of the novel).

Molina's first trick, then, is to identify with the figure of Irena. In a subliminal message to Valentín, Molina, too, belongs to a race of people who share something strange. Just as Tourneur's film sets up a game of hide and seek around questions of sexuality and shows us the double pull of sexual frigidity and desire, Molina creates this tension in the *mise en abyme* scene of the kiss (announced in the title of the novel), a symbol of submission and of the intimate connection between love and death.

Another interesting twist emerges from the situation in the jail cell. The two men kill time when one of them (and only one) decides to tell movie plots to the other. But the process takes an unexpected turn during the recycling of the second film described; after having identified with the cat woman in the first film, Molina now identifies with Leni, the French woman who collaborates with the Nazis. The film topic of double espionage introduces a new element in the jail cell (and in the novel) and complements the Hollywood repertoire with films of different national origins (European and Mexican). The film, which Molina calls *Destiny*, has a different formula from the first, principally because it is a Nazi propaganda film. The antihumanitarian charge of the film suddenly throws Molina and Valentín (as well as the readers of the novel) into the political realm, and the age of Hitler in Germany strangely touches on Argentine history in the 1970s. Beyond what is first made available to us through the narration of *Cat People*, in the Nazi film we have a decisive case of "communicating vases," as the surrealist André Breton used to say regarding the implicit connections among dreams and men that are always linked by desire. Here, we see the spaces of film and novel suddenly joined. It is not unexpected that Valentín is better equipped to interpret this film, given his experience in political analysis, and that his reading, different from Molina's, brings about the first clash between the two men. Valentín was not ready for the direct message of perverse seduction that formed part of the script of *Cat People*, but he is open to the message in the discussion of the Nazi film.[2] The two films, nevertheless, carry themes of betrayal and female protagonism that lie on both the superficial and hidden levels of narration.

Puig creates a pastiche of the Nazi film by taking his cues from the Third Reich productions starring the Swedish actress Zarah Leander (a star of 1940s German cinema). But when told through the voice of Molina, the political theme gives way to a critical irony about stereotypes of gender, an irony also observable in Molina's analysis of *Cat People*. These first two films belong to North American and German culture. Puig uses them, not unintentionally, as a springboard for echoing the discussions about gender and politics that were born in the United States and Germany in the 1960s and 1970s and left their marks in the following decades on an international map of gender debate. The fusion of national boundaries coincides indirectly with the criticism of the one-dimensional man who tries to ignore the political implications of his sexual preference.

Following an idea that is more evident in film and cultural criticism today, Puig reflected on the oppressive context for women and minorities of the 1930s and 1940s and the ways in which Hollywood cinema invented strategies to resist this oppression. Thus Hollywood, on one level, challenged the passivity of women. Even when they were surrounded by glamour, women in cinema of that period were always interesting characters, deserving of attention; they were presented as thinking persons entitled to certain rights (see, e.g., Cavell). The genre of film noir helps diffuse this image. Although noir was not managed strategically by Hollywood studios of the times, it is worth noting that films of this genre appeared en masse precisely in the oppressive years of the 1940s (Neale 151–64). These films reached Europe and France, in particular, as a complete package of Hollywood productions between 1945 and 1950 and caught the eye of continental critics who observed their common characteristics: a fatal sexual attraction, a perverse or sadomasochistic eroticism, and the characters' general sense of uneasiness in their world. Film noir revealed the fears, insecurities, and unhappiness of a whole generation (McCarthyism in United States politics would continue to fuel this disturbance). In its basic binary structure, film noir presented two types of women in conflict: the fatally attractive beauty and the respectable wife or girlfriend. One can also see in these films a repeated enactment of sexual desire that is built on stereotypical expectations of men and women, evolving from the asphyxiating climate of the gothic genre and transposed on a modern landscape.

Molina manages to create a common denominator among the six stories that he tells: they all depend on a dark and shadowy environment resembling the film noir context. In turn, this context suits the ominous hallucinations experienced by the two protagonists under the effect of drugs administered by penal "experts." Molina thus homogenizes the story, transforming into film noir even those films that originally did not belong to the genre: his gaze darkens the luminosity of the "racing car" film presumably made for men and turns the lights down in the film devoted to Nazi propaganda. Molina appears to have sought out this uniform darkness in the films he narrates to cast an obscure shadow over the prison cell that he shares with Valentín. This preference for the lugubrious surpasses any interest in the genre of the comedy or drag queen film, which would have been more logically appealing to a figure such as Molina: the Hollywood musicals (in the style of *Ziegfeld Follies*) or the light farces of marriage and divorce among the wealthy (such as *The Women*).[3] Molina offers so many alternatives that he submerges the readers in thought, obliging us to compare the different levels of narration, which are further complicated by the footnotes appended to the text. Seen in this way, the recycled films are not simply a form of escapism, despite what the two prisoners claim. Indeed, while the secondary structure of the stories is basically ominous and dark, the relationship between Valentín (hero) and Molina (heroine) shapes itself almost like a romance, whose fixed schema has been described by Janice Radway:

> The heroine's social identity is thrown into question; the heroine reacts antagonistically to an aristocratic male; the aristocratic male responds ambiguously to the heroine; the heroine responds to the hero's behavior with anger and coldness; the hero retaliates by punishing the heroine; the

heroine and hero are physically and/or emotionally separated; . . . the hero treats the heroine tenderly; the heroine responds warmly to the hero's act of tenderness; the heroine reinterprets the hero's ambiguous behavior as the product of previous hurt; the hero proposes / openly declares his love for / demonstrates his unwavering commitment to the heroine with a supreme act of tenderness, . . . the heroine's identity is restored.   (150)

The difference between Puig's novel and this fixed codification of romance lies in the explicit causality (not apparent in the romance genre) seen in the rapprochement of Molina and Valentín. After all, when Puig's heroine Molina, almost in maternal fashion, cares for the ill hero, the regression to a basic corporeality takes their relationship back to a primitive state of dependency. Another difference separating Puig's novel from the romance genre is the lack of a happy ending, the basic ingredient of romance. In *Kiss of the Spider Woman*, the conclusion brings us to the kiss of death, taking us back to the horror film genre that was introduced at the beginning of the novel. This horror goes deeper still, especially as we read the "scientific" seriousness (more a pastiche than a parody) expressed in the footnotes, the only evidence of an outside narrator who might be pulling the strings of the story. These notes put us in touch with the controversy about the origins of homosexuality, an issue of concern to intellectuals in the 1970s. The controversy would end when researchers in the United States depathologized sexual difference.

The other problem lies with Puig's undermining of the rigors of binary thought. Puig constantly works to unravel binary structures in the novel, dissolving the tensions between form and content and the usual stratification of different levels of narration (film plots, hallucinatory visions, and footnotes filter through a number of conversations and confuse the dimensions of social truths that the characters explore). In addition, Molina and Valentín are presented throughout the novel with interchangeable features so that each one eventually becomes confused with the other and loses specific physical detail. The kiss and sexual encounter exemplify this fusion.

Puig's manuscripts reveal an insistence on this idea of fusion.[4] Through this principle, Puig manages to forge an encounter of ideas of social responsibility with values of literary form, as evident from the title of the novel: the kiss, as a metaphor—not by chance, the visual climax observable in Hollywood film—of the physical coupling of the protagonists, is also a symbol of the union exhibited in all textual levels of the novel. Even the special presentation of dialogue sustained by the two characters of *Kiss of the Spider Woman* shows that no omniscient mediator can diminish the ambiguity of voices that the two protagonists supply. The manuscripts left by Puig and recovered after his death give evidence of this intention.

A concrete example of Puig's intentions is provided by a sketch of *Kiss* found among Puig's draft materials (*Beso*, Archivos 265–327). This outline of a proto-novel not only shows an idea in gestation but also fixes a clear date for the time of composition of the novel (Puig wrote his preliminary ideas on the back of an invoice addressed to him by Editorial Sudamericana and dated 26 March 1973). Here, we have the seed of the novel published in 1976, including the *mise en abyme* schema of the narrated films (Puig calls them "stories" and "representations"). In this original plan, he also gives us an idea of the triangulations of characters:

F(olle)   M(an)

woman

(Puig takes the word *folle* from the French, meaning literally a "madwoman" but also, as a common colloquialism, referring to an excessively feminine homosexual.)

Adding to this schema, Puig draws a second sketch in which he outlines three positions: Molina (Folle), Valentín (Man), and Marta (woman). Subsequent sketches reduce the triad "Folle-He-She" to the binary "She-He." This condensation erases Marta's role as a figure in the triangle and justifies on a compositional plane the shift in perspective of Valentín, who—at the end of the novel and in a state of delirium—imagines a figure with two faces whom he alternately refers to as Marta and Molina.[5] But there's more. In the novel, the supposed opposition of Valentín and Molina almost calls out in Spanish for the words *varón* (man) and *mujer* (woman). Puig shows here how one can exploit the combinatory power of proper names while playing metonymically with the connotations of opposites in Latin: *mollis* (sweet, tender, without energy, effeminate) and *valens* (strong, robust, vigorous, powerful). Hence, we have the effeminate *Mol*ina linked with the strong *Valent*ín.[6]

Puig's concern for naming is everywhere made apparent. In the manuscripts, we see two erasures: the political militant could have been called Juan, but Puig later expressed a preference for Roberto. Note in this choice the termination in –*to*, which seems to bring us back to the masculine and feminine poles of meaning that accompany name choice in Puig's earlier novels (remember To*to* and Mi*ta* in *Betrayed by Rita Hayworth*). Although Puig later eliminates the name Roberto, he nonetheless insists on calling the militant protagonist by his first name. In this way, the names of the couple—Molina and Valentín—link together two different social orders: the surname for the one and the first name for the other. This is not a chance event; rather, the social power of naming—the style of addressing men by their surnames and women by their first names—comes into play, significantly enough, in reversal. Puig insists on this double order of meanings that are later fused.[7]

The drafts of the final chapter of the novel shed light on the growing interchangeability of characters and the novel's broader social reach. In his delirium, Valentín thinks of the death of his cell mate, considering him a man of valor, but when we read through the scratched out words in the manuscript, we get the idea of the glamour of death. In effect, the deleted words in Puig's preliminary drafts leave us with the idea of a fusion of roles: death is stylized to the point of creating a charmed illusion, allowing us to consider Molina a valiant man, both hero and heroine of the novel. This melding is seen even in the connotations of vowels in Spanish—*o* for the masculine case and *a* for the feminine. Clearly, the names of the characters Molina and Valentín produce an inversion of *a* and *o* and upset the usual economies of gendered meaning: V*a*lentín and M*o*lina. The manuscript material reveals Puig as an author in search of the hidden molecules of meaning in language that produce the prevailing sexual economies of social life.

Finally, Puig's novel shows a melding of characters in their thoughts and speech. In the manuscript, Puig marks these internal meanderings as "comments" without clear identification of the speakers. Deliberately ambiguous, these vague phrases fit into Puig's larger scheme of things so that we are left with a contagion of personalities that overrides particular identities. In the same vein, one might point to Puig's new technique (as he describes his innovations) of using the textual footnotes, which appear to supply the scientific basis of Molina's homosexuality as well as reveal the reasons why Valentín might be considered perverse in the strictly Freudian sense. In this respect, the footnotes are about both protagonists and refer to the psychological bisexuality that inhabits all individuals. Carefully distributed throughout the text by the author so that they progressively occupy more space on the page (Puig shows this plan in his draft notes), the footnotes also call our attention to a visual structure of top and bottom. This disposition on the page is one more image to make visible the cross between nature (the natural sexual encounter between human beings regardless of gender) and culture (the scientific explanation and repression of sexual instinct). Nature is the linear flow of the novel; culture is our interpretative resources. Puig's text is a place of coexistence and fusion in which neither nature nor culture wins in the final game.

NOTES

This essay, including all quotations, was translated from the Spanish by Francine Masiello, unless otherwise indicated.

[1] See the studio photograph of this scene in Newman.

[2] Valentín, against all expectations, also assumes a perverse role when he takes the lead and wants to have an active part in the re-creation of Molina's films. Here, he reverses the traditionally passive, feminine role assigned to the listener.

[3] In this way, Puig links his character to his own filmic preference for the bizarre. In a personal exchange with the author, Puig once said that the film that had most influenced his childhood was the French detective story cryptically named after the central police station of Paris, *Quai des Orfèvres*, directed by Henri-Georges Clouzot (1947). Thus we might claim that Molina appears to be a cross between the consciousness of the author (Puig, attracted by the strange French cinema of Clouzot) and the personality of a character attracted by the film noirs of Hollywood. At the same time, Molina's tastes are in

tension with the preferences of a possible drag queen and the stereotype of a drag queen that the reader might have. For the meaning of gender in French cinema of the 1940s, especially in relation to Clouzot, see Burch and Sellier, 233–35.

[4] See the critical edition of *El beso de la mujer araña*, published by Archivos.

[5] Given all this, we come to understand why Puig erased the third character, Marta. After all, her presence meddles with the binary scheme that served Puig's interests and that he had hoped to subvert.

[6] The name Valent*ín* hides a masculine diminutive, whereas Mol*ina* conveys the sense of a feminine diminutive. It is as if the characters were made for each other, if only by the conjunction of their names.

[7] Evidence in the manuscripts helps us think further about the names of characters. The opposition *-ta/-to* is evident in Puig's first sketches, but in later drafts "Rober*to*" is replaced by "Valentín," whereas "Mar*ta*" is displaced entirely in the activist's hallucination. In Valentín's final delirium, a new code is introduced (*-in/-ina*) through which we see that the derivatives disappear; the characters find themselves alone, face to face, without the support of their respective clans.

Kiss of the Spider Woman
and the Demise of the Lettered City
Juan Pablo Dabove

Ignoro si la música sabe desesperar de la música y si el
mármol del mármol, pero la literatura es un arte que
sabe profetizar aquel tiempo en que habrá enmudecido y
encarnizarse con la propia virtud y cortejar su fin.
                              —Jorge Luis Borges
                    "La supersticiosa ética del lector"

I do not know whether music can despair of music or
marble of marble. I do know that literature is an art that
can foresee the time when it will be silenced, an art that
can become inflamed with its own virtue and court its
own demise.

                              —Jorge Luis Borges
                    "The Superstitious Ethic of the Reader"
                          (trans. Francine Masiello)

Kiss of the Spider Woman was published in the midst of the protracted conflict
of hemispheric proportions that Jorge Castañeda called "the thirty-year war,"
the Latin American version of the global cold war.[1] As is well-known but never
fully acknowledged by all too forgetful postdictatorship governments, this war
claimed hundreds of thousands of lives and left an enduring mark on Latin
America. Manuel Puig was among the many to suffer the consequences of the

conflict.[2] This essay highlights some of the cultural repercussions of the cold war in Latin America[3] to point out several of the ways in which *Kiss of the Spider Woman* can be used as a privileged point of entry for classroom presentation of certain topics pertaining to Latin American cultural history. This approach is most useful in courses of Latin American literature or Latin American culture with a strong sociohistorical emphasis.

Kiss of the Spider Woman allows us to showcase a turning point in Latin American cultural history that Jean Franco aptly called the "decline and fall of the lettered city."[4] This demise, certainly not triggered by the cold war (it began before the war), was undoubtedly shaped and intensified by its denouement. It implies that literature, together with all forms of high culture, lost its position as the cornerstone of national culture. At the same time, the traditional intellectual lost his or her ground as a cultural hero and a guide of the national community.[5] From the 1950s on, the very idea of nation-state as the only (or at least privileged) political and cultural synthesis faced serious, perhaps insurmountable challenges.[6] Nevertheless, we can explain this process as a collusion of factors of a different nature:

1. Triggering the decline of the lettered elite, the culture industry emerged with its manifestations in film, radio, TV, newspapers, comics, and fashion. Driven primarily by international market forces, the culture industry became the dominant presence in the Latin American post–World War II cultural landscape, breaching the supposedly autonomous realm of high culture and ultimately absorbing it as yet one more product belonging to mass culture. This development consequently rendered the triad of high, popular, and mass cultures largely irrelevant.[7] Although this occurred globally, the unstable, cash-poor states of Latin America were unable to provide a safe haven for high art and its producers at public universities, museums, or art councils.[8]

2. A double process of cultural and economic globalization decisively undermined the nation-state as the ultimate policy maker and power holder and saw the rise of new social movements (gay rights, indigenous rights, etc., all of which have global components). Both developments forged new forms of affiliation and political practices that were incompatible with the model of citizenship supported by the nation-state.

3. The exhaustion by the mid-1970s of the postwar cycle of economic growth in Latin America marked the beginning of the crisis in which the area is still enmeshed, which made evident (except for the neoliberal elites) the lack of long-term sustainability of the dependent model of growth.

4. The revolutionary movements that sprang up throughout Latin America following the triumph of the Cuban Revolution were defeated. The lettered city had often supported these movements, and Latin America's most prominent intellectuals entertained revolutionary ideals at some point in their careers. In fact, the debates in the cold war left were perhaps disproportionately interested in the topic of the intellectual and his or her relation with revolution (be it

the relation of the intellectual to the party, the working class, the peasantry, or popular culture). This interest explains why in most countries of Latin America students, educators, and intellectuals of all kinds comprised a significant proportion of the victims of political violence during the period 1960–90. The eventual defeat of revolutionary movements dealt a fatal blow to the perception of intellectual elites as political guides of the nation. The cold war in Latin America also brought an end to the era of democratic reform and enhanced citizenship that began during the early decades of the twentieth century.[9] These reforms were led or at least sponsored by the lettered intelligentsia, and the destruction of these reforms signaled the need for a reformulation of the notion of politics sponsored by intellectuals.

5. The several currents of thinking that highlighted the solidarity between high culture and the various forms of colonial, class, race, and gender domination triggered a radical self-criticism in the intellectual left. This criticism offered a way to explain the left's defeat as well as to advance its agenda, which subsequently was further eroded. The rise of testimonial literature was, for a while, the answer to these challenges, since it seemed to be a way to legitimize the literary institution from a different viewpoint.

One can read these topics into *Kiss of the Spider Woman* by reading the dichotomies of the novel. These are founded principally on the differences between the characters of Valentín Arregui (an urban militant incarcerated because of his participation in a labor strike) and Luis Alberto Molina (a professional window dresser, or *vidrierista*, imprisoned for "corruption of minors," a euphemism that in 1970s Argentine official culture had little to do with pedophilia and everything to do with homosexuality). This dichotomy is essential to the dualisms emerging from the novel: straight/gay; masculine/feminine; rational/emotional; educated/uneducated; high culture / pop culture; written/oral; class consciousness / class unawareness; high class / lower middle class; Prometheus/Orpheus; study by day / stories by night; "reality"/ideology; and so on. Although critics do not always agree on what the novel does with these dichotomies, it is safe to say that most interpretations involve the enactment of some form of dialectics (Amícola, *Manuel*), through which the kiss that seals the cell mates' relationship becomes a symbol of a new synthesis, rendering Valentín sensitized and Molina politicized.[10]

There is, however, much more to add to this version. The dichotomy Valentín/Molina also embodies an opposition between two models of cultural dynamics in Latin America. Valentín is a revolutionary, but he is first (and maybe foremost) an intellectual. Valentín may therefore be understood as a revolutionary intellectual and as the last modern avatar of the "man of letters."[11] He is both an architect and a university-trained political scientist. This double affiliation intertwines art, technology, and social science as well as class struggle with high education. Thus Valentín derives his epistemological privilege[12] by belonging to a cultural elite that is letter-centered (he reads books), white (he is blonde), male, heterosexual, Europeanized (he knows the aesthetic differences between a French garden and a German one), urban, logocentric, and national (the Arregui Paz family is, as Valentín himself points out, a family with *apellido*— literally, "last name," which refers to his lineage and standing in society). Paz is, not by mere chance, the surname of the European-minded, stubborn Unitarian general who for Domingo Faustino Sarmiento embodied civilization itself: it is a name that speaks to the very core of the Argentine national project.

By contrast, Molina is a window dresser. His identity is thus linked with the market (he displays commodities to lure people into buying) and with a form of cultural production (fashion) that for the traditional intelligentsia does not amount to art. Molina, moreover, works not for Versace but for cash-poor neighborhood boutiques in Buenos Aires.[13] Fashion for Valentín is both superficial (addressing the senses, not the higher faculties of the mind) and politically dangerous (a form of cultural imperialism),[14] whereas fashion for Molina serves as a framework for subjectivity. He doesn't think of history as a grand scheme according to a master narrative (like Marxism for Valentín), endowed with the guarantees of science. On the contrary, he indulges in narratives that have a limited temporal and spatial scope—a cottage, an island, a plantation—the stuff of Hollywood B movies, the very paradigm of ideological mystification.[15] The Valentín/Molina dichotomy can thus be read as the dichotomy between a modern, national, materialist, class-based idea of culture and politics and a postmodern, postnational, textualist, identity-based concept.

In my classroom, I find it extremely successful to use *Kiss of the Spider Woman* as part of an effort to map Latin American cultural history. In this way it is possible to contrast the Boom's ideology and aesthetic with its idea of a totalizing novel (à la Gabriel García Márquez)[16] or the idea of the revolutionary intellectual as giving a voice to the dead (à la Pablo Neruda) with the post-Boom. This contrast goes beyond mere thematic or formal analysis or empirical remarks about how the post-Boom was the heyday of minority writing, and it shows how this transition was due to transformations in the position of literature as an institution in a larger cultural and social landscape. It is even possible to address the specificity of Latin American postmodernity not as a French- or American-induced fad but as a sociohistorical process emerging from a unique set of factors ranging from the status of the Latin American intellectual to the collapse of revolutionary projects.[17]

The political focus of the novel is obvious: state-sponsored terror, the experience of censorship, political and sexual oppression, imprisonment, torture, and revolution are all present. *Kiss of the Spider Woman*, however, can be read not only as a political novel but also as a novel about politics, a reflection on contrasting and changing political paradigms in Latin America. On the one hand, Valentín is a proponent of class-based politics, with wholesale (i.e., national) revolution and state takeover as the center of its political program. From this position (authorized in the books that he reads every day, with unflinching discipline), he decries Molina's opinions as having no political import, at best, or as prepolitical and dangerously flirtatious with authoritarian ideologies, as evidenced by the Nazi film that Molina enthusiastically retells (Eng. 56, Span. 63, Archivos 51). Valentín tries to indoctrinate Molina and bring him over to class-based politics. This line of persuasion has a long history: the definition of what constituted politics was (and is) an essential part of the political struggle (Brunner, "Notes"). According to this definition, the man of letters saw himself as an exclusive political subject vis-à-vis the larger population, which was considered immature, ignorant, and given to criminal instinct (political labels with which the lettered elite excluded other forms of politics from its arena). Molina offers a different version of political experience. On the surface, he agrees with and respects Valentín. Molina appears to acknowledge the bourgeois gendered division of the social sphere: whereas Valentín engages in politics and serious study, Molina controls domesticity, comfort, and leisure time. In the fashion of an adoring wife, he repeatedly expresses his admiration for Valentín's knowledge, he misnames the disciplines (he says "political government" [76] instead of "political science"), and he manifests his derision toward politics, using a well-known bourgeois commonplace: "Así va el mundo, con los políticos" ("What's the world coming to, with all your politicians" [78]).

These points notwithstanding, I argue that throughout the novel, Molina is the true political subject. Unlike Valentín, Molina has the ability to stage a transforming intervention in a given reality. He is able—albeit temporarily—to fool the warden into accepting him as an informant. In the process, Molina is able to improve the living conditions for him and Valentín and to shield Valentín temporarily from further torture. One of the police reports transcribed in the novel tells us that Valentín has a bad reputation in the jail because he organized a (failed) protest against the mistreatment of inmates. Molina thus proves successful in cases where Valentín fails.

Molina is also able to build a community based on shared interests and values. Valentín is grudgingly brought into dialogue with Molina, which eventually leads to an intimate relationship between them. During the first half of the novel, however, Valentín indulges in a sort of ghost dialogue with his revolutionary comrades. For him, the vanguard party is the remedy to solitude. Valentín thinks of dialoguing with this imagined community as a way to establish a break with his individualist bourgeois past. Ángel Rama reminds us how the idea of a vanguard party prolongs a century-old practice in which intellectuals reaffirmed their superiority over civil society through exclusive membership in lodges or clubs (*Ciudad* 144). This belonging to an imagined vanguard community is directly related to Valentín's inability to relate to his actual community, his cell mate. Molina is the one to go above and beyond securing that community that Valentín cannot imagine.

Molina articulates a collective identity as opposed to a hegemonic identity. In effect, he provides the condition of possibility for both cell mates to become "we," and through his narratives a common identity begins to be imagined and negotiated. By contrast, Valentín, despite his abstract diatribes against individualism, lacks all sense of solidarity in the cell.

Molina, in this regard, may be called a full political subject, although not in the same way that Valentín is one. Indeed, Molina's and Valentín's ideas of politics are incommensurable in several respects. For example, Molina's idea of politics is not based on a grand narrative of emancipation that functions as a blueprint for history. Even the ending of the story is left open: Molina dies, and the meaning of his death (fashioned after the death of Molina's film heroines, in particular Leni's)[18] is not clear from the point of view of a national-partisan struggle. He is killed not by the state-sponsored death squads but by Valentín's own comrades. Nor is it clear that his death will benefit any cause. Molina dies by accident (following the destiny of his heroines), and no clear historical figure is shown: no epic, no tragedy, no sacrifice that might restore the order of the community (since the community disappears with Molina). This debunks the search for any higher meaning or links to a master narrative, and, in this respect, Puig is clearly positioned as a representative postmodern author.

Another point deserves attention. Molina's idea of politics does not have the nation-state as its center and goal. *Kiss of the Spider Woman* is clearly a love story. The romantic relationship is, as the novel makes clear, a reenactment of the stories that Molina tells. At the same time, it follows (and decisively transforms) a long pattern of "foundational romances" (Sommer). The kiss that reunites Molina and Valentín is linked to numerous kisses throughout Latin American literature. The sexual-marital metaphor was a guiding trope in Latin American nationalist fiction. In particular, love that crossed racial, class, linguistic, or legal boundaries was a metaphor used by the lettered elites to depict their utopia of national integration or, conversely, their anxieties regarding the lack thereof.

In these cases, the kiss is a powerful metaphor of reconciliation between two supposed adversaries under the guarantee of nation. In Puig's presentation, to the contrary, the romance does not have a nationalist dimension (out of love, Molina reluctantly agrees to participate in revolutionary struggle, only to be killed for his efforts). The nation-state is the place where genocide takes place. Puig accordingly looks for another space where a different definition of politics is possible, thus heralding the postmodern emphasis on forms of affiliation outside state interpellation and on the task of constructing these new identities. Molina's politics is a local politics, unlike Valentín's world-scale political designs. While Valentín wants to change the world, Molina wants only to change his cell. Yet he shows much generosity, shrewdness, and courage in doing so, demonstrating that local does not necessarily mean minor. For him, local means real.

Molina's idea of politics is based on abject materials such as fiction and pop culture. Throughout the novel, Molina uses the narration of movies to describe the situation in the cell and to actively intervene in that situation. In the process, he is able to rescue the political and ethical component present in kitsch (Bacarisse, *Impossible Choices* 81). Narration is far from being second to reality. It is distinct from ideology or the deceiving representation of reality that serves the interests of the dominant class (thus equating ideology to false consciousness and opposing it to scientific knowledge). Rather, narration is a part of that reality, an active and productive factor in it. The narration is fictional, but Molina knows and uses the powers of fiction not to delude but to illuminate. A fitting metaphor is found when Valentín realizes the beauty of the shadows cast on the wall by the heat of the stove. Molina "always watches them" because they help "pass the time" (Eng. 181, Span. 185, Archivos 157). Fashioned after the Platonic myth of the cave, but with a completely opposite meaning, this episode tells us of the change in the ethical consideration of fiction. The topic of the primacy of fiction (not defined as opposed to reality in a metaphysical way, of course) as linked to politics impregnates most of political reflection nowadays (see, e.g., Laclau and Mouffe).

Molina's politics are not a politics of self-consciousness. Molina intervenes in reality but without resorting to any sovereign language. He takes the language of passion from movies and puts it to use in another sphere. Molina's last words indicate his acceptance to carry Valentín's message outside: "Then I'll do whatever you tell me" ("Entonces voy a hacer todo lo que me digas") (Eng. 263, Span. 267, Archivos 239). These are not the words of a political subject in Valentín's sense of the term. These are the words of a woman in love (the woman who populates Molina's films), and Molina, at the same moment that he seems to be reaching class consciousness, is still inhabiting his film world. He is not deluded (he takes the necessary precautions; he foresees his own death and makes arrangements for when he is gone), but his politics are framed in a different language. His politics are no less successful (or failed) than those sponsored by Marxism. This distinction is important since it is linked to a line of thought that produced some of the most celebrated works of the post-Boom era (a classic example, though one whose literary value has been questioned by critics, is Laura Esquivel's *Como agua para chocolate* [*Like Water for Chocolate*], where the heroine pursues her agenda through cooking).

Molina's ideas of politics are detotalizing and open to contradiction. Valentín thinks of his political values as having universal currency, belonging to a language that can successfully translate any other language and explain any reality without gaps or contradiction. Molina, on the other hand, knows from the very beginning that his attempts are not going to be successful in the long run. He does not think of a new order, but rather he tries to survive and love and stand for his right to happiness and enjoyment. Molina turns this not into an escape but into a search for a space of freedom. Just like Puig, who chose a novel to present a powerful indictment of lettered culture, Molina represents a contradiction that we should not attempt to ignore or solve, one that invites us to reflect on the paradoxical status of literature in the last quarter of the twentieth century.

Molina is disengaged from power, but he uses weakness as a weapon. His appropriation of the feminine is part of this strategy. Molina perceives the commonality between Valentín and his captors, since they are both immersed in what Roland Barthes called "discourses of power" (*Rustle*) defined as discourses that create a lack in the other. To a certain extent, there is a greater difference between Molina and Valentín than between Valentín and his torturers. Even though Valentín and the military are on opposite sides of the political divide, they are on different sides of the same political paradigm. Despite an enormous amount of suffering and physical pain, Valentín and his enemies understand each other, which is something that Valentín painfully feels (Eng. 144, Span. 147, Archivos 125).

Kiss of the Spider Woman can be successfully used in courses with a strong political emphasis to show how the mid-1970s signaled a turning point in Latin American culture. This watershed was due to a change in Latin American society and politics at large and, in particular, to a change in the position of the literary institution vis-à-vis society. A major literary work produced during that period, Puig's novel reflects these social changes through a fictional dichotomy, which in turn stands in for the cultural schisms of the decade. In this way, we can approach *Kiss of the Spider Woman* by valuing its aesthetic specificity as we also value its place as a landmark in Latin American culture, embodying as it does the promises, shortfalls, contradictions, and failed dreams of a generation.

NOTES

[1] A preamble to the cold war in Latin America occurred in 1954, when a coup backed by both the CIA and the State Department overthrew the democratically elected president of Guatemala, Colonel Jacobo Arbenz, on false charges of communist leanings. The cold war, however, officially began when the Cuban Revolution adopted a more decisive turn toward Marxism-Leninism. It lasted until about 1990, when the electoral defeat of the Sandinistas in Nicaragua heralded the beginning of the end for Central American revolutions. The bibliography for this era is extensive, but for introductions to these topics well suited for use in undergraduate courses, see *Latin America: A Concise Interpretive History*, by E. Bradford Burns, in particular the chapter "The Revolutionary Option," and *A History of Latin America*, by Benjamin Keen.

[2] The first edition of Puig's third novel (*The Buenos Aires Affair*) was confiscated by censorship agencies as soon as it was released in 1973. Shortly thereafter, he was threatened by the AAA (Alianza Anticomunista Argentina) and forced to leave the country. When released in July 1976, *Kiss of the Spider Woman* was immediately banned by the recently installed military government in Argentina. The novel did not circulate fully in Argentina (in stark contrast with its international success) until the early 1980s.

[3] Important books on the subject are Jean Franco's *Decline and Fall of the Lettered City* and María Eugenia Mudrovcic's *Mundo nuevo: Cultura y guerra fría en la década del 60*.

[4] "Lettered city" (*ciudad letrada*) is a concept put forward by the Uruguayan critic Ángel Rama. It refers to the institutional cluster that depends on the exclusive administration of a particular technology (the written word) as the basis for its social and cultural prominence (the state; the church; the educational, artistic, commercial, or financial corporations; newspapers and publishing houses; etc.); the group of individuals that acquires a distinctive identity owing to its affiliation with these institutions (from state

officials, lawyers, and engineers to priests and poets); and the ideology and rituals that support that predominance. The concept is integral to our understanding of the relation between lettered practices and the state in Latin America, since it defines a unique mode of production and reproduction of a power elite that crosses (without ignoring) class, race, and gender determinations. The concept is also important for establishing patterns of change or continuity in certain paradigms from colonial times to the present. For a discussion of the possibilities and problems in the notion of the lettered city, see *Ángel Rama y los estudios latinoamericanos*, edited by Mabel Moraña.

[5] For an account of the formation of the idea of the intellectual as the cornerstone of national culture, see *Literatura y cultura nacional en Hispanoamérica*, by Mabel Moraña.

[6] These challenges were posed from the very beginning of the nation-state in Latin America. The notion of sociocultural heterogeneity, put forward by Antonio Cornejo Polar, and the analysis of Andean literatures that he presents in his masterful *Escribir en el aire* address emphatically the ways in which dreams of dominance were, to a significant degree, ideological fantasies concocted by the lettered city to legitimize its own problematic standing. Only recently has it been observed that this heterogeneity was not an accident, a product of Latin America's backward nature, but the very paradoxical core of a Latin American culture.

[7] In *Culturas híbridas*, the Argentine cultural critic Néstor García Canclini outlines the modern triadic division of the cultural realm between high culture (studied by literary and art criticism), mass culture (studied by sociology and communications), and folk culture (studied by anthropology and folklore). García Canclini shows how this triad (that certainly involves a hierarchy) is essential to the constitution of the nation-state, since it functions as a guide for the national community. High culture, he explains, is conceived as an autonomous realm, and as such it is free from the blind forces of the market and localism.

[8] For an insightful analysis of how the rise of the culture industry affected the cultural landscape, see García Canclini's *Culturas híbridas*.

[9] By the mid-1970s, most countries in Latin America were under a form of authoritarian rule.

[10] For a complete list of works on *Kiss of the Spider Woman*, see the excellent bibliography prepared by Guadalupe Martí-Peña in the critical edition of the novel published by Archivos.

[11] For a view of revolutionary culture in Latin America as a prolongation and revamping of a centuries-old paradigm, see the chapter "The Revolutionized City" in Rama's *La ciudad letrada*, as well as John Beverley and Marc Zimmerman's *Literature and Politics in the Central American Revolutions*.

[12] Epistemological privilege is a notion that names the authority embedded in discourse when this authority depends not on its truth-value but on the position that the producer of discourse holds in a given context. This notion can be linked to the Foucauldian positions of enunciation (see Foucault's *Archaeology of Knowledge*).

[13] I am following here the suggestion of Francine Masiello's article "Fuera de lugar," where she points out that "Manuel Puig pone sobre el tapete las dimensiones políticas y filosóficas del debate identitario" (574; "Manuel Puig puts forward the political and philosophical dimensions implied in the debate on social identities").

[14] More than once, Molina's film narrations digress into details on the clothing or hairdos of the heroines. Valentín usually reacts with impatience or indifference.

[15] *How to Read Donald Duck*, the brilliant book by Ariel Dorfman and Armand Mattelart, is a crucial example from the 1970s on how media culture was considered inherently fraught with a dangerous and misleading imperialist ideology.

[16] It is well known that Gabriel García Márquez considered *One Hundred Years of Solitude* a totalizing metaphor for Latin America (Alvarez Borland 89).

[17] For a discussion on Latin American postmodernity, see *Culturas híbridas* and *La globalización imaginada*, by García Canclini, and *The Postmodernism Debate in Latin America*, a collective volume edited by John Beverley, José Oviedo, and Michael Aronna.

[18] Even though Valentín longs for a heroic death as a fitting end for his struggle, following a well-established nineteenth-century pattern (from José Martí to Ernesto "Che" Guevara), it is Molina who has one.

Revolution and Sexuality in Argentina in the 1960s and 1970s: "May Love and Equality Reign"

José Maristany

> The cultural institutions cannot be used as a forum
> for the proliferation of false intellectuals who wish
> to convert snobbery, extravagance, homosexuality, and
> other aberrations into manifestations of revolutionary
> art, divorced from the masses and the spirit of our
> revolution.
> —Fidel Castro

At the exhibition *Experiencias 1968*, organized in May of that year by the Instituto Di Tella in Buenos Aires, Alfredo Rodríguez-Arias, who was involved in directing theatrical projects there, presented a giant image of Sigmund Freud, which the artist stated he had asked "those who design movie marquees" to paint. The artist explained his work in a popular magazine as the "Freud-Guevara Movement for Sexual and Social Liberation" (Longoni and Mestmann 89). Here we can see the emergence of a crossroads where avant-garde artistic and political movements of the day were mobilized and mixed in the cultural arena. The idea of a liberation movement in the 1960s and 1970s was based in some quarters on class revolution, but in others it was driven by a challenge to patriarchal society, demanding rights for women and sexual minorities. These two visions caused fractures and rifts among social activists. Although there were attempts to link these movements together, as the Di Tella exhibit shows, often those interested in sexual rights found little satisfaction. The tensions between political and sexual liberation in the militant groups in Argentina resulted in the exclusion of the utopia imagined by sexual minorities, whose behavior was severely censured as bourgeois, decadent deviance. This scene allows us a starting point for analyzing the conflictive relations that developed between different liberation movements and that were later incorporated in fictional form by Manuel Puig.

Marxism and Homosexuality: An Initial Abyss

For an understanding of the controversy provoked by sexuality in Latin American revolutionary movements in the 1960s, it is useful to return to Karl Marx's critique of production. Andrew Parker, writing about Marx's *Eighteenth Brumaire of Louis Bonaparte*, observed "an aversion to certain forms of parody that prevent sexuality from attaining the political significance that class has long monopolized" (28). In other words, as long as Marxism held the notion of production as its central paradigm, it could not "think" sexuality[1] in political terms or conceive of a political dimension to what it considered a private and distant territory, subordinated to class struggle. In any event, as a consequence of the socialist revolution, the transformation of bourgeois institutions would eventually bring the liberation of a sexuality repressed by capitalist society.

In Marx's work, production is modeled on the idea of procreation: productivity and fertility are equivalent concepts, two modes of the same vital process (Parker 41). This model leads to a marked division between public and private in terms of gender: the domestic sphere is not only the place where a natural sexual division prevails but also a place that forbids a political stance insofar as it does not include the experience of exploitation inherent in collective identities that spring from class consciousness.

In *The Eighteenth Brumaire*, Marx identifies the masses represented by Louis Bonaparte as the pseudoclass of the lumpen proletariat, a basically unproductive group. In discussing that group, he uses the same tone as that of the discourse popularly applied to the gay underworld: the lumpen is "a phenomenon that occurs in more or less developed form in all the so far known phases of society" (Parker 40), characterized by unhygienic living conditions, promiscuity, and licentious and unhealthy tastes. But perhaps even more important, the lumpen proletariat is assigned the typically feminine characteristics and qualities of theatricality, parody, posing, and inauthenticity.

For Marx, revolution is serious, and in this context it is important to distinguish the imaginary from the real, representation from what is being represented, the theatrical from the authentic, essences from appearances. Parker reminds us that the roots of Marx's aversion to theatricality have their origins in what Eve Kosofsky Sedgwick defined as homosexual panic: the fear that men have held since the nineteenth century that leads them in the company of other men to demonstrate in some explicit way that they are not homosexual.

In this way, a sexuality that does not adopt the approved gender norms falls into the category of suspicious theatricalization, similar to what occurred in France: both Bonaparte and the masses are seen as transvestites, parodies of the authentic relations of production who systematically confuse the inside with the outside. Homosexual panic is panic at the confusion of categories, panic caused by the fear of incorrect labeling. Parker's article helps explain how left political movements in Latin America also failed to think sexuality, instead acting out their sexuality in ways sanctioned as normal. Here we can find commonalities between left and right: conventional codes of masculinity and femininity are followed and are never questioned or examined from a political perspective by either position. Left and right converge in their struggle against the threat of abnormal desire.

The Argentine Gay Movement and the Revolutionary Left

In a hostile environment, in terms of both official policies and revolutionary resistance, a movement emerged that sought to think sexuality in these liberation movements. The poet and activist Néstor Perlongher chronicles the emergence of the first group who tried to create a state of consciousness of the conditions of oppression that gays experienced around 1969.[2] This development occurred a year after the avant-garde experiences at Di Tella, in a working-class environment very different and distant from that modern artistic intelligentsia:

> In 1969, a group of homosexuals, meeting in a tenement house in a Buenos Aires neighborhood, gave birth to the first attempt to organize homosexuals in Argentina: the Grupo Nuestro Mundo [Our World Group]. Its members, mostly lower middle-class union activists led by an ex-communist militant demoted in the party for being homosexual, spent two years dedicating themselves to bombarding the editorial offices of the Buenos Aires media with mimeographed pamphlets trumpeting homosexual liberation.
> (*Prosa* 77)

It was the first attempt in Argentina to bring the hidden world of homosexuality into the public sphere to denounce the political and legal repression under Juan Carlos Onganía's government and to question heteronormative constructs of homosexuality.

For its part, the Argentine Communist Party followed Stalinist policies that viewed homosexuality as a sickness that could be cured. Not even the New Left, however, managed to overcome this painful blind spot in Marxist thought.

As a second stage, Perlongher mentions the creation of the Frente de Liberación Homosexual de la Argentina (FLH [Front for Homosexual Liberation of Argentina]) in 1971, when the Grupo Nuestro Mundo joined with a group of gay intellectuals inspired by the North American gay power movement (*Prosa* 77–78). The writers Puig and Juan José Hernández, among others, participated in the initial meeting (Rapisardi and Modarelli 145).

In March 1972, according to Perlongher, a group of university students (including Perlongher), the Eros group, joined the FLH. The incorporation of these young militants trained in political action had an impact on the gay movement, expressed in two opposing documents in the first FLH *Bulletin*, published in March 1972:

> [O]ne stated that the objective of the FLH was to see that the left incorporated homosexual demands into its programs; the other gave greater emphasis to the role of sexuality and spoke skeptically of "fifty years of socialist revolutions."
> (*Prosa* 78)

In these two positions the utopian vision appears prominently, and despite their different objectives, there were points of agreement. Both positions demanded the repeal of repressive police edicts and the freeing of imprisoned homosexuals, called for an end to the oppression arising from the "compulsory and exclusively heterosexual system" springing from capitalism, and urged alliances with movements for national and social liberation, including feminist groups (*Prosa* 78).

The FLH defined itself as an alliance of autonomous groups that coordinated common actions among themselves (*Prosa* 78–79). It published a lone issue of *Homosexuales* in June 1973 and eight issues of the bulletin *Somos* between 1973 and January 1976 (*Prosa* 82). *Somos* critiqued the bourgeois ideology of the family as part of the capitalist ideological superstructure. *Homosexuales* affirmed that it was necessary to combat heterosexist oppression in the context of "social, political, cultural, and economic oppression," so that "all those who are exploited and oppressed by the system that marginalizes homosexuals could unite together in a program of liberation" (Rapisardi and Modarelli 150–51). Marxists believed that the transformation of the economic and political superstructure would necessarily produce a change in power relations at the social base as well as in the family. Therefore, women and homosexuals would achieve their liberation when the revolution triumphed and bourgeois patriarchy disappeared with the emergence of what Che Guevara had called the "new man."

Reading Michel Foucault, Gilles Deleuze and Félix Guattari, and Herbert Marcuse and Wilhelm Reich allowed these young militants to integrate debates over the gender system with plans for revolution. The attempt by the FLH to form alliances with leftist groups was difficult, and the relationship uneasy.[3] Although the FLH sought an alliance with the Montoneros and tried to collaborate in marches and protests, their efforts were consistently rejected. Graffiti linking the left, homosexuals, and drug addicts was quickly repudiated by the Montoneros with the slogan "No somos putos, no somos faloperos, somos soldados de Evita y Montoneros" ("We're not drug addicts, we're not queers—we're soldiers of Evita and Montoneros"), which became part of the repertoire chanted at rallies and demonstrations (Bazán, *Historia* 365). In that climate of mounting paranoia, the Montoneros severed any alliances that implied identification with the militant homosexual groups. The Soviet experience under Stalinism and the Cuban repressive stances on the place of homosexuals in a revolutionary society were not the best models for leftist groups in Argentina to follow: "In that context, the attempt to incorporate the left into a discussion whose goal was to link desire and politics—a 'politics of desire'—as a revolutionary tool became basically impossible" (Rapisardi and Modarelli 156).

Manuel Puig: The Limitless Space of Fiction

According to various witnesses, in 1971 Puig participated in the initial gatherings out of which the FLH grew. Juan José Sebreli observes, "That first session was organized by a group of writers. Manuel Puig was present, but he informed them that he would not participate in the movement because of his literary career" (322). Others offer a different version of events:

> Sebreli's reference to Manuel Puig is annoying. The publication of the FLH journal *Homosexuales* was financed in part with his money. Furthermore, he donated money for a campaign we held for gay prisoners at the Devoto prison.   (Rapisardi and Modarelli 145)

Similarly, Hernández, who participated in those first gatherings, insists, Puig "was completely open about his sexuality. . . . [E]ven if he wasn't a permanent militant, through the footnotes he adds in *Kiss of the Spider Woman* . . . he clearly supports the cause" (qtd. in Rapisardi and Modarelli 146). In 1973 Puig was working on *Kiss of the Spider Woman*, and a few months before leaving the country for Mexico he interviewed political prisoners who had been freed in May by the Peronist government of Héctor Cámpora. The genesis of this work occurs shortly after the formation of the FLH and its attempts to gain visibility in the area of national revolutionary militancy.

Kiss of the Spider Woman is the space for investigating this political reality. In an interview with Jorgelina Corbatta, Puig indicated that his writing sought to clarify aspects he found obscure, "a line of inquiry into the Argentine error . . . political error, sexual error" (603–04). In the novel, Puig examines part of this "error" in the tensions and misunderstanding that existed between the political vanguard and homosexuals.

Sharing space and conversation, Puig's characters bring together discourses that in reality seemed impossible to reconcile. Valentín explains that his "life is dedicated to political struggle" and therefore that gratification of the senses is "secondary" (Eng. 27–28, Span. 33–34, Archivos 28). The world of the senses, to which Molina belongs, and the world of reason, where Valentín's revolutionary ideals lie, appear contradictory and mutually exclusive. The world of the senses is identified with the feminine and the emotional, and Valentín says, "[T]hat kind of behavior can get in a man's way" (Eng. 29, Span. 35, Archivos 29). After that initial point, not only does Valentín get closer to Molina, but the closeness begins to soften him, in a different sense, allowing him to recognize his own desires, repressed under the weight of the prejudices of the sexist society in which he has been living. Valentín reevaluates a series of "truths" about sexuality and emotions on which he has based his militant actions and ideology. Thus, in a paradoxical way, the cell in which they find themselves confined becomes a utopian space in which consciousness can be modified and distanced from bourgeois and patriarchal order.

Molina is not the militant homosexual with the raised consciousness of groups such as Nuestro Mundo or the FLH, and yet it was people like him that such groups tried to represent, give a voice to, and mobilize at the same time. It is revealing that in the manuscripts for the novel, Molina is identified as the "Folle" ("queer"), or simply with the initial "F," whereas Valentín is "He."

"Folle," queen, queer, faggot Molina embodies the archetype of the effeminate homosexual, expansive and provocative, who feels like a woman and wants to be conquered by a real man. According to Perlongher, the model corresponds to a type of homosexuality where the man has sex with the queer without being considered homosexual ("Sexo" 638). When Valentín has managed to overcome the barriers of prejudice and distrust that have kept him from getting closer to his companion, he questions Molina and the model of identification that governs Molina's sexual conduct, in which desire is inextricably linked to submission. Valentín is concerned that Molina is resigning himself to "a form of exploitation": "if it weren't for the fact that it must hurt a hell of a lot, I'd tell you to do it to me, to demonstrate that this business of being a man, it doesn't give any special rights to anyone" ("si no fuera porque debe doler mucho te pediría que me lo hicieras vos a mí, para demostrarte que eso, ser macho, no da derecho a nada") (Eng. 244, Span. 246–47, Archivos 222).[4]

Valentín seems to be aware of the political implications of gender roles and tries to convince Molina that the way he experiences his desire is not natural, that it is the result of a social creation in which the feminine is the subaltern element necessary for masculine exploitation to occur. For the first time, then, it seems that Valentín's Marxist formation has been able to consider the unthinkable, formulating relationships not only between social classes but also between genders in terms of exploitation and ideology.

This dialogue recalls Perlongher's observation about a "Mediterranean" type of sexuality: the condition of being the "man" is directly identified with the active role of penetration (638). Molina, "physically . . . a man as much" ("físicamente tan hombre") as Valentín is (Eng. 243, Span. 246, Archivos 222), can conform to this condition only insofar as he assumes this role. The possibility of exchanging roles and "acting"[5] different parts would be a way of bringing the revolution to the relationships between homosexuals and distancing them from the patriarchal models they have imitated in their distribution of power. This great utopia, though verbalized in the dialogue, is not acted on: Valentín preempts this possibility with the excuse that it would hurt, and Molina abruptly ends the discussion and refuses to continue talking.

Thus *Kiss of the Spider Woman* acknowledges the polemics, misgivings, and impossibilities that developed in those years: Puig returns to the discussions that took place at the center of groups such as the FLH. A debate in the FLH at the time had to do with "the status of the flaming fag," who was considered to reproduce uncritically patterns of repression from normative heterosexuality (Rapisardi and Modarelli 165–66). Molina, in this regard, confesses to Valentín that he is attracted to a man who inspires fear (Eng. 244, Span. 247, Archivos 222); like a woman, his dream is to find a superior man whom he could serve, thus reproducing the stereotype of the traditional heterosexual relationship. Valentín's solid convictions about sexuality and emotions and the need to negate the gratification of the senses all start to become shaky.[6] Molina's dreams and desires also come under scrutiny from the logic of liberation inherent in Valentín's Marxist discourse.

One stereotype that Puig questions and that was a commonly accepted belief of the left was the incapacity of homosexuals to commit themselves and be true to their word. Before getting out of prison, Molina promises Valentín that he will get in contact with Valentín's revolutionary cell and pass on his message. Chapter 15 of the novel recounts Molina's movements to carry out that mission, thus reversing the idea of the homosexual as traitor.

Puig performs a didactic role in the footnotes on homosexuality. In the last of these, in chapter 11, using the pseudonym Anneli Taube, he gives his own position on the role of homosexuals in revolutionary society.[7] The doctor Taube celebrates the boy who chooses sensitivity and femininity and calls this choice revolutionary (Eng. 207, Span. 209, Archivos 187).

Puig's citation of the imaginary doctor anticipates what Valentín observes later. Valentín's "whoever filled your head with that nonsense" ("los que te llenaron la cabeza con esas macanas") (Eng. 244, Span. 247, Archivos 222), part of his critique of Molina's ideas, corresponds to Taube's reference to "slow brainwashing" ("lento lavado cerebral"), in which heterosexist models influence homosexual conduct (Eng. 212–13, Span. 211, Archivos 189).

Taube recognizes that this "prejudice, or perhaps truthful observation, concerning homosexuals" ("prejuicio, u observación justa, sobre los homosexuales") (Eng. 213, Span. 211, Archivos 189) was the reason they were marginalized in movements for class liberation and in political action in general. She also points out that, fortunately, this situation was changing: homosexual and women's liberation groups were evidence of the left's capacity for a wide-ranging social critique (Eng. 213–14, Span. 211, Archivos 189). Here the political and sexual dimensions of the conflict being played out in the text above appear in condensed form. Reviewing the rejection and exclusion of homosexuals that existed in the left, the footnotes culminate in the only mention of movements for sexual liberation, both for women and for homosexuals.

The big question would be where to root a homosexual identity that is now left without models. And perhaps Puig's answer aims to question the necessity of rooting an identity in a fixed role: he postulates an "original bisexuality" ("bisexualidad original"), as Taube puts it (Eng. 211, Span. 211, Archivos 188), that should not be erased in favor of one end of the spectrum. Puig defines his position on those movements that assume an identity and proudly stand for it. Although in interviews and talks Puig recognized that the liberation movements achieved important victories in terms of the rights and visibility of minorities, he questions an identity based on sexuality and later speaks not of a "political and/or sexual error" but of a "gay error" ("Error" 32).

Already in *Kiss of the Spider Woman* Puig had let slip the idea, in the voice of Valentín after his first sexual encounter with Molina, that "sex is innocence itself" ("el sexo es la inocencia misma") (Eng. 221, Span. 224, Archivos 204), an idea that would reappear in a lecture Puig gave in 1984 on his relationship with censorship:[8]

> [S]ex has no moral weight, it is an activity of the vegetative life, such as eating and sleeping. . . . The moment you give sex a moral dimension it is adulterated, since its nature is innocence itself, pure instinct of pleasure.
>
> (J. Romero, "Delito" 323)

Puig's article "El error gay" concludes a dossier in *El porteño* on "new masculinity" and appears after an article by activists in the Comunidad Homosexual Argentina (Argentine Homosexual Community), in which they critiqued the incendiary revolutionary discourse of the groups they saw as their predecessors:

> No one changes their sexual identity because others "supposedly promote a different one"; sexual identity is formed through the combined processes of socialization and sexualization, and the results do not entirely correspond to established models. . . .   (Zalazar and Freda)[9]

On the very next page, Puig begins his article with this categorical and transgressive judgment: "Homosexuality does not exist." The author of *Kiss of the Spider Woman* critiques the idea that there could be a homosexual movement that would gain legal recognition from the state. If homosexuality does not exist, then any organization that tries to represent homosexuals and speak for them would be absurd. Later in his article Puig affirms once again his belief that "[o]ne's sex has absolutely no moral or transcendent significance. Furthermore, sex is innocence itself, it is a game invented by creation to make people happy" (32). He affirms that he admires and respects the work of gay liberation groups but sees in them "the danger of adopting, of claiming homosexual identity as a natural fact, whereas it is actually nothing more than a historical-cultural product, as repressive as the heterosexual condition." Puig advocates integration and warns of the dangers of creating a ghetto that, in the end, would not remove the original error of maintaining an identity rooted in sexuality, from which the categories of hetero- and homosexuality are derived, a dichotomy that limits the immense range of nuances of human sexuality.

Puig recognizes that his position is utopian: "I think it's impossible to foresee a world without sexual repression" ("Error" 32). He maintains to some extent the revolutionary and antibourgeois perspective that stimulated discussions in the FLH and allied groups in the early 1970s, groups for whom a new society would involve a questioning and a transformation, not only of the economic base, but also of gender relationships, inasmuch as both aspects are intimately related.

The leaders of the Comunidad Homosexual Argentina, interested in gaining recognition from the state and the public, seem to be in step with a new stage of Argentine society, distant from the revolutionary approaches of the 1970s: they propose a struggle in the courts and strive to improve the public image of homosexuals as citizens.[10] For Puig, however, this position postpones a more radical questioning of the relation of gender, sexuality, and power in Western society and a true politics of liberation. Thus the legacy of the 1960s is not lost; it resonates in the voice of Manuel Puig.

NOTES

The epigram is taken from "Palabras de Fidel Castro en el Primer Congreso Nacional de Educación y Cultura." This passage and all translations of cited texts are by Susan Benner, who translated this essay, unless otherwise indicated.

[1] I am using "thinking sex" in the ways suggested by Gayle Rubin's famous article.

[2] See Perlongher's "Historia del Frente de Liberación Homosexual" in *Prosa plebeya*. In *Fiestas, baños y exilios: Los gays porteños en la última dictadura*, Rapisardi and Modarelli indicate that, according to recently discovered documents, by 1967 there were already secret gatherings of homosexual militants at the University of Buenos Aires (142–43).

[3] This relationship is the subject of a novel by Osvaldo Bazán, *La más maravillosa música* (2002), based on a romance between a gay liberationist and a leftist Peronist, with obvious echoes of *El beso de la mujer araña*.

[4] In comparing the edited text of this sequence with the manuscripts from the preediting phase, in their notes to chapter 13 of the Archivos edition of the novel, José Amícola, Julia Romero, and Graciela Goldchluk point out the change that has occurred in Valentín: "Successive modifications in Valentín's speech indicate how Puig has gone about constructing a character whose conceptions change. At this point in the plot, he [Valentín] can no longer think about homosexuality as an essential trait (to either 'be' a man or to 'be' a homosexual) because his own behavior has put that possiblity in doubt" (225).

[5] This word is used by Valentín just before the line cited above: "—Sure, you're not in any way inferior. Then why doesn't it occur to you to ever be . . . to ever act like a man?" ("—Sí, no tenés ningún tipo de inferioridad. ¿Por qué entonces, no se te ocurre ser . . . actuar como hombre?") (Eng. 243, Span. 246, Archivos 222).

[6] In the midst of the crisis, Valentín never questions the legitimacy of the revolutionary struggle of which he is a part. He does, however, question the biases of a revolution that does not manage to shake the sexual as well as the economic foundations of oppression in bourgeois society.

[7] On the sources Puig uses for these footnotes, see Balderston, "'Sexualidad y revolución.'"

[8] For a geneticist version of the typescript for this lecture in English, "Loss of a Readership," see J. Romero, "Delito."

[9] Legal status was denied the Comunidad Homosexual Argentina by the Justice Ministry in 1986, and their appeal was denied, first in the appellate court and then in the Supreme Court. These are the verdicts referred to by Zalazar and Freda in their article in *El porteño*. See Sebreli (360–61) and Bazán (*Historia* 422–24).

[10] For more on these sudden changes in gay conduct and models in recent years, see Perlongher's article "La desaparición de la homosexualidad" in *Prosa plebeya* (85–90) and Rapisardi and Modarelli (211–22).

The Writer as Smuggler

Graciela Speranza

> We have listened too long to the courtly muses of Europe.
> —Ralph Waldo Emerson
> "The American Scholar"

It should be no surprise that the Hollywood movie based on *Kiss of the Spider Woman* firmly established Manuel Puig's literary reputation, for this subtle, political story, based on the melodrama of love and sacrifice, is also his greatest tribute to film as the secret desire of literature. From the beginning, the dimly lit cell becomes a screen on which Molina "projects" his stories: these narratives fill the static vacuum of the prison, lighten the monotony of the prisoners' wait, invite a more intimate dialogue, and, in the end, entrap the distanced spectator, Valentín Arregui, in ethereal fantasy. Molina is thus Puig's perfect double, having learned the art of narrative seduction in the movie theater. Captivated by the realist obsession of the screen, Puig erases the distance between fiction and reality. Since the novel begins with the plot of a movie (Molina's voice occupies the void left by the narrator), the distinction between the beginning of the novel and the beginning of the movie is deliberately unclear. In this brief story, appropriations, inversions, and misunderstanding shape the complex relations between Puig's literature and film.

What led Puig from film to literature is well known. It all started in the matinees with his mother in their provincial town; it continued with a scholarship to study film in Rome, where he wrote his early film scripts; and finally there was the voice of an aunt that overflowed the boundaries of a discarded filmscript that would become the opening of his first novel, *Betrayed by Rita Hayworth* (*La traición de Rita Hayworth*). These biographical incidents, however, are nothing more than superficial versions of a more hidden and daring aesthetic adventure. His legendary substitution of a film or video library for the traditional writer's library produced an unprecedented and personal mix of film and literature. The dialogue goes beyond a mere renovation of the arsenal of film techniques that is common to literary adaptation. The substitution of film for literature speaks to a productive tension between the two; it announces the inadequacy of traditional boundaries set for literature and heralds the promise of literary change by a young, popular art form destined for mass consumption. The three thousand titles in Puig's video library, the hundreds of cinematic allusions, explicit and implicit, that appear in his novels, and the six films recounted in *Kiss of the Spider Woman* all specifically define the privileged place of film in his narrative world. But what does Puig seek in film that he doesn't find in literature?

Fate decreed that Puig's cinematic initiation (he saw his first movie, *Bride of Frankenstein*, from the projection booth of the movie theater in his native town, General Villegas, in 1936) coincided with the publication of two essays central to aesthetic theory, both of which examined the impact of film on the history of modern art: Walter Benjamin's "The Work of Art in the Age of Mechanical Reproduction" and Erwin Panofsky's "Style and Medium in the Motion Pictures."

It was Benjamin who first commented on the most notable artistic consequences of the invention of film—its ability to modify the relation of art, the public, and the means of mass artistic participation. If film, as Benjamin suggests, is the most powerful agent in the destruction of the aura of the artistic work, mechanical reproduction not only disrupts tradition but also allows one to bring things closer to the masses (223). Its "shock effect" (238) radically changes the conditions of reception. As a dialectical moment, film brings new social and aesthetic possibilities for reconciling high art and art for the masses, experimentation and comfort, an unthinkable feat in painting or literature.

Puig's literature exploits these new potentialities that Benjamin sees in film.[1] Reproduction, as a formal principle that seeks to achieve objectivity in the cinematic medium, works in Puig's novels to dilute the value of tradition (hence his freedom from literary history); it also produces the same ambiguous relationship between author and public, between real subject and character, and thus destroys the categories of authority and narrative originality. Note Puig's proposal on the back cover of his second novel, *Heartbreak Tango* (*Boquitas pintadas*): "Without renouncing the stylistic experiments that I began in my first book, I hope to develop a new form of popular literature in this serial novel."[2] For Puig, film is also a kind of entertainment. If, through the "shock effect," film leads to an inseparable mixture of criticism and reception, then literature can try to reproduce the conditions that permit that dual function. But beyond the technical objectivity inherent in reproduction, what are the particular attributes of this new medium that produce this effect on the masses?

Panofsky, an art historian and a witness to the evolution of film from a mere technical curiosity to an art and an industry, attempted to respond to that question through a social and aesthetic analysis of cinema's new possibilities with respect to the traditional forms of great art. His essay alludes to two distinctive features that define the medium (122).[3] Created as popular entertainment without any aesthetic pretensions, film managed to reestablish the dynamic contact between artistic production and artistic consumption that had become weakened, if not absent, in other spheres of art. For that reason, according to Panofsky, film in 1936 was the only "entirely alive" visual art that reflected mass tastes, habits, and practices (94). Even when elevated to the status of art, it still maintains a popular appeal. The other essential feature of film corresponds to the aesthetic and technical aspect implicit in the idea of movement that stands behind the movies. Because of its capacity to record the real world in motion, only film can attempt both the dynamization of space and the spatialization of time.

Film's biggest innovation is its interdependence on two unprecedented relations—the relation with society, based on film's commercial character, and the relation with physical reality, derived from film's technical character. The communicability required by the relation with society and the realism required by the relation with physical reality define the conception and effectiveness of the style of the new medium. While other representational arts struggle to fit more or less an idealist conception of the world, film can do justice to the materialist interpretation that pervades contemporary society. Film is the only medium that can manipulate reality in motion without branding it with a particular style but can still produce an artistic object with its own style.

Puig also recognizes in film that double social and aesthetic value to which literature can aspire. If the vitality of film springs from its popular origins and its communicability, it can provide a useful model for restoring the interrupted dialogue between literature and the mass public. Puig comments, "I am interested in direct communication with the public, and I try to write in a way that reproduces those conditions a little. Film is immediately accessible. Image; narrative interest . . . " (qtd. in Sosnowski 72). But the major lesson of film as a new language is not social but formal, as seen in Puig's attempts at narrative hyperrealism. Developed as a realization of the myth of "primordial realism"—an expression from André Bazin (qtd. in Andrew and Ungar 377)—film produces, as Panofsky suggests, the illusion of a more objective record of reality, before the mediations of personal style. Puig finds therein a purer, more immediate language, one less tied to the authority and personal mythology of the artist; he attempts a similarly neutral manipulation of reality through the recording and montage of voices, altering conventional notions of proprietary claims (copyright) in literature. Driven by the specificity of the medium, film offers an alternative point of departure to speak about style in modern literature. Reproduction—full of reminders of previous uses, in contrast to literary language—promises a degree zero of writing (Barthes, *Writing*), a reality independent of the language and style and the weight of possible modes of expression that writing entails. The integral realism of the new medium renews the utopia of an authorial absence (without refuge or secrets) that both exceeds the limits of personal language and captures the naturalness of living speech.

Puig's distancing of literature from film is deceptive. The voice of the aunt that went on for over thirty pages and became the beginning of *Betrayed by Rita Hayworth* carries the reproductive impression of film: "The only thing that interested me," Puig confesses, "was to capture voices. It wasn't just a question of recording. I manipulated the material afterward; I edited it, I used it to carry out the experiment I wanted, but the material was always spoken language" (qtd. in Sosnowski 71). That capturing of voices clearly corresponds to the realist obsession of the camera. The process described by Puig is the literary transposition of cinematic montage, the principle film has used, since D. W. Griffith, to turn itself into art.

Of the six movies that Molina recounts in *Kiss of the Spider Woman*, four of them are clear references to Hollywood films: more or less faithful renditions of *Cat People*, by Jacques Tourneur, and *The Enchanted Cottage*, by John Cromwell; a personal re-creation of the "auto racing" genre ("those films men usually go for" ["de esas películas que les gustan a los hombres"] [Eng. 114, Span. 118, Archivos 101] according to Molina); and a version of *I Walked with a Zombie*, by Tourneur, with shades of Alfred Hitchcock's *Rebecca* (1940) and Robert Stevenson's *Jane Eyre* (1944). The two others are Puig's inventions, and, while they may be based on a different kind of film model, they cannot resist a Hollywood touch: a Nazi propaganda film, *Destiny*, inspired by the expressionist cinema of the German film studio Universum Film AG[4]—in particular, *The Great Love* (1942)—with clear references to spy movies of the 1930s starring Marlene Dietrich and Greta Garbo, and a collage of Mexican cabaret melodramas of the 1940s influenced by the celebrated MGM version of *Camille* (1937), by George Cukor, and by Cukor's Mexican remakes.

Looking at Molina's choices of movies in *Kiss of the Spider Woman*, as well as at the cinematic allusions in Puig's other novels and the catalog of Puig's video library, one can conclude that cinema, for Puig, is above all the cinema of Hollywood. As Michel Foucault said, to talk about North American cinema is redundant. Puig's novels broaden the narrative terms of that pronouncement. If we consider Puig's childhood trips to afternoon matinees as well as his first real contact with film production in Rome, the primacy of Hollywood in his narrative world is motivated not only by biographical coincidence but also by aesthetic and cultural choice. Puig's time at the Centro Sperimentale di Cinematografia di Roma, directed by Cesare Zavattini in 1956, left him face-to-face with a dilemma that would soon be at the center of the polemics surrounding the "auteur cinema":

> My heart was divided. On the one hand, I liked the idea of popular movies, as well as ones of protest; but I also liked films with well-told stories, which seemed to be exclusive to the reactionaries. . . . One of Hollywood's principal characteristics was the care it took with narrative framework, and, given that for this new critical perspective all of Hollywood was synonymous with reactionary cinema, knowing how to narrate well came to

be considered a reactionary trait. Any attempt at dramatic structuration was considered suspect, contaminated with the poison of serial novels or *pièces-à-ficelles*.   (Prologue 10)

The films of the late 1950s reformulated the tension between high and mass culture: on the one hand, there were art films, politicized and experimental, represented in Italy by Italian neorealism; on the other, there were North American films, tied to a system of genres and to entertainment.

But it was precisely in Hollywood where Puig would find a model for resolving this cultural tension:

I don't have any literary models; that space is taken by cinematic influences. If someone were to try, they would find influences from Lubitsch in certain structures of mine, von Sternberg in my passion for very Hitchcockean atmospheres.   (Corbatta 605)

Puig has chosen as the fundamental model for his literature Hollywood's pioneering auteurs, who, faced with the demands of the cultural industry, produced an artistic and personal version of popular forms long before the post–avant-garde era. The great European masters demonstrated in the 1930s and 1940s that art film could also flourish in the major studios and that genre films did not have to be synonymous with commercial cinema. But how did they manage to reconcile the effectiveness of impersonal popular forms with their own formal creativity?

In his documentary history of North American cinema, Martin Scorsese (with Michael Henry Wilson) has created a personal journey centered on the same dilemma: how does one find one's own forms of expression in a system of fixed rules subject to the demands of the public?[5] To answer that question, he examines the guises developed by the great masters of the century for keeping art film prospering in the industry: the director as storyteller, as illusionist, as smuggler, as iconoclast. Because of Scorsese's practical rather than theoretical approach to the lessons of Hollywood, his subjective gaze is not very different from Puig's apprenticeship. If we examine that history, keeping Scorsese's choices in mind, it should come as no surprise that the central figures of each chapter of *Kiss of the Spider Woman* coincide with Puig's most admired directors and obey the strategies that Scorsese detects in those classic films.

First, there is the primacy of the director as storyteller. Ever since Griffith, the cinema of Hollywood has been the genre cinema par excellence, opposed to fixed formulas, clichéd narratives, and the stereotypical high culture traditions of an original and unique work of art. Even so, North American cinema has managed to extend the limits of the genres, using gaps in convention to propose new innovations, as in the work of Raoul Walsh and Howard Hawks, as well as Vincent Minelli, Cukor, and Hitchcock.

Narrative interest and the creative use of genres are two major lessons that we can take from Puig's literature. We see the narrative voracity of his characters;

the exasperating repetition of the word "tell"; the subtle economy of suspense and narrative seduction that moves the narrative along; and the deliberate re-occurrence of popular genres, such as serial, melodrama, detective, spy, and science fiction. "The careful intrigue," Puig asserts, "the anecdotal interest, the *coup de scène* all seem valid to me. What I find immoral is boredom" (qtd. in Muñoz 136). And furthermore, Puig says, "I never read Sue's *The Mysteries of Paris*, for example. I never read a serial novel in my life, but I watched a lot of serial-like movies" (qtd. in Rodríguez Monegal, "Folletín" 28).

Second, we have the director as illusionist. To give form to their gaze, Hollywood directors invented a visual language exploring the specific techniques of the medium: close-ups, tricks of montage, fade-ins and fade-outs, changes in focus, lighting effects, changes in perspective, special effects. In addition to the great inventions of Griffith, Cecil B. DeMille, and King Vidor, we have Friedrich Murnau's sumptuous visions, Frank Borzage's melodramatic pantomime, the illusive genius of Tourneur's shadows, and the contributions of Hitchcock.

In the creativity of these directors, Puig found a source of inspiration for exploring new possibilities of point of view and montage, re-creating fantastic or dreamlike atmospheres, and enriching scenic description. Indeed, Puig's formal experiments at the beginning of *The Buenos Aires Affair* are inspired by Hitchcock's camera: the discursive montage, the close-up shots, the tones of voice, the visual texture of the scenes narrated, the framing and lighting effects, the magical resonance of a fade.

To illustrate the third and most daring strategy of art cinema in the industry—the director as smuggler—Scorsese chose the two directors whom Puig most admired, Tourneur and Max Ophüls (from among other European exiles who challenged Hollywood's conventions and imposed their own personal visions, such as Fritz Lang, Hitchcock, Billy Wilder, and Douglas Sirk). Scorsese begins with the two films by Tourneur that Molina retells in *Kiss of the Spider Woman—Cat People* and *I Walked with a Zombie*—and finds there perfect examples of how to turn the very real limitations of the industry—low budgets, the rigid demands of the genre—into the impetus for a personal language. In *Cat People*, Tourneur reduces the ominous presence of the panther woman to a shadow, for reasons that go beyond the low budget: "The less seen, the more you believe. You must never try to impose your views on the viewer, but rather you must try to let him see in, little by little" (qtd. in Scorsese and Wilson 98). In this indirect approach, Scorsese finds the perfect definition of the director as smuggler; he sifts through to find original touches, unexpected motifs, and even radical political perspectives: esoteric thought in Tourneur's horror films, philosophical skepticism in Ophüls's melodramas, the oppressive omnipresence of violence in Fritz Lang's detective movies, political irony in Ernst Lubitsch's comedies, and paranoia in Hitchcock's thrillers.

What better definition than "smuggling" for Puig's subtle intrusions masked by the seductive trappings of popular forms? Like the movies that Molina recounts, Puig's novels always talk about something else. If genres are social contracts between an artist and a public whose function is to specify the appropriate use of a particular cultural artifact, Puig accepts the benefits of that contract but calls into question the limits of appropriate use. Thus in *Heartbreak Tango* he chooses the enigmas and dramatic intrigues of the serial novel to examine Argentine machismo; in *The Buenos Aires Affair*, Puig turns to the stereotypical model of a whodunit to encode the violence in the struggles for legitimacy in the artistic sphere; in *Kiss of the Spider Woman*, he prefers the classic melodrama of sacrifice made for love to talk about homosexuality and sexual politics as an unfinished chapter in the process of Argentina's social transformation in the 1970s. In *Pubis angelical*, with the same subtlety of form, he again resorts to melodrama, along with the spy novel, parapsychology, and science fiction, to explore feminine fantasies subjected to a masculine gaze. On the sly, Puig's novels offer a firsthand account of post–World War II Argentine political history—from the first period of Peronism to the repression of the dictatorship and Juan Perón's exile to the revolutionary militancy and leftist Peronism of the 1970s.

This strategy of smuggling allows a subtle form of social and sexual pedagogy, even through its most mystifying figures, the movie stars. Through its fantasized women, and especially through its exaggerated women—Dietrich, Bette Davis, Barbara Stanwyck, and Katherine Hepburn—Puig finds an ambivalence that allows them to momentarily embody a covert process of liberation, an enigmatic blurring of the lines of their traditional gender roles, a dream of power and freedom. In this ambiguity, North American cinema is not only the ubiquitous space of consolation but also a possibility for mass consumption of a liberating introspection.[6] Trained in the tradition of Hollywood contraband, Puig creates his own political use of popular forms—one that goes beyond the narrow limits of parody, mere consumption, and consolation—and explores a spectrum of possible narrative translations. What textual translation could be more evident of the smuggling strategy than the footnotes in *Kiss of the Spider Woman*? Through a series of brief texts in the footnotes that carry on a dialogue with the main text of the novel and bring other resonances to the protagonists' dialogues, Puig presents theories about homosexuality in a new stylization. He uses the discourse of scientific or philosophical inquiry, which has a long tradition in the popular magazine genre. He thus condenses the principal psychoanalytic and sociological theories of Sigmund Freud and Herbert Marcuse in a dialectics of sexual oppression and liberation. As he said in an interview,

> Since little is known about sexuality—the scientific studies are very new, sparse, and generally presented using a terminology difficult to understand—I wanted to solve the information problem usually kept so repressively hidden.   (qtd. in Coddou 12)

In the interplay between what is written above and what is written below, we can find new, formal resolutions of the problem of narrative authority and a dialectical materialization of fact and fiction (see Balderston, "Sexuality"). The asterisk, we could say, is the conspiratorial wink of the smuggler to his seasoned readers and a subtle invitation to legalize the contraband for unsuspecting readers.

The smuggler, however, is merely the strategic double of a more anarchical figure that openly challenges the system, defies its conventions, and expands artistic forms. In the last chapter of Scorsese's journey, dedicated to the director as iconoclast, Eric von Stroheim and Josef von Sternberg (the director for whom Puig had a fascination) occupy a central position. Von Sternberg's baroque stylization turns out to be as subversive for Hollywood as von Stroheim's extreme realism. Persistently dogged by the censors, threatened by producers and traditional editorial canons, the iconoclasts nevertheless took the cinematic form to its highest artistic levels. There is a lineage that runs from the European pioneers to Orson Welles, Stanley Kubrick, and John Cassavetes.

Puig admires the possibility of direct subversion in von Sternberg, as well as the scandalous audacity of his diva, Dietrich: "What would I save from the fire if I had to choose one film from the history of the cinema? I suppose that the aficionados of Antonioni and Godard would find my choice a *dishonored* one" ("Homenaje" 149).[7] This comment closes "Homenaje a von Sternberg," written by Puig in 1969 for the Spanish journal *Bazaar*, in which, from among all the Viennese director's films that he considers, he chooses the Hollywood tetralogy starring Dietrich produced between 1931 and 1934: *Morocco, Dishonored, Shanghai Express,* and *Blonde Venus*.

Two extreme features sum up the attraction for Puig of the von Sternberg–Dietrich alliance. Von Sternberg's magic creates an artificial world, "a heterocosmos of lights and shadows," and can be seen as a modernist critique of Hollywood's "illusion of realism" (Baxter 102); the enigmatic and androgynous figure of Dietrich, with her emphasis on sexuality as representation, frees women from the rigid imposition of traditional gender roles. Von Sternberg's plots, relatively tame in comparison with the intense passions of melodrama or the exoticism of adventure films or the double identities of spy movies, find the possibility of a more daring challenge in Dietrich's feminine force. Spy or cabaret singer, androgynous and mysterious, Dietrich is the emblematic woman who confronts the masculine world and the social conventions imposed on the feminine world, surrendering only to the dictates of the heart.

But the most lasting lesson learned from von Sternberg can be found in the subtle difference between style and stylization, evident in the contrast between his first films (*The Docks of New York* [1928], *Blue Angel* [1930]) and the tetralogy. Puig finds in these films a particular mixture of "humor and sincerity," a model of ironic distance and ambivalence that, despite his resistance to critical labels, for the first and only time he refers to as "camp":

> That vision, both cynical and compassionate at the same time, is perfectly coherent and full of hidden dimensions behind the tulle, the gold lamé,

and the false eyelashes. *Dishonored* is a metaphor for the conflict between the individual and patriotism; *Shanghai Express* is a subtle gibe at abuses of authority.   ("Homenaje" 148)

That vision, "both cynical and compassionate at the same time," "full of hidden dimensions"—the typical ambivalence of a camp stylization (Sontag, "On Style" 19)—allows him to endow his writing with his own aesthetic weight, without renouncing his social and political interests, retaining the distance he has chosen for his narration.

Von Sternberg's extravagant aestheticism brings us back to *Kiss of the Spider Woman*. If the movie plots that Molina chooses to recount refer us back to the cinematographic models that inspired the narration, his narrative art—his personal style of recounting them—is also inherited from Hollywood and has an eloquent genealogy in Puig's literature. In chapter 13 of *Betrayed by Rita Hayworth*, Puig includes a school essay written by the protagonist Toto for the annual literary essay competition—modestly titled "My Favorite Movie"—a personal version of the Hollywood-like biography of Johann Strauss, *The Great Waltz* (1938). The choice of this film as Puig's first conversion of film to literature is not a coincidence. It is the first film for MGM directed by Julien Duvivier, one of the "five greats" of the French poetic realism of the 1930s and the director of the classic film *Pepé, le Moko* (1937). The final sequences—melodramatic and artificial re-creations of several biographical scenes from Strauss's life—carry the unmistakable mark of the true director, von Sternberg, who replaced Duvivier in the final scenes without being mentioned in the credits. A fervent disciple of von Sternberg, Puig's alter ego Toto copies various sequences, freely re-creates others, and invents wild swings in fortune for the plotline, accentuating the emotional effects, the romantic fatalism, the camp extravagance, and the visual mannerisms of *The Great Waltz*:

> When Johann appears, the salutes are fired, everyone was waiting for him, it is the homage the emperor prepared for him in secret, and the cheers little by little take on a rhythm, a waltz rhythm, the multitude sings those old love stanzas about dreams coming true and beautiful faces that can only exist in the imagination, and suddenly Johann seems to see, way up high, above the multitude, a creature of the blue yonder, and the vision becomes clearer and clearer, it's a beautiful young woman, yes, it is Carla singing his verses, and her lips aren't coral nor her eyes green like the emerald sea, her face is transparent over the sky of Vienna and Johann anxiously tries to think what color that heavenly vision is.
>
> (*Betrayed by Rita Hayworth* 196)

Al aparecer Johann estallan las salvas, todos lo esperaban, es el homenaje que el emperador le preparaba en secreto, y las voces que vitorean poco a poco toman un ritmo sostenido, un ritmo de vals y todos corean aquellas

estrofas de amor: "Sueños de toda una vida pueden hoy ser realidad, el
rostro que yo veía cuando mis ojos cerraba . . ." y sin cerrar los ojos Johann
cree ver allá en lo alto, por encima de la multitud a una criatura del éter, y
la visión se hace más y más nítida, es una hermosa mujer joven, sí, es Carla
que canta sus versos y su piel no es blanca ni sus labios de rojo coral ni sus
ojos de verde esmeralda, sobre el cielo de Viena su figura ahora se refleja
transparente, y Johann se afana pensando de qué color es esa sublime
visión.   (*Traición* 263)

The cinematic passion that up to this point was expressed as a childish game
of copying, collage, and montage (Toto cuts, traces, paints, and puts together
a series of little books) is now turned into literature. In the story of the adoles-
cent artist that is suggested in *Betrayed by Rita Hayworth*, Toto moves from
practicing a craft that is distant, flat, and typical of the pop tradition to practicing a literary celebration of the baroque artifice and stylization typical of
camp. Those two artistic gestures that spring from film are expanded in Puig's
work and resolve the dilemma of style. He uses a double strategy: the objective
reconstruction of anonymous voices to the point of hyperrealism (as if they had
been recorded) and the daily fantasies, the dreams, the unconscious murmurs,
the stories within a story, modeled on the most extravagant aestheticism of
camp cinema.

Thus it is not surprising that in his notes for writing *Kiss of the Spider Woman*,
Puig insists on the importance of different distancing techniques (a "dispassion-
ate" story told "not from within" and theatrical dialogues), and he saves the sensitive transparency of his desires—his splendor and his prison—for Molina. The
secret refuge of a "queer art" (*arte Folle*) is Puig's special tool. "Avoid all similarities with the author," Puig writes in his notes on Molina, and, immediately
after that, "[h]is whole art lies in his narration" ("Fase" 275). Molina, always
diligent, gives himself away in the theatrical nature of his gestures, the affected
mannerisms of his personality, and the artificial excess of the plots he chooses
to recount. A successor to Toto, he gets lost in the play of light and shadow, in
sensual surfaces, in textures:

And when the chorus number's finished, the stage gets left in total darkness until, up above, a light begins to rise like mist and the silhouette of
some divine-looking woman, who's very tall, absolutely perfect, but still
just a hazy outline, slowly emerges sharper and sharper, because she steps
forward through layers and layers of hanging tulle, and you obviously get
to see her more and more clearly, wrapped in a sliver lamé gown that
fits her like a glove. The most divine woman you can imagine. And she
sings a song, first in French and afterwards in German. She's way high up
over the stage, and then all of a sudden some lightning flashes under her
feet and she makes her way downwards and with each step, zap! another
streak of lightning, and finally the whole stage is left crossed by horizontal

lines, because actually each line of light is on the edge of a step, and takes
the form of a staircase all in lights without your realizing it.   (50)

Y cuando termina ese número queda el escenario todo a oscuras hasta
que por allá arriba una luz se empieza a levantar como niebla y se dibuja
una silueta de una mujer divina, alta, perfecta, pero muy esfumada, que
cada vez se va perfilando mejor, porque al acercarse va atravesando colga-
jos de tul, y claro, cada vez se la va pudiendo distinguir mejor, envuelta en
un traje de lamé plateado que le ajusta la figura como una vaina. La mujer
más divina que te podés imaginar. Y canta una canción primero en francés
y después en alemán. Y ella está en lo alto del escenario y de repente a los
pies de ella como un rayo se enciende una línea recta de luz, y va dando
pasos para abajo y a cada paso, ¡paf! una línea más de luz, y al final queda
el escenario todo atravesado de estas líneas, que en realidad cada línea
era el borde de un escalón, y se formó sin darte cuenta una escalera toda
de luces.   (57, Archivos 47)

Silenced to hear other voices, Puig's most secret style reappears in Molina's
story with the ingenious and ambiguous excuse of re-creating a queer art: a
generous aestheticism, tender, theatrical, intense without being heavy, happy
without excessive forethought or prejudice, camp. Molina's queer art emerges
as the author recedes, inaugurating *Kiss of the Spider Woman*. Toto's artistic
education finds its felicitous corollary here. Doubly inspired by film, almost
renouncing literature, Puig finds a personal way, democratic and liberating, to
confront the absolute sovereignty of style.

NOTES

This essay, including all quotations, was translated from the Spanish by Susan Benner,
unless otherwise indicated. The original Spanish essay appears in José Amícola and Jorge
Panesi's critical edition of *El beso de la mujer araña*.

[1] "Benjamin is perhaps the one who has best anticipated Manuel Puig's literary practice, and is perhaps his most insightful theorist" (Pauls 65). We should add that Benjamin's essay is not one-sided in its analysis of the potentialities of the new media. While in
his central argument he speaks in auspicious terms of the possibilities for destruction of
the aura made possible by film, in the epilogue, Benjamin discusses the risk that it could
be used as a vehicle for fascist propaganda.

[2] Translator's note: This commentary by Puig occurs only on the cover of the original
Spanish version of the novel, *Boquitas pintadas*.

[3] For the title of the first version of the essay, "On Movies" (1936), Panofsky chose
to use what was then the less familiar North American term for the medium. The third
version of Panofsky's essay, "Style and Medium in the Motion Pictures," was published
in 1947 and is reproduced in Panofsky, *Three Essays on Style*.

[4] Translator's note: Universum Film AG was Germany's major film studio both before and during the Nazi era.

[5] Scorsese and Wilson's text is based on the documentary film produced in honor of the first hundred years of cinema, *The Century of Cinema, A Personal Journey with Martin Scorsese through American Movies*.

[6] Italo Calvino agrees with the characterization of Hollywood as a particular form of pedagogy: "North American cinema at that time . . . was a particular mystification. Just as for a psychoanalyst it doesn't make a difference whether a patient lies or tells the truth because either way he reveals something of himself, so I, a spectator belonging to a different system of mystifications, can learn something from that bit of truth and that mystification that Hollywood's products provided me. . . . The most important model of female characters in North American cinema was that of men's rival in decision making and in stubbornness. . . . For a society such as ours, for the Italian customs of that era, especially in the provinces, that autonomy and initiative on the part of North American women could be a lesson, which somehow reached its audience."

[7] Translator's note: Here Puig is using a play on words in the Spanish that is impossible to reproduce exactly in English. This movie, known in English as *Dishonored*, is titled *Fatalidad* in Spanish, which is perhaps best translated in this context as "misfortune." Thus Puig is saying, "I suppose that for the aficionados of Antonioni and Godard, my choice would be a *misfortune*," but of course the title in English is different. Puig's original Spanish reads, "Supongo que para los aficionados a Antonioni y Godard, sería una *fatalidad* mi elección."

An Impossible Love:
Film and Literature in
Kiss of the Spider Woman

David Oubiña

If mass culture has defined new narrative forms that create tension with high literary tradition, Manuel Puig's work represents an emblematic effort to relate them to one another and thus to reshape the connection between popular culture and high culture that has constituted the novelistic genre. Puig constructs his writing from an accumulation of heterogeneous and underrated materials: boleros, tangos, serial novels, radio dramas, B movies. His aesthetic (or lack of an aesthetic) is built on literary appropriation of the imaginary of mass culture. "There have been attempts at repression by arbiters of good taste for centuries," Puig declared. "I am afraid that the cultured forms of art have exercised a great deal of repression and that there are fascinating possibilities in those discarded expressions" (qtd. in Torres Fierro 509–10).

Puig collects and appropriates those discarded materials and then gives them novelesque forms: personal diaries, legal documents, forgotten letters, newspaper clippings, résumés, shopping lists, classroom compositions, fragments from an engagement book, job applications, or airline records. For him, all discourses have the same literary rights. His novels function as collages, not only because they are created from pieces of other texts, but also because they listen to all voices. Puig dispenses with the cohesive and totalizing figure of the omniscient narrator who establishes hierarchies and puts things in a certain perspective. At one point, the author stated that he was terrified of the grammatical third person because it created an objectivity that does not correspond to the "real" (Catelli 26); his texts instead lean toward the partiality and distortion of individual points of view. The empty space left by the omniscient narrator is occupied by diverse voices that take on, in their pronouncements, the representation of their own context, as in the beginning of *Eternal Curse on the Reader of These Pages* (*Maldición eterna a quien lea estas páginas*): "My name is Larry. Yours is Ramírez. And Washington is the name of this square," Larry recites to Ramírez—and also to himself (*Eternal Curse* 3). We could say that, like Ramírez, Puig's novels are aphasic: they retain the names of things but not their concepts, and therefore the writer's task is to reconstruct the relation that should unite them.

Thus the story cannot pass the truth test and is never as reliable as a ubiquitous and transparent narrator. We stand no longer before the facts but before versions of the facts—self-interested, malicious, dubious, or uncertain versions that are always skewed in terms of what happened. In *The Buenos Aires Affair*, the narration also includes its own potentialities as possible bifurcations that never occur (be they imagined actions or actions that would have happened if fate had not intervened); in *Heartbreak Tango* (*Boquitas pintadas*), all speakers are by definition liars who are hiding something; in *Pubis angelical*, Ana contradicts herself constantly in her personal diary; in *Blood of Requited Love* (*Sangre de amor correspondido*), Josemar inconsistently reconstructs his past; in *Eternal Curse on the Reader of These Pages*, discursive intermittency is marked by Larry's cat, which capriciously dies and then reappears in his stories; and in *Tropical Night Falling* (*Cae la noche tropical*), we read a circle of transmissions in which Silvia tells Nidia about things that happen to a third person.

In *Kiss of the Spider Woman* (*El beso de la mujer araña*), Molina gives his version of the films he loves. His movie stories, which take on the form of a narration in installments, place the gaze of a naive storyteller before the ear of a hypercritical listener. Serge Daney has asserted that if film allows us to see, it is to some extent because it obliges us to see: to see a movie is to see something already seen by someone else (83). And in this sense, any gaze involves a kind of cutout that reveals as much as it hides. This dialectic between what a discourse expresses and what it simultaneously represses always governs the relation between different statements in Puig's work. But while in his other novels movies are part of the great imaginary of mass culture to which the writer continually refers, in *Kiss of the Spider Woman* they constitute most of the central material.

Puig's first three novels function on the basis of an oscillation between the rhetorical subjectivity of interior monologue and a naturalistic objectivity in the reproduction of documents. His constructive principle consists of isolating the discourses to articulate them in a polyphonic structure. Like the pictures of movie stars that Toto cuts out in *Betrayed by Rita Hayworth* (*La traición de Rita Hayworth*), the narrative movement comes from the montage of fragments. But beginning with *Kiss of the Spider Woman*, dialogue becomes the privileged form of pronouncements (even though various kinds of documents and texts continue to appear throughout his novels). Structured as a kind of minute record of the conversation, the story has no other movement than the alternation between two interdependent voices. In the cell where Molina and Valentín are imprisoned, everything flows through that orderly situation that conversation tends to take on in films, the canonical recourse of shot / reverse shot that allows us to see and hear each interlocutor alternately in a dialogue.[1]

The development of sound in movies led to transformations in interpretation and staging methods. In the talkies of the 1930s and 1940s we can see the abandonment of some of the techniques of silent films (such as depth of field), the affirmation of a certain static state of the image, and the consolidation of what Gilles Deleuze calls the system of human interactions:

> It was inevitable that the talkie took what appeared to be the most superficial social forms as its privileged object: encounters with the other, other sex, other class, other region, other nation, other civilization. The less of

> a pre-existing social structure there is, the better is revealed, not a si-
> lent natural life, but pure forms of sociability necessarily passing through
> *conversation.*   (230)[2]

Like the talkies of Hollywood's golden age, *Kiss of the Spider Woman* is a dialogued novel. It's not that the text unfolds without any action but that the action
is only apparent through the resonances it creates in conversation. What the
characters do must be reconstructed from their allusions, their inflections, their
pauses, and in their silences. The whole plot of the novel is constructed through
the succession of these long scenes of retelling movies. And in this sense, the
movies that Molina recounts are not a metaphor or a digression, nor are they
stories that merely accompany a central history, interspersed with its telling; on
the contrary, the relationship between the two prisoners develops through or
around the comments and opinions that each movie elicits.

The character of the dialogue in *Kiss of the Spider Woman* stems from the
nature of its interlocutors. It is a question of connecting two opposites, that is,
two discourses in which the communication between the two is blocked a priori
and is destined to be mutually exclusive, each annulling the other rather than
creating interaction between the two. Valentín objects that it is impossible to
talk with Molina, but he also recognizes that he himself does not know how
to listen.[3] It is a dialogue between two deaf people: two solitary persons put in
contact by their forced cohabitation. The films function as an arena where the
points of view of two opposing spectators confront each other. The conflicts
between a political mystic and a mystic of romance novels (or, as Silvia says in
Tropical Night Falling, "an attitude toward life which revolves around emotions
and imagination as opposed to rationality" [146]) are delineated there in the different interpretations of the same object. In discussing the Nazi movie, Valentín
states, "It interests me as propaganda, that's all. In a certain sense it serves as a
document" ("Me interesa como material de propaganda, nada más. Es un docu-
mento en cierta forma") (Eng. 79, Span. 85, Archivos 70), whereas for Molina,
"when it came to the love scenes the film was divine, an absolute dream" ("tené
bien claro que la película era divina por las partes de amor, que era un verdadero
sueño") (Eng. 89, Span. 98, Archivos 79).

The films would seem to show a glamorous world far from the prison reality, but it is through them that an artful continuity is established and the relationship between Molina and Valentín is presented under different terms. The
stories in the films concern impossible love where the lovers are invariably condemned to unhappiness: a man and a woman who should never have found each
other must live out the fatal course of a torturous passion. The panther woman
and the architect, the French chorus girl Leni Lamaison and the Nazi official, the scarred young man and the ugly servant woman, the race car driver
and the director of a fashion magazine, the young couple trapped in a voodoo
spell, the passionate reporter and the lover of a Mafia magnate—they all dare
to cross the barriers that separate them but later pay for their audacity. When

Valentín asks Molina whom he identifies with in the film about Irena, the panther woman, Molina replies, "With Irena, what do you think? She's the heroine, dummy. Always with the heroine" ("Con Irena, qué te crées. Es la protagonista, pedazo de pavo. Yo siempre con la heroína") (Eng. 25, Span. 31, Archivos 21).[4] It does not matter to Molina that Irena is a monster, just as it does not bother him that Leni Lamaison is a traitor to her country, because the heroine is always guided by the loftiest intentions of a romantic passion. In this code of ethics, love only needs answer to itself; for those who give themselves completely to love, there is no other judgment than that of their fidelity to that sentiment.

Thus Molina dies like a heroine of one of his films: although he is shot during a skirmish between the police and a guerrilla group, the motive of his mission is love. One might ask whether *Kiss of the Spider Woman* is a political novel or a melodrama. But the text seems to question the essentialism of those two categories in order to evolve from the fusion of the two.[5] It is true that in the melodramas of industrial culture, as Max Horkheimer and Theodor Adorno proclaim, the tragic becomes "an institution for moral improvement": "tragedy is reduced to the threat to destroy anyone who does not cooperate, whereas its paradoxical significance once lay in a hopeless resistance to mythic destiny" (152). Puig, however, restores to the notion of the tragic that potential for resistance. Molina's dreams of becoming a *bourgeois señora* lead him to his heroic destiny. The political nature of his rebellion arises from a promise he makes for love, not from a militant conscience. In Puig we find a politics of sentiment.

The narrative scheme Molina uses in recounting his versions of the films is a scale model of the mechanisms of representation that organize the novel. Molina narrates as if in the theater. He not only recounts the plot but describes the phenomenological materiality of the film. He has a cinematic imagination, and thus his story is organized as if it were a decoupage.[6] When he needs to describe a montage sequence, he clearly specifies the succession of shots:

> And afterwards the applause, and then some short scenes with the two of them very happy: an afternoon at the horse races, with her all in white, wearing a sheer picture-hat and with him in a top hat; and next a toast together on some yacht sailing down the River Seine; and then in a private room of a Russian nightclub, he's in tails, blowing out the candelabra and he opens a jewel case and takes out a necklace of pearls, and you don't know how but even in the darkness they shine fantastically, through some movie trick. (73)

> Y después siguen aplausos y escenas cortas de ellos dos que son muy felices, de tarde en las carreras de caballos, ella toda de blanco con una capelina transparente y él con galera, y después brindando en un yate que corre por el río Sena, y después él de smoking en el reservado de una boîte rusa apagada los candelabros y en la penumbra abre un estuche

y saca un collar de perlas que no se sabe cómo pero aunque esté oscuro brilla bárbaramente por trucos del cine.   (80, Archivos 67)

When there is an ellipsis, Molina indicates the visual form in which the passage of time is presented:

In the meantime, the officer is giving orders for a candlelight dinner for two, and afterwards you see the candles all look twice as short as they did before, but he's still playing the piano, a sort of very slow, very sad waltz. (80)

Mientras tanto el muchacho está dando las órdenes de la cena para dos, con candelabros, y después se ve que las velas ya están consumidas por la mitad, y él está tocando el piano, esa especie de vals lento, muy triste. (86–87, Archivos 71)

In referring to the nondiegetic use of music, he naturalizes the absence of a source for the sound, as if it were a physical property of the surroundings: "and at this point the whole invisible orchestra starts to accompany her as loud as can be and she, she belts it out" ("y allí la orquesta invisible empieza a todo volumen y larga ella toda su voz") (Eng. 237, Span. 240, Archivos 218). If the description of the shot is from a subjective camera angle, Molina describes the image literally through the eyes of the character:

impossible to determine his features, only an image distorted by the glare from the candelabras or even like through eyes filled with tears, his face seen through eyes filled with tears, tears drying up, face seen with absolute clarity. (108)

imposible distinguir sus rasgos, la visión distorsionada por reflejos de los candelabros, o también como a través de los ojos cargados de lágrimas, la cara de él vista por ojos cargados de lágrimas, las lágrimas se secan, la cara de él vista con toda claridad. (112, Archivos 92–93)

And when there is a voice-over, the sound of the words echoes fantastically in his own discourse: "the magnate's threat is still ringing in her ears: 'I'll wreak my vengeance on any man that dares to go near you'" ("en los oídos todavía le silban las palabras del magnate: 'me vengaré con la vida del hombre que se haya atrevido a acercársete'") (Eng. 228, Span. 231, Archivos 208).

Puig has stated that his writing took from film "the speed of the story, a dose of intrigue, and the manipulation of information" (Torres Fierro 512). In *Kiss of the Spider Woman*, there is effectively an expository mode that seems to come more from cinematic narration than from literary tradition. Puig has learned this from B movies, to which he continually returns and which were Molina's favorites as well:

> that category of North American films from the 1940's, defined by a rigidly contractual mode of production (they were made to order), created on a small budget, shot at a breathtaking pace, and marked by a singular practice of quotation. The B movies copy the genre (detective, melodrama, spy, romantic), though never the style, of a particular film maker. (Pauls 79)[7]

What interests Molina is the serial novel or soap opera, that is, the genre defined as a frame of representation and a horizon of expectations. In B movies, the genre-related mechanisms and procedures can be clearly seen in their greatest transparency (Valentín recognizes this—although in a critical manner—when he comments on how coherent the film *Cat People* is [Eng. 20, Span. 26, Archivos 18]). This kind of film, then, is like a catalyst that acts on those genre-related conventions, forcing them to reveal the origin of the classic narrative model: a storytelling machine resting on an infallible structure of action-reaction and an impeccable dramatic logic.

We often hear of the parody in Puig's work, yet his narration never casts a distanced gaze over his characters and materials. If the films discussed are reconstructed through Molina's idealized telling, they are only made an issue through Valentín's point of view. And while Valentín can never abandon for a moment his Marxist doctrine, Molina identifies to such a degree with the world of the movies that he is quickly offended by his cell mate's ironic commentary. Their opinions are thus set in sharply delineated perspectives: they establish the space from which they are spoken, and, at the same time, they reveal their blind spots. This development of the spectator function avoids any parodic intention in the novel.[8] Stereotyped points of view full of prejudices and clichés end up being complementary and interdependent and move the narrative along. There is no psychology in Molina or in Valentín, because in reality each functions as a medium being spoken by a different sociolect. The importance of what they say lies not so much in its status as individual expression as in the fact that what they say functions as a vehicle of cultural discourse in which certain dogmatic conceptions of politics, love, loyalty, honor, and sexuality confront each other.

This explains, at least in part, the problems that plagued Héctor Babenco's cinematic adaptation of the book. In Puig's novel, there are no sharp, unmistakable images or precise profiles of people's bodies. In Babenco's version, those stereotyped discourses are constrained by objective narration. In trying to accommodate the text so that it conforms to the concrete materiality of the image, the filmmaker contextualizes the action, individualizes the characters, and concretizes the discourses in flesh and blood. Look at the differences that are established at the beginning of the novel and the beginning of the film:

while in Puig's novel, it is at first impossible to assign the discourses to anyone or to determine their location (only very slowly are we able to infer the bits and pieces of information that allow us to put together the situation and the characters), in Babenco's film we know from the very first that the two men are talking in a prison cell. Forced to take the form of concrete individuals, those schematic discourses are absorbed by the characters; they are no longer voices inhabited by prejudices and crystallized notions but commonplace, one-dimensional subjects. The same thing happens with the films that Molina recounts. Babenco has chosen to condense all the movies into just one story: the tragedy of Leni Lamaison. But then how to show the film? Or, at any rate, is it necessary to show it? The film itself is not really a main part of the novel; rather, Puig only presents Molina's oral version. Babenco understands that Molina's version is the only one that matters, but in the process of translating it into images, Babenco's film inevitably gives it a parodic tone that is completely alien to Molina's character.[9] In trying to reproduce Molina's gaze, the film shows what he recounts, but from a distance that seems to observe everything over his shoulder. While in the novel there is only the alteration caused by putting events into words, the film shows those words as deformations and cannot avoid judging them. In this way, the film eliminates the dialogical circuit in which Puig lets the voices interact.

It is worth pointing out that these problems are not unique to Babenco's film— they have occurred in all other attempts to adapt Puig's work.[10] Puig's texts have always had a powerful seduction for film producers: his writing, which does such a beautiful job of capturing the tone of everyday speech, his use of certain processes typical of screenplays, and his constant reference to movies or to the cinematic imaginary—all foster the belief that these books could be easily transferred to the big screen. Nevertheless, they invariably turn out to be traps for the filmmakers. While Puig's novels find a microcosm of social codes in popular cinema, in the reverse direction the narration loses its resistant dimension. Puig wrote:

> I didn't decide to move from film to the novel. I was planning a scene of a screenplay where the voice of one of my aunts, as a voice-over, was introducing the action in the washroom of a house in the village. That voice was supposed to say no more than three lines of the script, but it kept going on without stopping for thirty pages. There was no way to stop her. She had only banalities to tell, but it seemed to me that the accumulation of banalities gave a special significance to the account.   (Prologue 10)

The script eventually turned into his first novel, *Betrayed by Rita Hayworth*. This anecdote indicates the exact moment that Puig made the change from filmmaker to author of fiction and thus from working with images and sound to working with words. What Puig understood early on is that beyond whatever possible exchange there might be between one medium and the other, there is no negotiation between their expressive languages.

Film is a synthetic medium that operates in an instantaneous and simultaneous manner; literature, on the other hand, functions analytically, by linkages and succession. Concerning the film version of *Boquitas pintadas*, Puig wrote that he did not feel comfortable in the role of adapter because "I had to condense the novel, prune it, find ways to synthesize what had originally been presented analytically" (Prologue 11).[11] It is precisely when Puig's work seems the most cinematic that it is as remote from film as that of any other writer. It seems significant that after his incursion into film adaptation, Puig returned to literature and wrote *Kiss of the Spider Woman*, almost as if it were a reaction to that experience.

The presence of film is obviously central to Puig's work. The writer himself has indicated that his influences have been more cinematic than literary, and it is clear that behind his texts there is a video library rather than a library of books. But it would be mistaken to think that his novels have only dealt with film when in fact they are concerned with a literature that has managed to process films in written terms and has made a literary style out of cinematic processes. In this sense, if *Kiss of the Spider Woman* can be considered a cinematic novel (as *Heartbreak Tango* was subtitled "a serial" and *The Buenos Aires Affair* a "detective novel"), it is because cinema has been converted in its own way to literature.

NOTES

This essay, including all quotations, was translated from the Spanish by Susan Benner, unless otherwise indicated.

[1] In his previous novels, the dialogues generally appear in a recessive or atrophied form. *Betrayed by Rita Hayworth* is mostly composed of monologues of voices that bring to mind other voices. When dialogue is presented, it only registers half the conversation (such as the telephone conversation between Choli and Mita), or it is presented as a confusion of voices, more of an intertwining than an interchange (as in the first chapter). In *Heartbreak Tango* the dialogue is maintained through the exchange of letters and thus involves an absence. When people speak, one of the voices is held in check (as when Mabel confesses to the priest), or the dialogues are dominated by a double discourse to such an extent that what matters is the counterpoint between what the speakers say and what they actually think rather than the conversation (as in the dialogue between Mabel and Nené or between Celina and the Widow Di Carlo: the characters speak "actor to actor"). In *The Buenos Aires Affair*, the dialogue seems mutilated: either only one voice remains (as in Leo Druscovich's musings during a visit to the doctor and in the reports María Esther files with the police), or the voices are separated and scattered to describe the emotions the speaker feels at the moment of speaking, such that the dialogue becomes diluted (as in the conversation between Leo and María Esther when the former resolves to kill Gladys).

[2] For a discussion of the characteristics of dialogue in sound films, see Deleuze's ninth chapter, "The Components of the Image." For a discussion of the stylistic figure of shot / reverse shot in classic cinema, see Bordwell.

[3] Puig always chooses situations that prevent the ideal conditions for dialogue. In *Pubis angelical*, there is a political barrier between Ana and Pozzi and a sexist barrier between Ana and Beatriz; in *Eternal Curse*, Larry and Ramírez are confronted with differences in age, nationality, experience, and language; in *Tropical Night*, Luci and Nidia, despite their common past, suffer from "technical" impediments: deafness and arteriosclerosis respectively. *Blood of Requited Love* is special because its dialogue directly entails the destruction of an interchange: a person assailed by an uncontrollable memory and invaded by voices that act as interferences and rebel against his story.

[4] Molina recounts six movies modeled on Hollywood pictures: a version of *Cat People*, quite faithful to the original (Tourneur); a Nazi propaganda film titled *Destino* (*Her Real Glory*), inspired by the productions of Universum Film AG (UFA), Germany's major film studio both before and during the Nazi era, with a Marlene Dietrich–like heroine; a re-creation of *The Enchanted Cottage* (Cromwell); a film about auto racing that mixes the jet set of Europe with South American colonialism; a film about supernatural appearances and events based on *I Walked with a Zombie* (Tourneur) that also incorporates elements of other films; and a Mexican melodrama similar to those of George Cukor.

[5] Néstor Perlongher says of *Kiss of the Spider Woman*, "Through the figures of Molina and Valentín, the connection between two different forms of confronting the social order is realized: that is, the political and the sexual—the vehemence of discourse and the eloquence of bodies" ("El sexo" 4). Also, Piglia recognizes the subversive character that homosexuality and communism carry for society in *Betrayed by Rita Hayworth* (357).

[6] In a limited sense, the decoupage technique is the shooting script. By extension, Noël Burch states, "*découpage* also refers to the more or less precise breakdown of a narrative action into separate shots and sequences *before filming*" (3).

[7] For a recent study of the relation between Puig's work and the cinema, see Speranza.

[8] Severo Sarduy and Margery Safir have wanted to find a parodic intention in Puig, and Héctor Schmucler has even pointed out the judgmental nature of this supposed parody. Puig himself, however, has stated, "I looked up the word 'parody' in the dictionary and it said 'a mocking imitation.' I don't wish to mock anything" (qtd. in Catelli 24).

[9] In the theatrical version, written by Puig himself, the only film Molina tells is *Cat People*. Given that it is not possible to include all the films that appear in the novel, both the film and the play opted for just one. The decision is not a completely misguided one, but it does reduce Molina's complex cinematic universe to an excessively allegorical use of film. For an analysis of the relations among the novel, the play, and the movie, see Santoro. For a critique of Babenco's film, and especially the character of Molina and William Hurt's interpretation, see Foster.

[10] Besides Babenco's film, with screenplay by Leonard Schrader, Leopoldo Torre Nilsson filmed *Boquitas pintadas* (1973), and Raúl de la Torre adapted *Pubis angelical* (1982). The filmmaker Wong Kar-Wai, who traveled to Argentina to shoot a film loosely based on *The Buenos Aires Affair*, had problems with the rights to the novel and ended up filming *Happy Together* (1997) instead.

[11] Later on, Puig would return to writing for film, but it would be original screenplays (such as *Recuerdo de Tijuana* [1978]) or adaptations of other people's texts (such as *El lugar sin límites*, by José Donoso, in 1976, or the story "El impostor," by Silvina Ocampo, in 1977, both for the director Arturo Ripstein). See Lorenzano and Domenella.

Kiss of the Spider Woman: The Adaptations

Suzanne Jill Levine

The Play

A wandering exile from Argentina—still under dictatorial rule—Manuel Puig moved from New York to Rio de Janeiro in 1980. After the Argentine military coup in 1976, (relatively) gay-friendly Brazil had become home to many gay Argentines such as the poet Néstor Perlongher, fleeing an intolerant and unstable situation. As in most Latin American countries (except for his native Argentina), Puig was highly regarded as an important and innovative writer in Brazil, where, after writing plays and scripts in Mexico and New York for the last decade, he had his first major success as a playwright. Soon theatrical productions of *Kiss of the Spider Woman* began to crop up all over the globe; the first stage adaptation of the novel had been performed in Milan, in 1979. But he felt that in this production "the word got lost. . . . It was modern theater—projections, music, very visual" (qtd. in Manrique 16). There was too much multimedia and not enough emphasis on the language; it was more like a musical than a dramatic play. The production, a resourceful, if free, adaptation was well received, however, and played for over a year. Marco Mattolini, the director, had tried to respect the dialogue and the setting and used a lavish set made in Cremona, home to the Stradivarius and Puig's maternal grandmother.

Meanwhile in New York a professor at Rutgers, Ronald Christ, was eager to write the play directly in English for appreciative West Village audiences, but again Puig was dubious: the book seemed too unwieldy to adapt to the temporal constraints of a play because the plot development was "too long and splintered," especially the film narrations, the characters' fantasies, and those extensive footnotes (qtd. in Christ, "Interview" 26). How could one trim what was integral? On the other hand, the novel led its reader from the very birth of a relationship to its final consequence, in the spare form of a dialogue between two characters, unfolding within a tight bubble of time and space. The almost Aristotelian unity of the novel's scaffolding lent itself very well to the medium of theater. Motivated by the success of the play in Milan, Einaudi, a prestigious press, published the novel as *Bacio della donna ragno*. Puig was pleased by this move: *Bacio* won him the award for the best Latin American novel of 1981 and, months later, a nomination for the Nobel Prize. This last news reached him in Rio, in early October, but he took it with a grain of salt, as he wrote to his mother, "I think it's a bit premature, but it's 150,000 dollars, not to be sneezed at, but now onto other matters . . ." (Puig, letter to María Elena Puig, 9 Oct. 1981).[1]

Writing from Caracas to a friend in October 1981, he realized how much publicity he was receiving because of the Nobel nomination—a stimulus for the proliferation of productions in theaters everywhere from Caracas to Stockholm (Levine, *Manuel* 320). But let us return to 1979: the Italian theater debut motivated Puig to begin working on his own adaptation and led to a first offer optioned with RAI2, educational TV in Italy, to make *Kiss* into a film. Top actors vying for the role of Molina included Gian-Maria Volonte, Giuliano Gemma, and even Marcello Mastroianni; if France had signed on, Phillip Noiret would have played Molina and Gerard Depardieu would have played Valentín, the young Marxist. This project did not come to pass, however.

Although the abridgement of his novels into movies or plays would always involve disappointing compromises—an experience common to many writers—the rewards of glamour, fame, and, above all, money were too tempting to pass up. When Puig began work on the theater version of *Kiss* he was finishing his sixth novel, *Eternal Curse on the Reader of These Pages*. The outrageous title (with an irony not captured by many) insinuated his anger at reviewers who mostly misunderstood Puig, a writer who in so many ways was ahead of his time. He was taking a big risk—for the first time writing a novel directly in English, about a non-Argentine character in New York—and he felt that working simultaneously on a theater or film team project would be a relief from the solitude of writing (Levine, *Manuel* 321).

Puig's theatrical version of *Kiss* in Spanish was first produced in Madrid for the Teatro Martín and directed by José Luis García Sánchez, an esteemed Spanish filmmaker. The very first performance, a dry run, was staged in April 1981 in a small theater (Sala Escalante) in the coastal city of Valencia. *Kiss* the novel had been published first in Spain, just after Franco's death in 1975: the recently liberated Spain had received the daring novel with enthusiasm. If initially the friendship between the window dresser and the Marxist had been offensive to the intellectual left, it was now a welcome jolt to Spain in its sexual revolution, the *destape*. The Madrid production was a big hit, and the critics all agreed that the Argentine author was politically in tune with the times. On opening night, the theater was packed with national art and entertainment bigwigs, among them Fernando Rey, Luis Buñuel's lead actor and a longtime friend of Puig's, famous in Hollywood for his suavely sinister role in *The French Connection*; another admirer of Puig's was the young trendsetter of the new Spanish cinema, Pedro Almodóvar. Puig was now fully recognized as the writer of an accessible litera-ture that produced pleasure without compromising artistic originality or political idealism. The Spaniards, sentimentalists under their new racy veneer, went for the play's wishful romanticism; all over town the billboards were papered with Molina's climactic words to Valentín: "ahora yo . . . eras vos" ("As if now, some-how . . . I . . . were you") (Eng. 219, Span. 222, Archivos 196).

Meanwhile Puig was working with his translators in Rio de Janeiro, New York, and Paris (from his home in Rio he traveled frequently to Europe and the United States) on theater versions of *Kiss*, which, as a novel in dialogue, seemed ready-made for the stage. But this format was deceptive. Already, in his own Spanish-language theater adaptation, Puig reinstated his words but had to pare down the text by clipping Molina's six film narratives to one, *Cat People*; he managed to eliminate twenty-five percent of the original dialogue to present the play in a more abbreviated format. The dialogues in the play were livelier but also less ambiguous and more superficial.

The Changes

The Italian production had also inspired the minimalist notion of a single set: the prison cell. Molina's interviews with the warden were taped and played as a voice-over that, at the play's end, like a contrapuntal Greek chorus, vocal-izes each character's final monologue. The play, published in various languages, is almost a kind of blueprint of the novel, more straightforward but with less reflective characters. Puig's Molina was much more of an ordinary man; the Molina who evolved from the play to the film was more a caricature of a stereo-typical gay man.

Puig's play, an abridged version of the novel, was the basis of the screenplay that eventually turned into the Hollywood movie. Subordinating the novel's dense and subtle weave of movie plots, fascist politics, sexuality and the imagi-nation to the spider woman's stratagem, the successive commercial interpreters of the work made seduction, the love that conquers all under generic patriarchal oppression, take center stage. Set in a Latin American prison, *Kiss of the Spider Woman*, one film reviewer remarked, "is essentially a homosexual wish fantasy about how the love of a real man, however brief, can be transforming—purifying (Russo 285). *Kiss*, more than his other novels, reflects Puig's painful realiza-tion that such a fantasy could only be fulfilled in fiction, yet the film leaves out the novel's most crucial aspect. When William Hurt masculinizes Molina at the end of the Hollywood movie, when he dies heroically for a political cause, he defeats the whole thrust of Puig's argument. Molina doesn't have to conform to manly manners to be heroic, effeminate doesn't have to mean cowardly.

Of the six film narratives in the novel, Puig chose to retain in his theatrical adaptation *Cat People*, the horror film recounted in the novel's opening scene, because it was the most familiar—hence recognizable to the widest audience— and because it deliberately illustrated repressed sexuality and its outlet, violence. The principal characters of this 1940s Hollywood classic are a frigid, foreign bourgeois woman (played by the feline-featured Simone Simon) and her virginal American fiancé, played by the mild-mannered Kent Smith. The theme of the film is summarized in a tagline Puig and I used as an epigraph in our translation into English of Puig's novel *Boquitas pintadas*: "She was one of the dreaded Cat People—doomed to slink and prowl by night . . . fearing always that a lover's kiss might change her into a snarling, crawling killer!" Simon's enigmatic foreignness stressed, grotesquely, the "flawed" woman—different, possibly dangerous, metaphorically a queer, a man who cannot quite be a woman.

The Brazilian production of *Kiss* was a major event: opening night at the Ipanema theater, 14 August 1981, was attended by local and international celebrities. Among those present were the local *carioca* director and producer Flavio Tambellini and Héctor Babenco, who was already impressed by his compatriot's fame in Brazil. It was a thrilling evening, and the production was the best thus far, Puig told friends, because the Brazilians had infused it with their eros and playful humor. The play's sensationalism, political relevance, and success spurred Babenco to approach Puig about making a film based on his literary material. At the same time, the play drew negative press from militant gays—"Stalinist queens" as Puig called them—politicized by AIDS, which by 1982 was spreading like wildfire (Levine, *Manuel* 324). (Puig's first friend to be hit was in the United States, a cultural attaché in Washington.) Gay critics were particularly offended by the portrait of Molina as a frivolous queen instead of a hero. While Puig shared the gay community's fears and sympathies regarding the horrifying epidemic, he defended himself in "Losing Readers in Argentina," published in Amnesty International's *Index on Censorship*, insisting that he "shows gays as unexceptional human beings, in this case gentle and muddled, but at the same time courageous and loving." Once again, as often occurred in Puig's career as a writer, prevailing politics, despite Brazilian openness to all forms of sexuality, resisted his idiosyncratic art.

The Film

Early in 1982, Babenco, an Argentine documentary director living in exile in São Paulo who had just finished his first successful feature film, *Pixote*, met the American producer David Weisman through a mutual acquaintance, Arnaldo Jabor, a young Brazilian director whose sexy hit *Eu te amo* had also recently opened. Babenco was hoping to make his next film in Hollywood and had just been with the New York translator and agent Thomas Colchie, who represented several Brazilian writers as well as Puig. Out of this meeting Babenco optioned *Kiss of the Spider Woman*. Both he and Weisman knew that the time was ripe for Latin American themes to make it into the movies and that coproductions south of the border could be cost-effective. Their primary challenge was the gay theme, which Babenco thought might be too radical for mainstream audiences. They needed big-name actors to transmute this unlikely love story about a political prisoner and a gay window dresser, who were, in essence, the only characters. Signing stars meant not only big bucks but also another worry for Babenco: as an Argentine expatriate working in Rio's film industry and as a Paulista—Babenco had married into an affluent Jewish family in Rio's rival cosmopolis, São Paulo—he was fearful of arousing xenophobic reactions to the project by hiring American actors. After a tortuous process (see Levine, *Manuel*), Hurt was signed on as Molina, and the Latin Hollywood star Raúl Juliá as the Marxist; Sonia Braga, the leading Brazilian film diva at that time, was also cast in the film.

Puig first met Weisman on 15 September 1983, in Babenco's office and production headquarters, a suite at the newly built Maksoud Plaza Hotel in São Paulo. On this occasion Puig was explaining to Braga and other members of the crew his vision of Leni, the glamorous chanteuse in the Nazi movie narrated by Molina to Valentín. By acting the scene, Puig showed Braga that she should have both hands on one hip, in an arch 1940s kind of gesture, rather than a hand on either hip. Shooting was scheduled to start that month, on location at an abandoned prison in São Paulo. Puig's presence, his warm wit and intelligence, was a welcome diversion considering the tensions already evolving between the director and his producer and scriptwriter. Braga and Puig got along well too: in Puig's eyes she was the picture of glamour but also a simple Brazilian girl from humble origins, flattered to be treated as an equal by a great Latin American writer.

Puig appreciated Weisman's intelligence, and Weisman encouraged Puig's input; the two even composed together the lyrics of an absurd cabaret song performed by Braga as Leni. Puig's influence on the script was felt also in autobiographical nuances not explicit in the novel, as in the scene after Molina is released from prison, when Hurt watches a movie on television with his mother. Molina's constant worries about his mother's ill health in the novel had been reduced to one remark, so Puig added this touch, a typical scene from Puig's everyday life—almost like an Alfred Hitchcock walk-on.

The scriptwriter, Leonard Schrader (who had studied with the Chilean novelist José Donoso at the University of Iowa and was acquainted with Puig's novels in English), was nervous about meeting Puig. The author, after all, might look at him as the culprit betraying the original, even though Schrader had based the screenplay on Puig's stage play (the only version Babenco knew when he took on the project) instead of adapting it directly from the novel. Puig was reassuring to Schrader as he was to everyone he came in contact with on the set. Putting everyone at ease by joking around and feminizing all the men's names—La Hurt, La Juliá, La Great Babenko—was Puig's way of dispelling the tension.

It was also his way of trying, gently, to regain some control over the making of each scene, which, like a latter-day Scheherezade, he would dramatize for those willing to listen. Behind Puig's humor was pain, probably, as one observer recalls: "Puig was sweet and patient, almost as if he were the wise parent dealing with spoiled children, but the stress he went through must have been terrible" (Levine, Personal interview).

The art of screenwriting consists of reducing everything to its essence. What happens in several pages in a novel needs to happen in thirty seconds in a movie. At least once a page in the *Kiss* script one of the relationships in the movie needed to change: Molina's relationship to Valentín and Valentín's to Molina and the spectator's relationship to the two characters as well as to their relationship. Twice a minute, in well-wrought films, a relationship grows, or you see another dimension. Dialogue has to be minimalist, as Puig understood when rewriting the dialogue in his stage version of *Kiss*, but cutting the dialogue to write the screenplay was a challenge since the novel was already minimalist—there are only two characters in a cell. How was Schrader to write a film about bored characters without boring the audience? The cinematographer's solution was to shoot each new scene in the cell from a different corner. Despite its minimalism, the novel did have moviemaking potential, partly, according to Puig's own ideas about the differences between novels and movies, because the novel's structure is allegorical. The novel condenses the basic plot of all human relationships in which two people meet, their relationship grows, is consummated, and ends with death.

Schrader had been as faithful as he felt he could be to the original dialogue, beginning the movie as Puig began the book, with Molina's voice. At the same time he had to translate a specific historical and regional frame into a more generic one, starting the film so that the English-speaking audiences, at first puzzled that the characters were in a Latin American prison where everybody was speaking English, would come to accept this convention.

What holds the reader of the novel—the storyteller Molina's elaborations and suspensions of his film plots designed to whet Valentín's appetite—had to be presented in compressed form through Zen-like concoctions, as when Molina gives Valentín the avocado, saying simply, "enjoy what life offers you." Puig took a whole page, if not the whole book, to say this in the novel, having Molina teach Valentín, little by little, the aesthetic pleasure of enjoying the fictional world of movies. Thus the Zen seed was already in the novel.

Faced with two guys talking about old movies in a prison cell, the writers needed to liven things up. They decided to accent the spider woman motif, since Braga required her role to be more substantial. Through visual storytelling, the film projected not only the seductiveness of Woman, who spins Man in her web—whether she's male or female—but also the idea that all women are Greta Garbo, Rita Hayworth, or Braga to the men who desire them. This interpretation would please Braga and would be faithful to the novel's pervasive underlying thrust: Woman as Muse, Love, Death—fantasy, filmic, or flesh and blood. To the men who either dreamed about or identified with them, all women fit one ideal. Braga played Valentín's girlfriend in the flashbacks, as well as Leni in Molina's Nazi film and the fantasy spider woman. Spotlighting Woman would also suit most audiences by softening the gay male focus, which, in transit from novel to film, would lose subtlety and complexity anyway because of the exclusion of the footnotes, which Puig himself had excised from the stage adaptation.

The film was originally going to begin with Molina's narration of the last scenes of *Cat People*, under the assumption that the producers would obtain the rights because the scriptwriter's brother Paul Schrader had directed the 1982 remake. After negotiating with Universal for almost a year, they received the news—a week before they were to start shooting—that Universal had refused to grant them rights to use *Cat People* footage or even to reshoot any scenes from the original classic. They would have to begin instead with the French Nazi propaganda movie, originally woven into the script twenty-five pages later. This change meant a last-minute scramble to eliminate the first twenty-four pages and introduce the Nazi movie on page 1.

In the first five minutes of the movie the audience had to be introduced to Molina; to make general audiences laugh and get over their embarrassment and then start to appreciate Molina as a human being, scriptwriter, director, cameraman, and actor had to get the audience to accept or empathize with someone who was different. Circling his hand over his head, Puig suggested that Hurt could hide his all-American football player look if he wore a turban and a kimono, as if he imagined he was some sort of geisha or odalisque. It worked, *grosso modo*, as Pauline Kael noted in her *New Yorker* review: "William Hurt . . . is just about the only thing to look at. . . . He first appears wrapping a red towel around his head as a turban—a Scheherazade flourish—and wearing the thick, coquettish makeup of an aging vamp" (62). As Kael put it, Hurt's presence captured the spectator in part because he was so "physically miscast"; he made a "showy feat" of his performance, or, as a friend of Kael's jested, "Hurt as Molina is like having a basset hound playing a Chihuahua" (62).

From the very start of the shoot Hurt seemed justifiably nervous about this dicey role: it would be awkward to fail, and if he succeeded he might be typecast. Kael noticed this reserve in the performance: "Hurt holds back; he has a knotted, bunched-up presence" (62). As a spectator prejudiced by Puig's Molina, when I saw the movie in 1985, I agreed with Kael's observation, though as the movie proceeded I found myself growing used to watching Hurt playing Hurt playing Molina. Because Puig had definite ideas about the kind of actor who should play Molina—his first choice was Jean-Louis Trintignant—his presence behind the scenes appeared to cause Hurt further anxiety. The chemistry was not there, Puig decided early on, after meeting Hurt over dinner with the director, the producer, the screenwriter, and Juliá at a restaurant near the hotel. Hurt and Puig did not share the same sense of camp, evidently, which bode ill: Molina was a caricature, a certain kind of uneducated queen, and, as such, streetwise but with a frilly touch of Carmen Miranda. Puig saw that between Molina's earthy levity and Hurt's neurotic intensity yawned an abyss.

Babenco, whose English was limited, felt beleaguered by Puig's and Weisman's constant revisions of the script and was on uneasy ground attempting to direct Hurt, an English-speaking Hollywood movie star. The director was in conflict not only with his producer and screenwriter but also with his star. After the first week of shooting, Babenco and Hurt got into a violent altercation and nearly came to blows; they did not speak to each other again. Puig described the tension on the set in a letter to his mother:

> Every change suggested became a full-scale battle, but I've accomplished quite a lot; after New York [the first cut] there will be more things to change, but a lot was accomplished. We'll see. The fights between the American producer and Babenco are a scream; they're always at each other's throats. The movie world is a HORROR.   (19 Oct. 1983)

To a friend in New York he wrote, "Now it seems la Hurt is really directing the film, they say she does a very bad pathetic believable queen but not funny, and that's bad news" (letter to Howard Mandelbaum). Hurt had taken over the direction of both himself and Juliá, and, without the light humor of the original novel, Puig thought the whole film would turn into a pointless cliché.

After the first edits the film was three hours, but it needed to be two; to boot, early in 1984, Babenco, who had not been feeling well, was diagnosed with lymph cancer. Thinking that he was going to die soon (it was a false alarm), Babenco wanted to be with his family and disappeared for the next ten months; Weisman and Schrader had to handle the final cut. Back in Los Angeles, they recruited the editor Lee Percy, who worked intensely with Schrader in an editing studio that summer, sometimes dubbing new dialogue that went along with the actors' facial expressions. Schrader also flew to New York during this period to work with Juliá and Hurt. With Braga, who was flown from Rio to Los Angeles, the dubbing was arduous because of her English; once it took a whole day to work on one line, the last, and in a way most important, line of the movie (and the book): "This dream is short but this dream is happy." In her thick accent, she kept mispronouncing "short" as "shirt." Percy and Schrader had to tape her repeatedly and finally, after multiple takes and infinitesimal sound splicing, produced the final cut.

The film's heavy-handed naturalism irked Puig. The last scene was a case in point: the stage play ended with the famous kiss good-bye and a hallucinatory voice-over much like in the novel, a less brutal ending than in the movie, in which Molina's dead body is dumped in an alleyway and one of his assassins utters, "You fucking fag." In a letter to Emir Rodríguez Monegal, the Uruguayan literary critic and Puig's close friend, Puig summarized his reaction to the film with damaging wit:

> The movie: A hodge-podge, without the slightest subtlety. Babenco was a nightmare; no sooner did I give over the rights he vanished and to avoid

my influence he fell into the claws of the U.S. scriptwriter (Paul Schrader's brother, boring and heavy-handed like him) and finally W. Hurt who completely colonized the idiot Babenco, and a typical "Schraderade" was the outcome, slow and lugubrious. Hurt playing the sad, tortured and neurotic New York queen he is in real life. In the end, they excised the core of the story, which was the fag's joie de vivre and the humor. Julia is better, despite the fact that the character [the Marxist] no longer exists. Nor did they leave the motivations that make the story believable. The way it ended, Valentín could be bisexual or who knows what. In any case, what little was left appears to have touched people in a big way, so may it serve at least to sell more books.   (30 May 1985)

Puig modulated his opinion for public consumption, responding to interviewers with an author's fatalism, alluding to the nasty old Hollywood story in which writers often felt cheated fiscally as well as creatively. To the *Boston Globe* he remarked:

> I did not like the movie; I found it too grim, too severe, but I liked the effect it had on audiences, so it is all right. What I like is that it presents the "queen" as a human being. Molina comes to think of himself as the quintessential queen. When I sold it, I knew the vision in the final work would be that of the director, and not mine. The best thing is not to get too upset.   (Puig, Interview)

Puig's opinion found further articulation, again, in the words of Kael. In her insightful review, she compared the movie to the novel, describing the novel's vision: "More than a defense of escapism—it's an homage to escapism. The glory of the book is that the reader feels the power of fantasy." She stressed that Puig was not a "sentimentalist" and noted that the lack of an "authorial voice" (typical of Puig's novels) leaves the reader to guess at the characters' "elusive" motives, the "subversive hints" that the movie was not clever enough to pick up on. She confirmed that the movie turned the story into a cliché about two men "who give to each other and learn from each other," a story of "Molina's transfiguration through the power of love and happiness and a new self-respect— that is, his shedding of his effeminate mannerisms," a "redemptive drama . . . as phony as the forties screen romances that Molina is infatuated with." Kael conjectured that Babenco may have been trying to make the film politically correct, but its "squareness" ultimately betrayed "movie-loving gays" who carry "a personal theater of romantic fantasy inside themselves." While Puig's "Molina is the moviegoer as *auteur*," Babenco wanted to express "something larger, something tragic and aggressively moral." For Babenco, in Kael's words, "[t]he picture makes a show of its commitment to the highest human values," whereas the novel says, Kael believed, "queens may be useless, silly window dressing, on the order of movie romances, but that can be lovely fun, can't it? It enhances life, makes it more rapturously giddy." Kael concluded glumly, "Gay groups may consider this politically incorrect"—but inserted prophetically "right now, anyway" (62). She added:

> Puig's plea for the indulgence of romance is much like that of Tennessee Williams, and the novel speaks to that part of us which wants more than is strictly essential—wants the delirium of excess. Babenco . . . has steamrolled the romance and absurdity out of the material.   (62)

In 1985, the film *Kiss of the Spider Woman* was released. Contrary to Puig's expectations, it received kudos at Cannes in May and at the Tokyo Festival and was nominated in February 1986 for four Academy Awards: Best Film, Best Actor, Best Screenplay Adaptation, and Best Director. This unlikely production, with only two characters, "the queer and the commie," came up like a dark horse (Levine, *Manuel* 331). Babenco, relatively unknown except for *Pixote*, was nominated over Steven Spielberg, who that year had directed his dazzling war epic *Empire of the Sun*. Hurt, in what is widely considered the crowning performance of his career, was awarded the Cannes Palme D'Or as well as an Oscar, becoming the first American to win the award for best actor for the portrayal of a homosexual. *Kiss of the Spider Woman* broke more than one ground rule: it was the first independent film not only to receive four Oscar nominations but also to win an Academy Award. Whether because of Babenco's charismatic energy, because the film was a ticket to Hollywood, or out of idealism, everyone who worked on this difficult and challenging project stayed with it, even those who did not reap material profit. The effect on Puig's reputation as a writer was enormous—finally "la Metro," as he campily referred to Hollywood, had rolled out the red carpet. If Puig had been courting the movies for the first forty years of his life, the cameras were rolling for him now.

NOTES

This essay is a version of part 6 of my book *Manuel Puig and the Spider Woman: His Life and Fictions*.
[1] All translations of Puig's letters are mine.

A Poetics of Discomfort:
Teaching Puig with Babenco

Idelber Avelar

> It does not matter that the mode of life portrayed by
> Hollywood is false. It has taught you to have hope.
> —Manuel Puig

Manuel Puig is sexy, readable, fun to teach. The same students who suffer through the twenty pages of Alejo Carpentier's "Viaje a la semilla" or the eighty pages of Carlos Fuentes's *Aura* finish the nearly three hundred pages of Puig's *Kiss of the Spider Woman* without much complaint, at times quite enthusiastically. This reaction is due to Puig's insight that experimentation and formal innovation are not contradictory with the use of popular forms such as the detective story or the melodrama. Puig's recourse to popular narrative forms—along with his use of a full array of modernist, experimental techniques and his depiction of a host of contemporary political themes—accounts for his unique status in the Latin American canon. His melodrama and suspense make him an irresistibly popular writer, but his experimentalism and social content endow him with the legitimacy of serious fiction, worthy of inclusion in survey courses, introductions to Latin American literature, and the like. The potential and the traps of teaching Puig at the undergraduate level hark back to this ambiguous double status of the author as a novelist who can be both experimental and catchy, explosively political and irredeemably pop.

Whereas teaching the high modernist Boom novels of Carpentier or Mario Vargas Llosa requires a constant exercise in creating and sustaining student interest, teaching Puig often demands a diametrically opposed strategy. Teachers must interrupt uncritical student identification with the text to shed light on the prejudices that the identification might be concealing. Students from the United States—at least those students in elite, research institutions—often come to the classroom with firm assumptions about Latin American machismo. Unskilled handling of that assumption by the college teacher can often, for a novel such as *Kiss of the Spider Woman*, turn out to re-create and reinforce uninformed stereotypes precisely when he or she believes to be critiquing gender hierarchies presumably typical of Latin America. How can teachers start from the immediate fascination sparked by Puig's novel and move toward a critique of the conditions that make that fascination possible? Written in the light of my experience teaching *Kiss of the Spider Woman*, the novel and the film, in introductory Latin American literature and culture courses (both in Spanish and in English translation), this essay suggests ways to articulate that double bind in the classroom.

Puig's fourth novel takes us to Argentina in the mid-1970s, a period of intense political violence preceding the military coup of 1976. Already controlled by the right, the political apparatus was increasingly used to carry out repression and torture. Valentín, a Marxist activist (whose connections—or lack thereof—with Peronism remain ambiguous), shares a prison cell with Molina, a gay man incarcerated for alleged sexual relations with minors. Depicted in agile dialogue, their relationship evolves primarily out of Molina's accounts of films with which he is fascinated for sentimental, romantic reasons. Valentín, jailed as part of a wave of repression against left-wing activists, listens to Molina's film stories with a mix of voyeuristic curiosity and guilty rejection of their "propagandistic" or "reactionary" content. This tension is most visible in Molina's narration of the second film, which relates the love affair between a French woman and a German officer during the Nazi occupation of Paris. Over time these narratives become Valentín's fundamental source of enjoyment, as much as they become Molina's primary form of empowerment. Héctor Babenco's film adaptation erases that dialectic by overemphasizing Valentín's rejection of Molina's alienated films, to the point of making Valentín repeatedly utter insults or even shove and push Molina onto the floor—scenes that would be out of place in Puig's subtle portrayal of their relationship, where displeasure is more delicately expressed.

In the first half of the novel, Molina's narratives are interrupted by Valentín's tentative mentions of his fiancée, as well as by his insistence of his loyalty to the political cause. He voices his loyalty with a dogmatism that makes the reader suspicious of his commitment, as if his fortress of belief were being set up only to be dismantled later. The growing intimacy between the two men leads Molina to relate details about his fascination with a waiter with whom he had intermittent encounters before his arrest. First Molina and then Valentín suffer from diarrhea caused by prison food. Molina's caring for Valentín during his illness brings the two men closer together as Valentín progressively allows himself to become vulnerable to Molina's affective language. Sleep visits Molina and Valentín alternately. When in vigil, Valentín emphatically demands that the film retellings continue. At no moment is the political activist Valentín fully impermeable to the fascination of melodrama.

The first half concludes with a dialogue between Molina and a prison official. We learn that the poisoned food had been destined for Valentín but was eaten by Molina, who was worried that the two portions were too unequal and therefore could have aroused Valentín's suspicion, or at least so Molina tells a jail official. Police tempt Molina with an early release in exchange for information from Valentín about his militant group. The reader approaches the second half hanging in suspense about Molina's allegiances: are police manipulating Molina to betray Valentín? Or is Molina playing with the officials and gaining time? Could he be up to something else? By then the reader also has questions about Valentín: Will he dismiss the fascination provoked by Molina's narratives and maintain his allegiance to an orthodox, fixed, heteronormative take on the world? Or will he be seduced by the freer and gayer sensibility with which he is coming into contact? Moreover, will he ever have a chance to choose between those two ways of being? Or will the choice have already been made for him?

The novel's second half offers to these riddles answers that are not quite unequivocal. The challenge of teaching the novel with Babenco's film is that the film often eliminates that "not quite," thereby erasing the ambiguity constructed in the novel. Teachers should not encourage in students the perception that the more explicit nature of cinematic, visual language stands in opposition to the presumed opacity and ambiguity of literary, verbal language. While the differences between cinema and literature must be kept in mind and explored when teaching novels and their film versions, these differences should not function as a deus ex machina to explain phenomena that must be explained for what they are. Here the contrasting treatments of those questions in the novel and in the film reveal different takes on narrative and on gayness by Puig, on the one hand, and by Babenco, William Hurt, the producer David Weisman, and the scriptwriter Leonard Schrader, on the other. The formal differences between filmic language and literary language interact with the political and cultural differences between Puig and Babenco's team in a variety of ways, but teaching *Kiss* is, sometimes, primarily an exercise in preventing students from collapsing those two sets of problems into each other.

When approaching the question of how to cast the film of a novel structured as a play in which one inmate recounts films to the other, teachers should try to avoid the facile answer that the ideological and political differences between Puig's novel and Babenco's film hark back to the differences between literature and cinema. Instructors should also prevent students from judging Babenco's film in terms of how faithful it is to the novel (a no-win situation for the genre doing the adapting and a sterile exercise for the instructors teaching film adaptations of literary works). After instructors address the problems of contrasting codes of film and text and of critiquing for faithfulness in film adaptations, Puig's and Babenco's versions of *Kiss of the Spider Woman* still leave us with the interesting questions of the choices made by each man. More productive than the debates on faithfulness are the questions, What filmic means were available to Babenco to face the considerable challenge of shooting a story that takes place almost entirely in a prison cell? What means did Babenco choose to create a cinematic narrative out of a dramatic text? As I read the film, Babenco responds superbly to the challenge of creating dynamic cinema out of a fairly static theatrical situation, although he responds poorly to the challenge of recasting in film the subtlety, ambiguity, and gender politics of Puig's text.

While the second half cancels the hypothesis that Molina is simply being manipulated by the police into betraying Valentín, it does not make as clear where exactly Molina's heart and plans reside. Questions also remain about Valentín's trajectory. In chapter 9 (the first chapter of the second half, in Puig's typical sixteen-chapter, rounded, coherent narrative scheme), Molina tells the story of *I Walked with a Zombie*, a film about an eerie love triangle set in the Caribbean and portrayed in stereotypical, seductive Hollywood style. Inspired by the sentimental language of melodrama, Valentín allows himself to dictate a letter to his lover, in which his desires for freedom begin to struggle with his repressive

Marxist superego. The shared letter writing further humanizes Valentín as some-one who is coming to a painful acceptance of his feelings. The administration of the jailhouse periodically confers with Molina, but Molina never delivers any-thing other than a request for an abundant basket of food and beverage like the one that his mother would bring him on her visits. This food was necessary, Molina convinces the jailhouse administrators, in order for Valentín not to be suspicious (Eng. 152). Molina's elegant sharing of the food with Valentín further eroticizes their relationship. A moment of mutual touching eventually leads to a night of sex, presented by Puig as an intense experience of affect, love, and self-discovery for both.

Abandoning their attempts to get Molina to extract information from Valentín in exchange for the promise of freedom, the police decide to grant Molina his freedom and follow his footsteps in the outside world in the hopes that he will deliver a message for his former cell mate. As the police tactics change, Molina argues with Valentín that it would be safest not to tell him anything about his political group. Not counting on the police following Molina after his release, Valentín convinces him to deliver a message. The next chapter is a police report that reflects the espionage and surveillance of Molina immediately after his leav-ing jail. According to that report Molina visits friends, spends days with his mom, and withdraws all his money from the bank. He then makes a suspicious phone call and agrees with someone to meet and deliver the message. Police officers circle in, and Molina ends up dead in a drive-by shooting. The report on Molina ends by saying that Molina's plan "may in fact have been one of the following: either he expected to escape with the extremists, or he was ready to be elimi-nated by same" ("pudo huber sido uno de los dos siguientes: o pensaba escapar con los extremistas, o estaba dispuesto a que estos lo eliminaran") (Eng. 274, Span. 279, Archivos 251). The final chapter features Valentín's delirium after a horrific torture session at the hands of the military. Both characters have, in a way, been destroyed, but the reader finishes with the sense that they were agents of their destiny, that they chose their paths.

Students of Latin American culture should be encouraged to go beyond the facile reading of Valentín as the prototypical Latin American macho and Molina as the force of renewal. When students assume that Molina represents the entire transgressive or anti-*machista* stance in the novel, it is worthwhile to remind them that it is he, not Valentín, who assumes an automatic association between the arts and the feminine (ch. 3). It is he, not Valentín, who insists that a good woman should cook and take good care of her man. It is Molina who insists on the fundamental inequality of male and female roles. Thus he is the character who defends unashamedly the *machista* division of sexual labor that Valentín—as a man completely entrapped in the heteronormative logic—ultimately supports as well, as much as he cannot defend it explicitly without betraying his Marx-ist belief in equal rights for men and women. Certainly, Puig is making a point about the inability of a certain politicized Latin American middle class to go beyond a heterosexist norm, and in that sense Molina represents the force of subversion in the novel. The association of Valentín with a certain image of Latin American machismo, however, ends up denying Molina's transformation by denying Valentín the ability of affecting him.

If one does not assume Molina to be a character that changes, one has to see his death, while delivering a political message, as a fatality rather than a conscious and clear choice to fight a battle and endure the consequences. Yes, Valentín's heteronormativism is being profoundly transformed by Molina, but if one does not see how Molina's sensibility and politics are also changed by the interaction with Valentín, one is only getting half the dialectic. By the same token, if one sees politics entirely on the side of Valentín and sees Molina's narratives as purely romantic, sentimental, apolitical, or politically neutral fictions—that is, if one separates gender constructions from politics—one only captures half the dialectic. Molina is the force of renewal of gender constructs in the novel, but under his influence Valentín comes to unsettle a sexist and heteronormative model of sexuality as much as Molina does. Conversely, Valentín is the force of political and social awareness, but it is Molina whose sentimental romances turn out to be political—they expand the definition of the political—in ways that had not yet become clear to Valentín.

For Puig the film failed the moment it chose to portray Molina's political mission at the end (the delivery of the message requested by Valentín) as the culmination of a process whereby he had become a reasonable, respectable character, redeemed by politics away from a world of triviality. Puig indicated on more than one occasion that he found this implicit evolution of Molina's character in the film to be a betrayal of the spirit of the novel, a betrayal that erased the joy, the gayness of Molina's character throughout. The last diegetic scene in the film is the murder of Molina by a woman activist who shoots from a taxi when she realizes that police are following Molina. The cab driver stops, blocking passage at a corner, as Molina runs toward the vehicle. The woman shoots him three times in the lower chest. The camera captures his slow death with a close-up from above as he falls to his knees, while Muzak plays in the background, finalizing the image of Molina as a martyr and redeemer. This choice of imagery to portray Molina's death draws on an aesthetic that is profoundly antagonistic to the joyfulness and guiltlessness that Puig cultivated throughout his work.

Babenco's film seems to cast political struggle and gender subversion as separate endeavors. In choosing to deliver the message and die like a martyr, Molina rejects the life presented in the film's exaggerated and parodic depiction of his gay friends' cabaret culture. The film trivializes his friends in a cabaret scene with a caricatured fat chanteuse dressed in scandalous red, singing and blowing balloons, while Molina's friends chat at a table. The narrative sequence cannot but suggest that in deciding to deliver the message Molina is moving away from a subversive but ultimately trivial world toward the real realm of politics. In Babenco's film what upsets gender hierarchies does not upset the political order. Not so in Puig's novel, where we are not even sure whether Molina delivered a message at all or who killed him.

Whereas in the film the scene of Molina's death is shot as if it were the true and uncontested reality, in Puig's novel our only source of information about Molina's release and ultimate death is a police report. As any reasonably well informed Latin American over thirty will attest, in the recent dictatorships the falsification of police reports and death certificates was common practice, a practice that was certainly part of the historical background of Puig's writing. Fraudulent reports were regularly used to conceal police crimes, usually cold-blooded murder, and to suggest suicides and accidental deaths. Puig's phrasing of the report—"shots were fired from a passing automobile" ("dispararon desde un auto en movimiento") and "Molina expired before arriving patrol unit could administer first aid" ("Molina expiró antes de que la patrulla pudiera aplicarle primeros auxilios") (Eng. 274, Span. 279, Archivos 251)—makes it impossible to tell if the report is true. All we can infer is that Molina's death occurred in such a way as to elicit from the police the narrative we read. But there is no textual or historical basis to suggest that the police are telling the truth. While some might suggest that such ambiguity is impossible to reproduce in cinema, others might argue that the elimination of this ambiguity was Babenco's deliberate choice, rather than some sort of fatality embedded in the medium. Students here should be reminded of the vast array of recourses available for cinema to represent a version of reality without necessarily assuming that version to be true.

Yet *Kiss of the Spider Woman* is still a remarkable film. Full appreciation of it can actually shed light on its questionable choices in the terrain of gender politics. Babenco responds to the difficult challenge of filming such a theatrical text by resorting to agile camera work that uses all imaginable angles within the cell's scarce space. Molina's narratives are performed on screen by a cast led by the Brazilian actress Sonia Braga, who plays the French woman in love with the German officer; the paradisiacal spider woman; and Marta, the woman who populates Valentín's dreams. Braga thus becomes a sort of omnipresent femme fatale, a counterpoint to the story's male homoerotic energy. Although Babenco predictably resorts to darkness to represent Molina and Valentín's sex scene, the caressing that leads to it is depicted sympathetically, with respect and intensity. Raúl Juliá is a convincing 1970s Latin American Marxist, and Hurt's turban added—at Puig's suggestion—a slightly orientalist touch to Molina, who begins to appear like a modern Scheherazade, weaving tales to keep death away.

Puig's text and Puig himself (from what we know based on the available biographical information) imagined a Molina who was more exuberant, a "kind of uneducated queen, and, as such, streetwise, but with a frilly touch of Carmen Miranda" (Levine, *Manuel* 343). Testimonies such as those offered by Suzanne Jill Levine's biography of Puig are invaluable in setting for students the complex context of the film's production, from Puig's early rejection of Babenco as a compatriot filmmaker who could not possibly have too profound a knowledge about or even too sympathetic a gaze toward the gay world to his belated conviction that Hurt had dominated and imposed his particular aesthetic on the director. Levine relates how Puig had confided to a friend in France that Jean-Louis

Trintignant would be his first choice for Molina's role (423). Babenco's first invitation went to Burt Lancaster, who, then already past his prime, reportedly rewrote the script and made *Kiss* a sort of soft porn film. When Lancaster abandoned the project because of health problems, the news brought great relief. Puig actually celebrated it as the end, altogether, of the movie project with "la awful Babenco" (Levine, *Manuel* 336). Selling the rights to the production and then following the making of the movie were for Puig processes that were not quite compatible with the joy and freedom evoked by Molina's character in the novel. Puig's own distaste for the film has quite clear roots in the vicissitudes of those processes.

After reading the biographical information on Puig and his relation to the film, students of literature and cinema should be reminded of what biography cannot do, namely, replace formal, cultural, and ideological analyses either of the novel or of the film. Thus teaching the novel and film together is productive in many different pedagogical contexts. The novel is appropriate in courses on Latin American literature; Puig's unique insight into the power of melodrama as the narrative of gender politics marks a fundamental break with the earlier moment, the Boom. The film deserves a spot in courses on Latin American cinema, not only for its many achievements as a film but also for emblematizing, in 1985, new conditions of production in continental cinema. The film was a true Pan-American Hollywood flick: it was directed by an Argentine resident of Brazil who cast stars from Brazil, the United States, and Puerto Rico; was shot in Brazil with an American producer; and featured a story that presumably takes place in Argentina. Studying the novel with the film is also exemplary in courses on Latin American culture and history, provided that one complicates and questions certain immediate identifications between the two characters and two commonly held social stereotypes. The questions in the appendix have these contexts in mind and are designed to assist the teaching of Puig's and Babenco's works at the undergraduate and graduate levels.

NOTE

The epigraph is from Suzanne Jill Levine's *Manuel Puig and the Spider Woman* (284).

APPENDIX
Questions for Discussion

1. Except for police reports, footnotes, and the italicized streams of consciousness of Molina and Valentín, *Kiss of the Spider Woman* is entirely structured in dramatic form; dialogue occupies the entire text. How does the complete absence of an omniscient, third-person narrator condition and affect our perception of the text?

2. Valentín represents the Marxist activists of the 1960s and 1970s who gave their lives for the struggle for socialism and equal rights for all citizens. How does Valentín measure up to this ideal? Where does he fall short of it? To what extent is that ideal—and its proponents—being critiqued in the novel and in the film? How would you characterize Puig's representation of Valentín? And Babenco's?

3. Molina, a female-identified gay man who is not particularly worried about rules of decorum and who wears his sexual and aesthetic choices on his sleeve, represents the vibrant gay culture that came of age in many Latin American cities in the 1970s. What are the subversive potential effects and the limits of this character as he is represented in Puig's text? And in Babenco's film? Are there significant differences between the two?

4. Although Valentín is very critical of the Nazi propaganda film, he says he enjoyed the first film narrated by Molina (inspired by Jacques Tourneur's 1942 *Cat People*), about the woman who becomes a panther. Besides the fact that the imaginary romance of the French woman and the German officer is an explicit right-wing propaganda film, what other reasons does Valentín have to prefer *Cat People*? What does his enthusiasm for *Cat People* tell us about his evolution as a character?

5. The bulk of chapter 5 is dedicated to Molina's internal recounting of a movie (*The Enchanted Cottage* [1944]). Much of chapter 6 is devoted to a stream of consciousness as well, in which Valentín imagines a woman in a number of situations. Regardless of their differences, can you identify ways in which these two discourses parallel each other? Do you see any marks of Molina in Valentín's daydreaming? And vice versa? How do these marks situate the evolution of each character at that moment?

6. Would you agree with the criticism that although Puig endows a gay character with a voice and a centrality, rare in Latin American literature, the novel ultimately reproduces a traditional heterosexist scheme—a female-identified gay man sacrificing himself and caring for the more conventional male character? Is the tension between transgression and reproduction of the heterosexist paradigm played out differently in the novel and in the film?

7. Babenco chooses to represent the death of Molina exactly as the police report describes it in the novel but dramatizes it further by surrounding the death with the aura of martyrdom. Are there ways of representing the novel's police version without suggesting that it is the uncontested truth? Would it be legitimate to imagine endings for the film that incorporated other possibilities of reading the conclusion of the novel? If so, what would some of these other endings be?

8. In Babenco's film, analyze the cabaret scene where Molina is reunited with his gay friends and the scene where his married waiter friend asks him, on being told of his imminent departure, "Running away with another boy? Don't get arrested again. You're too old for it." How do these two scenes, not present in Puig's novel, portray the world to which Molina was returning after prison? Do they change the perspective of the novel in any significant way?

9. While heterosexual sex had been portrayed in literature and film in a wide range of registers in the 1970s and 1980s, homoerotic love was a relatively rare topic for canonical literature and commercial cinema, as it still is today, to a certain extent. How is Puig's literary portrayal of Molina's sexual encounter with Valentín (a man who thought of himself as purely heterosexual) innovative? How does Babenco choose to represent this crucial moment for both characters?

10. Babenco's adaptation casts Sonia Braga in three different femme fatale roles: Valentín's imaginary lover, the spider woman, and the French woman in occupied Paris. This range creates a recurrent, and highly sexualized, female character that has no counterpart in the novel. Does the prominence of Braga in the film add an object for the male heterosexual gaze absent in Puig's novel? How does this character fit in with, or interrupt, the homoerotic thrust of Puig's text? To what extent might the image of Braga also be a point of identification for the female viewer?

11. The critic Lucille Kerr has pointed out, "What *El beso de la mujer araña* develops is not so much a stable putdown of one side or the other (even though from a certain perspective it might seem that popular art and passion win out over a political ideology and action) but an interplay of and a turning between the poles of an opposition that, by the end of the novel, are brought together (*Suspended Fictions* 195). Would you agree that there is ultimately a dialectic between these two poles? Would you agree that they are "brought together" or reconciled in the end? Or would you say that there remains a breach, a rift between them? Explain your point of view.

12. The challenges for a director who films *Kiss of the Spider Woman* are manifold. One basic challenge was noted by the Puig biographer and translator Suzanne Jill Levine: "How do you write a film where the characters are bored but the audience is not?" (*Manuel* 341). What are the filmic procedures used by Babenco and his team to overcome that challenge? Discuss the possible role of embedded narratives, camera work, lighting, and music for accomplishing the task of representing boredom without boring the viewer.

NOTES ON CONTRIBUTORS

José Amícola teaches Argentine literature at the Universidad Nacional de La Plata. He is the author of *Manuel Puig y la tela que atrapa al lector* (1992), the coeditor (with Graciela Speranza) of *Encuentro Internacional Manuel Puig* (1998), and the coeditor of the critical edition of *El beso de la mujer araña* (2002) and of *Materiales iniciales para* La traición de Rita Hayworth (1996). He is the author of *Camp y posvanguardia* (2000) and of books on Mikhail Bakhtin (1997), the Gothic novel and the Bildungsroman (2003).

Idelber Avelar is professor of Spanish and Portuguese at Tulane University. He is the author of *The Untimely Present: Postdictatorial Latin American Fiction and the Task of Mourning* (1999), *The Letter of Violence: Essays on Narrative, Ethics, and Politics* (2004), and numerous scholarly articles published in Europe and the Americas. He is currently working on two books, "A Genealogy of Latin Americanism: Essays on the Disciplinary Uses of Identity" and "Timing the Nation: Rhythm and Nationhood in Brazilian Popular Music."

Daniel Balderston is professor of Spanish at the University of Iowa. Recent books include *Borges, realidades y simulacros* (2000) and *El deseo, enorme cicatriz luminosa: Ensayos sobre homosexualidades latinoamericanas* (2004). He coedited *Voice Overs: Translation and Latin American Literature* (2002) and the *Encyclopedia of Latin American and Caribbean Literature, 1900–2003* (2004). He is president of the Instituto Internacional de Literatura Iberoamericana.

Susan Benner, who translated four of the essays in this volume, coedited and translated a collection of short stories by Andean women, *Fire from the Andes* (1998), and translated *The Noé Jitrik Reader* (2005). She teaches at Iowa State University.

Juan Pablo Dabove is assistant professor of Spanish at the University of Colorado, Boulder. He is the author of *La forma del Destino: Sobre* El beso de la mujer araña (1994) and *Nightmares of the Lettered City: Banditry and Literature in Latin America, 1816–1929* (2007) and the coeditor of *Heterotropías: Narrativas de identidad y alteridad latinoamericana* (2003). His book deals with the literary use of banditry as a cultural trope in nineteenth-century Latin America. He has published articles in *Revista iberoamericana, Revista de crítica literaria latinoamericana, Latin American Literary Review, Estudios, Hispanic Culture Review*, and *Variaciones Borges*, as well as in several critical collections.

Lucille Kerr is professor of Spanish at Northwestern University. She is the author of *Suspended Fictions: Reading Novels by Manuel Puig* (1987) and *Reclaiming the Author: Figures and Fictions from Spanish America* (1992) and is among the international contributors to *Literary Cultures of Latin America: A Comparative History* (2004). She has published scholarly articles in *Criticism, Journal of Interdisciplinary Literary Studies, Latin American Research Review, MLN, Review of Contemporary Fiction, Revista de crítica literaria latinoamericana, Symposium*, and *World Literature Today*.

Suzanne Jill Levine is professor of Latin American and comparative literature at the University of California, Santa Barbara. She is the author of the literary biography

Manuel Puig and the Spider Woman: His Life and Fictions (2000; published in Spanish in 2002). Among the writers she has translated are Jorge Luis Borges, Julio Cortázar, Guillermo Cabrera Infante, Severo Sarduy, Adolfo Bioy Casares, José Donoso, and Puig. Her books also include *El espejo hablado: A Study of* Cien años de soledad (1975), *Guia de Bioy Casares* (1982), and *The Subversive Scribe: Translating Latin American Fiction* (1991).

José Maristany teaches Argentine literature and literary theory at the Universidad Nacional de La Pampa and at the Instituto Superior del Profesorado Joaquín V. Gonzales in Buenos Aires. He is the author of *Narraciones peligrosas: Resistencia y adhesión en las novelas del Proceso* (1999), the coeditor of *Mujeres y Estado en la Argentina: Educación, salud y beneficencia* (1997), and the coeditor of the journal *Anclajes*.

Francine Masiello is Sidney and Margaret Ancker Professor in the Humanities and teaches Spanish and comparative literature at the University of California, Berkeley. She is the author of *Lenguaje e ideología: Las escuelas argentinas de vanguardia* (1986), *Between Civilization and Barbarism: Women, Nation, and Culture in Modern Argentina* (1992), *La mujer y el espacio público: El periodismo femenino en la Argentina del siglo XIX* (1994), and *The Art of Transition: Latin American Literature and Neoliberal Crisis* (2001).

María Eugenia Mudrovcic is associate professor of Spanish at Michigan State University. She is the author of *Espejo en el camino* (1988) and *Mundo nuevo: Cultura y guerra fría* (1997). She is currently completing a book on literary memoirs in Latin America.

David Oubiña teaches film studies at the University of Buenos Aires and screenwriting at the Universidad del Cine. His books include *Filmología: Ensayos con el cine* (2000), which won the Premio del Fondo Nacional de las Artes; *El cine de Hugo Santiago* (2002); and *Jean-Luc Godard: El pensamiento del cine* (2003).

Rosa Perelmuter is professor of Spanish at the University of North Carolina, Chapel Hill. She is the author of *Noche intelectual: La oscuridad idiomática en el* Primero sueño (1982) and *Los límites de la femineidad en Sor Juana Inés de la Cruz: Estrategias retóricas y recepción literaria* (2004). She is currently at work on a book-length study of the representation of nature in epic poems written in the New World in the sixteenth and seventeenth centuries.

Ricardo Piglia is professor of Spanish at Princeton University, a novelist, and a critic. His fiction includes *Nombre falso* (1975; Assumed Name [1995]), *Respiración artificial* (1982; Artificial Respiration [1994]), *La ciudad ausente* (1992; The Absent City [2000]) and *Plata quemada* (1997; Money to Burn [2003]). He is the author of *Crítica y ficción* (1986) and *El última lector* (2005), a study of reading in Latin American literature.

Juan Poblete is associate professor of Latin American literature at the University of California, Santa Cruz. He is the author of *Literatura chilena del siglo XIX: Entre públicos lectores y figuras autoriales* (2003) and the editor of *Critical Latin American and Latino Studies* (2003). He is coediting "Andres Bello" (with Beatriz Gonzalez-Stephan) and "Redrawing the Nation: Latin American Comics and the Graphic Construction of Cultural Identities" (with Héctor Fernández-L'Hoeste).

Graciela Speranza teaches Argentine literature at the University of Buenos Aires. She is a novelist (*Oficios ingleses* [2003]), translator, and scriptwriter. Her work on Puig includes *Encuentro Internacional Manuel Puig* (1998, coedited with José Amícola) and *Manuel Puig: Después del fin de la literatura* (2000). She has also published *Primera persona: Conversaciones con quince narradores argentinos* (1995), *Razones intensas: Conversaciones sobre arte* (1999), and *Fuera de campo: Literatura y arte argentinos después de Duchamp* (2006). She is the coeditor of the magazine *Otra parte*.

Richard Young, professor emeritus of Spanish and Latin American studies at the University of Alberta, has published essays on Puig and other Argentine writers. He was the editor of *Revista canadiense de estudios hispánicos* between 1996 and 2003, and recent publications include the edited volume *Music, Popular Culture Identity* (2002) and *Contemporary Latin American Cultural Studies* (2004), coedited with Stephen Hart.

SURVEY PARTICIPANTS

Blanca Acosta, *Tougaloo College*
Idelber Avelar, *Tulane University*
Jorgelina Corbatta, *Wayne State University*
Juan Pablo Dabove, *University of Colorado, Boulder*
Robert Richmond Ellis, *Occidental College*
Eduardo Guizar, *Michigan State University*
Lucille Kerr, *Northwestern University*
Gwen Kirkpatrick, *Georgetown University*
Suzanne Jill Levine, *University of California, Santa Barbara*
Ignacio López-Calvo, *California State University, Los Angeles*
Carol Maier, *Kent State University*
Deanna Mihaly, *Emory and Henry College*
María Eugenia Mudrovcic, *Michigan State University*
Rosa Perelmuter, *University of North Carolina, Chapel Hill*
Juan Poblete, *University of California, Santa Cruz*
Kathryn Quinn-Sánchez, *University of Southern Maine*
José Quiroga, *Emory University*
Paul Julian Smith, *Cambridge University*
Richard Young, *University of Alberta*

WORKS CITED

Abrams, M. H. *A Glossary of Literary Terms*. 7th ed. Boston: Heinle, 1999.

Alvarez Borland, Isabel. "An Approach Using History, Myth, and Metafiction." *Approaches to Teaching García Márquez's* One Hundred Years of Solitude. Ed. María Elena de Valdés and Mario J. Valdés. New York: MLA, 1990.

Amícola, José. *Camp y posvanguardia: Manifestaciones culturales de un siglo fenecido.* Buenos Aires: Paidós, 2000.

———. *Manuel Puig y la tela que atrapa al lector: Estudio sobre* El beso de la mujer araña *en su relación con los procesos receptivos y con una continuidad literaria contestataria.* Buenos Aires: Latinoamericano-Emecé, 1992.

Amícola, José, and Graciela Speranza, eds. *Encuentro Internacional Manuel Puig.* Rosario: Viterbo, 1998.

Andrew, Dudley, and Steven Ungar. *Popular Front Paris and the Poetics of Culture.* Cambridge: Harvard UP, 2005.

Babenco, Héctor, dir. *Kiss of the Spider Woman*. VHS. Charter Entertainment, 1986.

Bacarisse, Pamela. *Impossible Choices: The Implications of Cultural References in the Novels of Manuel Puig.* Calgary: U of Calgary P, 1992.

———. *The Necessary Dream: A Study of the Novels of Manuel Puig*. Cardiff: U of Wales P, 1988.

Balderston, Daniel. "Los progresos de la doctora Anneli Taube." Amícola and Speranza 271–76.

———. "'Sexualidad y revolución': En torno a las notas de *El beso de la mujer araña*." Puig, *Beso*, Archivos 564–73.

———. "Sexuality and Revolution: On the Footnotes to *El beso de la mujer araña*." *Changing Men and Masculinities in Latin America*. Ed. Matthew C. Gutmann. Durham: Duke UP, 2003. 216–32.

Barthes, Roland. *Le plaisir du texte*. Paris: Seuil, 1973.

———. *The Rustle of Language*. Berkeley: U of California P, 1989.

———. *Writing Degree Zero*. New York: Hill, 1968.

Baudrillard, Jean. *De la séduction*. Paris: Seuil, 1973.

Baxter, Peter. *Just Watch! Sternberg, Paramount and America*. London: British Film Inst., 1993.

Bazán, Osvaldo. *Historia de la homosexualidad en la Argentina: De la Conquista de América al siglo XXI*. Buenos Aires: Marea, 2004.

———. *La más maravillosa música*. Buenos Aires: Perfil, 2002.

Benjamin, Walter. "The Work of Art in the Age of Mechanical Reproduction." *Illuminations*. Trans. Harry Zohn. New York: Harcourt, 1968. 217–51.

Bennett, Tony. "Texts in History: The Determinations of Readings and Their Texts." *Post-structuralism and the Question of History*. Ed. Derek Attridge, Geoff Bennington, and Robert Young. Cambridge: Cambridge UP, 1987. 63–81.

Benstock, Shari. "At the Margin of Discourse: Footnotes in the Fictional Text." *PMLA* 98 (1983): 204–25.

Beverley, John, and Marc Zimmerman. *Literature and Politics in the Central American Revolutions*. Austin: U of Texas P, 1990.

Beverley, John, José Oviedo, and Michael Aronna, eds. *The Postmodernism Debate in Latin America*. Durham: Duke UP, 1995.

Boccia, Michael. "*Versiones (Con-, In-,* and *Per-*) in Manuel Puig's and Hector Babenco's *Kiss of the Spider Woman*, Novel and Film." *Modern Fiction Studies* 32.3 (1996): 417–26.

Booth, Wayne C. *The Rhetoric of Fiction*. Chicago: U of Chicago P, 1961.

Bordwell, David. "Ideal Positionality: Shot / Reverse Shot." *Narration in the Fiction Film*. Madison: U of Wisconsin P, 1985. 110–12.

Borinsky, Alicia. *Ver/ser visto: Notas para una analítica poética*. Barcelona: Bosch, 1978.

Brunner, José Joaquín. "Notes on Modernity and Postmodernity in Latin American Culture." Beverley, Oviedo, and Aronna 34–54.

———. "Sobre el crepúsculo de la sociología y el comienzo de otras narrativas." *Revista de crítica cultural* 15 (1997): 28–31.

Burch, Noël. *Theory of Film Practice*. Trans. Helen Lane. New York: Praeger, 1973.

Burch, Noël, and Geneviève Sellier. *La drôle de guerre des sexes du cinéma français, 1930–1956*. Paris: Nathan, 1966.

Burns, E. Bradford. *Latin America: A Concise Interpretive History*. 1972. Englewood Cliffs: Prentice, 1994.

Calvino, Italo. "Autobiografía de un espectador." *Hacer una película*. Ed. Federico Fellini. Buenos Aires: Perfil, 1998. xv–xvii.

Campos, René. "'I'm Ready for My Close-Up': Los ensayos de la heroína." Puig, *Beso*, Archivos 535–49.

———. "Los rostros de la ilusión: Metamorfosis y desdoblamiento en la intertextualidad fílmica de *El beso de la mujer araña*." Puig, *Beso*, Archivos 259–70.

Carlson, Marifran. *Feminismo! The Woman's Movement in Argentina from Its Beginnings to Eva Perón*. Chicago: Academy Chicago, 1988.

Castañeda, Jorge. *La utopía desarmada*. Barcelona: Ariel, 1995.

Castillo Zapata, Rafael. *Fenomenología del bolero*. Caracas: Monte Avila, 1990.

Catelli, Nora. "Una narrativa de lo melifluo. Entrevista con Manuel Puig." *Quimera* 18 (1982): 22–26.

Cavallo, Guglielmo, and Roger Chartier, eds. *A History of Reading in the West*. Trans. Lydia G. Cochrane. Amherst: U of Massachusetts P, 1999.

Cavell, Stanley. *Pursuits of Happiness: The Hollywood Comedy of Remarriage*. Cambridge: Harvard UP, 1981.

Chambers, Ross. *Story and Situation: Narrative Seduction and the Power of Fiction*. Minneapolis: U of Minnesota P, 1984.

Chamorro, Eduardo. "Manuel Puig, secuestrado." *Cambio 16* 289 (1977): 83.

Christ, Ronald. "Interview with Manuel Puig." *Christopher Street* 3.4 (1979): 25–31.

Cleto, Fabio, ed. *Camp: Queer Aesthetics and the Performing Subject: A Reader*. Ann Arbor: U of Michigan, 1999.

Coddou, Marcelo. "Seis preguntas a Manuel Puig sobre su última novela: *El beso de la mujer araña*." *American Hispanist* 2.18 (1977): 12–13.

Cohn, Dorrit. *Transparent Minds: Narrative Modes for Presenting Consciousness in Fiction*. Princeton: Princeton UP, 1978.

Colás, Santiago. "Beyond Valentín's Dream: From the Crisis of Latin American Modernity." Colás, *Postmodernity* 100–17.

———. "Latin American Modernity in Crisis: *El beso de la mujer araña* and the Argentine National Left." Colás, *Postmodernity* 76–99.

———. *Postmodernity in Latin America: The Argentine Paradigm*. Durham: Duke UP, 1994.

Coover, Robert. "Old, New, Borrowed, Blue." Rev. of *Kiss of the Spider Woman*, by Manuel Puig. *New York Times Book Review* 22 Apr. 1979: 15+.

Corbatta, Jorgelina. "Encuentros con Manuel Puig." Puig, *Beso*, Archivos 601–24.

———. *Mito personal y mitos colectivos en las novelas de Manuel Puig*. Madrid: Orígenes, 1988.

Cornejo Polar, Antonio. *Escribir en el aire*. Lima: Horizonte, 1994.

Cortázar, Julio. *Hopscotch*. Trans. Gregory Rabassa. New York: Pantheon, 1987.

Cromwell, John, dir. *The Enchanted Cottage*. 1945. VHS. Los Angeles: Turner Home Entertainment, 1987.

Cuddon, J. A. *The Penguin Dictionary of Literary Terms and Literary Theory*. 4th ed. Rev. C. E. Preston. London: Penguin, 1999.

Dabove, Juan Pablo. *La forma del Destino: Sobre* El beso de la mujer araña. Rosario: Viterbo, 1994.

Daney, Serge. "Un tombeau pour l'œil (pédagogie straubienne)." *La rampe*. Paris: Cahiers du Cinéma, 1983. 78–85.

Débax, Michèlle, Milagros Ezquerro, and Michèle Ramond. "La marginalité des personnages et ses effets sur le discours dans *El beso de la mujer araña* de Manuel Puig." *Imprévue* 1 (1980): 91–112.

Dejong, Nadine. "Mutaciones de la mujer araña: Análisis comparativo de las versiones novelística, dramática y cinematográfica de una novela de Manuel Puig." *Tropelías* 9 (1998): 157–72.

Deleuze, Gilles. *Cinema 2: The Time-Image*. Trans. Hugh Tomlinson and Robert Galeta. London: Athlone, 1989.

Deleuze, Gilles, and Félix Guattari. *A Thousand Plateaus: Capitalism and Schizophrenia*. Trans. Brian Massumi. Minneapolis: U of Minnesota P, 1987.

D'Lugo, Carol. "*El beso de la mujer araña*: Norm and Deviance in the Fiction / as the Fiction." *Symposium* 44 (1990–91): 235–51.

Dorfman, Ariel, and Armand Mattelart. *How to Read Donald Duck: Imperialist Ideology in the Disney Comic*. 1971. New York: International General, 1978.

Echavarren, Roberto. "*El beso de la mujer araña* y las metáforas del sujeto." *Revista iberoamericana* 44 (1978): 65–75.

Eco, Umberto. *Apocalittici e integrati*. Milan: Bompiani, 1965.

Esquivel, Laura. *Como agua para chocolate: Novela de entregas mensuales con recetas, amores y remedios caseros*. 1989. New York: Anchor, 1992.

Fisher, Jo. *Mothers of the Disappeared*. Boston: South End, 1989.

————. *Out of the Shadows: Women, Resistance and Politics in South America*. London: Latin American Bureau, 1993.

Foster, David William. "*Kiss of the Spider Woman* (*El beso de la mujer araña*): Being Gay and Acting Protocols." *Contemporary Argentine Cinema*. Columbia: U of Missouri P, 1992. 123–35.

Foucault, Michel. *The Archaeology of Knowledge*. Trans. A. M. Sheridan Smith. New York: Pantheon, 1972.

————. *Discipline and Punish: The Birth of the Prison*. Trans. Alan Sheridan. New York: Random, 1979.

Franco, Jean. *The Decline and Fall of the Lettered City: Latin America in the Cold War*. Cambridge: Harvard UP, 2002.

————. "Narrador, autor, superestrella: La narrativa latinoamericana en la época de cultura de masas." *Revista iberoamericana* 47 (1981): 129–48.

Friedrich, Otto. *City of Nets: A Portrait of Hollywood in the 1940s*. 1986. Berkeley: U of California P, 1997.

Fuentes, Carlos. *La nueva novela hispanoamericana*. Mexico City: Mortiz, 1969.

García Canclini, Néstor. *Culturas híbridas: Estrategias para entrar y salir de la modernidad*. Mexico City: Grijalbo, 1990.

————. *La globalización imaginada*. Buenos Aires: Paidós, 1999.

García Ramos, Juan Manuel. *La narrativa de Manuel Puig: Por una crítica en libertad*. La Laguna: U de La Laguna, Secretariado de Publicaciones, 1993.

Genette, Gérard. *Figures II*. Paris: Seuil, 1969.

————. *Narrative Discourse: An Essay in Method*. Trans. Jane E. Lewin. Ithaca: Cornell UP, 1980.

Gimferrer, Pere. "Aproximaciones a Manuel Puig." *Plural* 57 (1976): 21–25.

Giordano, Alberto. *Manuel Puig: La conversación infinita*. Rosario: Viterbo, 2001.

Goytisolo, Juan. *El bosque de las letras*. Madrid: Alfaguara, 1995.

Gramsci, Antonio. *Selections from Cultural Writings*. Cambridge: Harvard UP, 1985.

Green, James Ray, Jr. "*El beso de la mujer araña*: Sexual Repression and Textual Repression." *La Chispa '81: Selected Proceedings of the Second Louisiana Conference on Hispanic Languages and Literatures*. Ed. Gilbert Paolini. New Orleans: Tulane UP, 1981. 133–39.

Hall, Stuart. "Encoding and Decoding." *Culture, Media, Language*. Ed. Hall et al. London: Hutchinson, 1980.

Halperin Donghi, Tulio. *The Contemporary History of Latin America*. Trans. John Charles Chasteen. Durham: Duke UP, 1993.

Harmon, William, and C. Hugh Holman. *A Handbook to Literature*. 10th ed. Upper Saddle River: Pearson-Prentice Hall, 2006.

Hodges, Donald. *Argentina, 1943–1976: The National Revolution and Resistance*. Albuquerque: U of New Mexico P, 1976.

Holladay, Kandace. "La imagen fílmica en *El beso de la mujer araña* de Manuel Puig como inversión del proceso ecfrástico." *Alba de América* 21.39 (2002): 309–15.

Horkheimer, Max, and Theodor W. Adorno. *Dialectic of Enlightenment*. Trans. John Cumming. New York: Herder, 1972.

Hutcheon, Linda. *Narcissistic Narrative: The Metafictional Paradox*. London: Routledge, 1991.

James, Daniel. *Resistance and Integration: Peronism and the Argentina Working Class*. Cambridge: Cambridge UP, 1988.

Kael, Pauline. "Tangled Webs." *New Yorker* 26 Aug. 1985: 61–63.

Keen, Benjamin. *A History of Latin America*. Boston: Houghton, 1996.

Kerr, Lucille. "Manuel Puig." Amícola and Speranza 329–40.

———. "The Politics of Seduction: *El beso de la mujer araña*." Kerr, *Suspended Fictions* 184–235.

———. *Suspended Fictions: Reading Novels by Manuel Puig*. Urbana: U of Illinois P, 1987.

King, John. *Magical Reels: A History of Cinema in Latin America*. London: Verso, 2000.

King, John, and Nissa Torrents, eds. *The Garden of Forking Paths*. London: British Film Inst., 1988.

Kiss of the Spider Woman. By Terrence McNally. Music by John Kander. Lyrics by Fred Ebb. Dir. Harold Prince. Broadhurst Theatre, New York. 3 May 1993.

Laclau, Ernesto, and Chantal Mouffe. *Hegemony and Socialist Strategy*. London: Verso, 1985.

Laplanche, Jean. *Life and Death in Psychoanalysis*. Trans. Jeffrey Mehlman. Baltimore: Johns Hopkins UP, 1976.

Leal, Néstor, ed. *Boleros. La canción romántica del Caribe, 1930–1960*. Caracas: Grijalbo Venezuela, 1992.

Lehmann-Haupt, Christopher. Rev. of *Kiss of the Spider Woman*, by Manuel Puig. *New York Times* 26 Apr. 1979: 17.

Lentricchia, Frank, and Thomas McLaughlin, eds. *Critical Terms for Literary Study*. 2nd ed. Chicago: U of Chicago P, 1995.

Levine, Suzanne Jill. *Manuel Puig and the Spider Woman: His Life and Fictions*. Madison: U of Wisconsin P, 2001.

———. Personal interview with Jolie Chain. 1995.

Lewis, Paul H. "Argentina: Intransigent's Paradise." *Latin American Politics and Development*. Ed. Howard J. Wiarda and Harvey F. Kline. Boulder: Westview, 2000. 95–126.

Longoni, Ana, and Mariano Mestman. *Del Di Tella a "Tucumán Arde." Vanguardia artística y política en el '68 argentino*. Buenos Aires: Cielo por Asalto, 2000.

Lorenzano, Sandra, and Ana Rosa Domenella, eds. *La literatura es una película: Revisiones sobre Manuel Puig*. Mexico City: U Nacional Autónoma de México, 1997.

Lukács, György. *The Theory of the Novel: A Historical-Philosophical Essay on the Form of Great Epic Literature*. Trans. Anna Bostock. Cambridge: MIT P, 1974.

Macchi, Yves. "Fonction narrative des notes infrapaginales dans *El beso de la mujer araña* de Manuel Puig." *Les langues néo-latines* 76 (1982): 67–81.

Manrique, Jaime. "A Remembrance of Manuel Puig, Author of *Kiss of the Spider Woman*: The Writer as Diva." *Christopher Street* 17.7 (1993): 14–27.

Manuel Puig. Spec. issue of *World Literature Today* 65.4 (1991).

Martí-Peña, Guadalupe. *Manuel Puig ante la crítica: Bibliografía analítica y comentada, 1968–1996*. Frankfurt: Vervuert, 1997.

Martin, Wallace. *Recent Theories of Narrative*. Ithaca: Cornell UP, 1986.

Marx, Karl. *The Eighteenth Brumaire of Louis Bonaparte*. New York: International, 1964.

Masiello, Francine. "The Spectacle of Difference." *The Art of Transition: Latin American Culture and Neoliberal Crisis*. Durham: Duke UP, 2001. 53–103.

———. "Fuera de lugar: Silencios y desidentidades en *El beso de la mujer araña*." Puig, *Beso*, Archivos 574–88.

———. "Jailhouse Flicks: Projections by Manuel Puig." *Symposium* 32 (1978): 15–24.

Meltzer, Françoise. "Unconscious." *Critical Terms for Literary Study*. Ed. Frank Lentricchia and Thomas McLaughlin. Chicago: U of Chicago P, 1990. 147–62.

Meyer, Moe. *The Politics and Poetics of Camp*. New York: Routledge, 1994.

Moles, Abraham. *El kitsch. El arte de la felicidad*. Trans. Josefina Ludmer. Barcelona: Paidós, 1971.

Molho, Maurice. "Tango de la madre araña." *Actes du Colloque sur l'oeuvre de Puig et Vargas Llosa*. Fontenay-aux-Roses: Fontenay, 1982. 161-68.

Moraña, Mabel, ed. *Ángel Rama y los estudios latinoamericanos*. Pittsburgh: Instituto Internacional de Literatura Iberoamericana, 1997.

———. *Literatura y cultura nacional en Hispanoamérica, 1910–1940*. Minneapolis: Inst. for the Study of Ideologies and Literature, 1984.

Mudrovcic, María Eugenia. *Mundo nuevo: Cultura y guerra fría en la década del 60*. Rosario: Viterbo, 1997.

Muñoz, Elías Miguel. *El discurso utópico de la sexualidad en Manuel Puig*. Madrid: Pliegos, 1987.

Neale, Steve. *Genre and Hollywood*. New York: Routledge, 2000.

Neruda, Pablo. "Ode to the Book." *Selected Poems*. Ed. Nathaniel Tarn. Trans. Anthony Kerrigan, W. S. Merwin, Alastair Reid, and Tarn. Boston: Houghton, 1990. 287–90.

Newman, Kim. *Cat People*. London: British Film Inst., 1999.

Norris, Margot. "Cinematic Self-Critique in *Kiss of the Spider Woman*." *The Scope of Words: In Honor of Albert S. Cook*. Ed. Peter Baker, Sarah Webster Goodwin, and Gary Handwerk. New York: Lang, 1991. 179–93.

Orovio, Helio, ed. *Trescientos boleros de oro. Antología de obras cubanas*. Mexico City: Presencia Latinoamericana, Instituto Nacional de Antropología e Historia, 1991.

Oviedo, José Miguel. *De Borges al presente*. Madrid: Alianza, 1995. Vol. 4 of *Historia de la literatura hispanoamericana*.

Panofsky, Erwin. "Style and Medium in the Motion Pictures." 1947. *Three Essays on Style*. Cambridge: MIT P, 1997. 91–128.

Parker, Andrew. "Unthinking Sex: Marx, Engels, and the Scene of Writing." *Social Text* 29 (1991): 28–45.

Pauls, Alan. *Manuel Puig:* La traición de Rita Hayworth. Buenos Aires: Hachette, 1986.

Perlongher, Néstor. *Prosa plebeya. Ensayos 1980–1992.* Ed. and introd. Christian Ferrer and Osvaldo Baigorria. Buenos Aires: Colihue, 1997.

———. "El sexo de la araña." *Tiempo argentino* 29 June 1986: 4. Rpt. in Puig, *Beso,* Archivos 637–40.

Piglia, Ricardo. "Clase media: Cuerpo y destino. Una lectura de *La traición de Rita Hayworth." Nueva novela latinoamericana II.* Ed. Jorge Lafforgue. Buenos Aires: Paidós, 1972. 350–62.

Poblete, Juan. "Literary Education and the Making of State Knowledge." *Literary Cultures of Latin America.* Ed. Mario Valdés and Djelal Kadir. Vol. 3. Oxford UP, 2004. 284–99.

Potash, Robert. *The Army and Politics in Argentina.* 2 vols. Stanford: Stanford UP, 1969–80.

Puig, Manuel. *El beso de la mujer araña.* Barcelona: Seix Barral, 1976.

———. *El beso de la mujer araña.* Ed. José Amícola and Jorge Panesi. Critical ed. Paris: Archivos, 2002.

———. *Betrayed by Rita Hayworth.* New York: Dutton, 1971.

———. *Boquitas pintadas: Folletín.* Buenos Aires: Sudamericana, 1969.

———. *The Buenos Aires Affair.* Mexico City: Mortiz, 1973.

———. *The Buenos Aires Affair: A Detective Novel.* New York: Dutton, 1976.

———. *Blood of Requited Love.* New York: Vintage, 1984.

———. *Cae la noche tropical.* Barcelona: Seix Barral, 1988.

———. "El error gay." *El porteño* 105 (1990): 32–33.

———. *Eternal Curse on the Reader of These Pages.* New York: Random, 1982.

———. "Fase preredaccional." Appendix. Puig, *Beso,* Archivos 265–384.

———. *Heartbreak Tango: A Serial.* New York: Dutton, 1973.

———. "Homenaje a von Sternberg." *Estertores de una década, Nueva York '78.* Buenos Aires: Seix Barral, 1993. 146–49.

———. Interview. *Boston Globe* 12 Aug. 1986: 49.

———. *Kiss of the Spider Woman.* Trans. Thomas Colchie. New York: Knopf, 1979.

———. Letter to Emir Rodríguez Monegal. 3 Jan. 1983. Papers of Emir Rodríguez Monegal. Firestone Lib., Princeton U.

———. Letter to Emir Rodríguez Monegal. 30 May 1985. Papers of Emir Rodríguez Monegal. Firestone Lib., Princeton U.

———. Letter to Guillermo Cabrera Infante. 26 Feb. 1977. Papers of Guillermo Cabrera Infante. Firestone Lib., Princeton U.

———. Letter to Howard Mandelbaum. 6 Nov. 1983. Puig Family Archive, Buenos Aires.

———. Letter to María Elena Puig. 9 Oct. 1981. Puig Family Archive, Buenos Aires.

———. Letter to María Elena Puig. 19 Oct. 1983. Puig Family Archive, Buenos Aires.

Puig, Manuel. "Losing Readers in Argentina." *Index on Censorship* 14.5 (1985): 55–57.

———. *Maldición eterna a quien lea estas páginas*. Barcelona: Seix Barral, 1980.

———. Prologue. *La cara del villano / Recuerdo de Tijuana*. Mexico City: Seix Barral, 1985. 7–14.

———. *Pubis angelical*. Barcelona: Seix Barral, 1979.

———. *Pubis angelical: A Novel*. New York: Vintage, 1986.

———. *Sangre de amor correspondido*. Barcelona: Seix Barral, 1982.

———. "Thomas Disch: Como un auto lanzado a fondo por una carretera vacía." *Crisis* 54 (1987): 35–38.

———. *La traición de Rita Hayworth*. Buenos Aires: Alvarez, 1968.

———. *Tropical Night Falling*. New York: Simon, 1991.

Radcliffe, Sarah A., and Sallie Westwood. *Remaking the Nation: Place, Identity, and Politics in Latin America*. New York: Routledge, 1996.

Radway, Janice A. *Reading the Romance: Women, Patriarchy, and Popular Literature*. Chapel Hill: U of North Carolina P, 1984.

Rama, Ángel. *La ciudad letrada*. Hanover: Norte, 1984.

———. *La novela en América Latina: Panoramas, 1920–1980*. Montevideo: Fundación Angel Rama, U Veracruzana, 1986.

Rapisardi, Flavio, and Alejandro Modarelli. *Fiestas, baños y exilios: Los gays porteños en la última dictadura*. Buenos Aires: Sudamericana, 2001.

Richter, David E., ed. *Falling into Theory: Conflicting Views on Reading Literature*. Boston: Bedford, 1994.

Rimmon-Kenan, Shlomith. *Narrative Fiction: Contemporary Poetics*. London: Methuen, 1983.

Rock, David. *Argentina, 1516–1982: From Spanish Colonization to the Falklands War*. Berkeley: U of California P, 1985.

Rodríguez Monegal, Emir. *El Boom de la novela latinoamericana: Ensayo*. Caracas: Tiempo Nuevo, 1972.

———. "El folletín rescatado." *Revista de la Universidad de México* Oct. 1972. 27–35.

———. "The New Latin American Novel." *Books Abroad* 44.1 (1970): 45–50.

———. "A Revolutionary Writing." *Mundus Artium* 3.3 (1970): 6–11.

Roffé, Reina. *Del "kitsch" a Lacan: Manuel Puig*. VHS. Hanover: Norte, 1984.

Romero, Julia. "Del delito de la escritura al error gay." *Revista iberoamericana* 187 (1999): 305–25.

Romero, Luis Alberto. *A History of Argentina in the Twentieth Century*. Trans. James P. Brennan. University Park: Penn State UP, 2002.

Rubin, Gayle S. "Thinking Sex: Notes for a Radical Theory of the Politics of Sexuality." 1984. *The Lesbian and Gay Studies Reader*. Ed. Henry Abelove, Michele Aina Barale, and David M. Halperin. New York: Routledge, 1993. 3–44.

Russo, Vito. *The Celluloid Closet: Homosexuality in the Movies*. New York: Harper, 1987.

Saer, Juan Jose. "Entrevista realizada por Gerard de Costanze." *Una literatura sin atributos*. Mexico City: Universidad Iberoamericana, 1996. 79–86.

Safir, Margery. "Mitología: Otro nivel de metalenguaje en *Boquitas pintadas*." *Revista iberoamericana* 90 (1975): 47–58.

Santoro, Patricia. "*Kiss of the Spider Woman*, Novel, Play, and Film: Homosexuality and the Discourse of the Maternal in a Third World Prison." *Framing Latin American Cinema: Contemporary Critical Perspectives*. Ed. Ann Marie Stock. Minneapolis: U of Minnesota P, 1997. 120–40.

Sarduy, Severo. "Notas a las notas a las notas: A propósito de Manuel Puig." *Revista iberoamericana* 90 (1975): 554–67.

Schmucler, Héctor. "Los silencios significativos." *Los libros* 4 (1969): 8–9.

Scorsese, Martin, and Michael Henry Wilson. *A Personal Journey with Martin Scorsese through American Movies*. New York: Hyperion, 1997.

Sebreli, Juan José. "Vida cotidiana: Historia secreta de los homosexuales en Buenos Aires." *Escritos sobre escritos, ciudades bajo ciudades*. Buenos Aires: Sudamericana, 1997. 275–370.

Sklar, Robert. Rev. of *Kiss of the Spider Woman*, dir. Héctor Babenco. *Cinéaste* 14 (1986): 38–39.

Smith, Paul Julian. "*La Mujer Araña* and the Return of the Body." *The Body Hispanic: Gender and Sexuality in Spanish and Spanish American Literature*. Oxford: Clarendon, 1989. 193–201.

Snow, Peter G. "Argentina: Politics in a Conflict Society." *Latin American Politics and Development*. Ed. Howard J. Wiarda and Harvey F. Kline. Boulder: Westview, 1996. 71–108.

Somers, Margaret R., and Gloria D. Gibson. "Reclaiming the Epistemological 'Other': Narrative and the Social Constitution of Identity." *Social Theory and the Politics of Identity*. Ed. Craig Calhoun. Oxford: Blackwell, 1994. 37–99.

Sommer, Doris. *Foundational Fictions: The National Romances in Latin America*. Berkeley: U of California P, 1991.

Sontag, Susan. *Against Interpretation*. New York: Farrar, 1966.

———. "Notes on Camp." Sontag, *Against Interpretation* 275–92.

———. "On Style." Sontag, *Against Interpretation* 15–37.

Sosnowski, Saúl. "Entrevista." *Hispamérica* 3 (1973): 69–80.

Speranza, Graciela. *Manuel Puig: Después del fin de la literatura*. Buenos Aires: Norma, 2000.

Tittler, Jonathan. *Manuel Puig*. New York: Twayne, 1993.

Torres Fierro, Danubio. "Conversación con Manuel Puig: La redención de la cursilería." *Eco* 173 (1975): 507–15.

Tourneur, Jacques, dir. *Cat People*. 1942. DVD. Los Angeles: Warner Home Video, 2005.

———. *I Walked with a Zombie*. 1943. DVD. Los Angeles: Warner Home Video, 2005.

Trachtenberg, Jeffrey A. "David Weisman: Producer, *Kiss of the Spider Woman*." *Millimeter* Dec. 1985: 134–35.

Turco, Lewis. *The Book of Literary Terms: The Genres of Fiction, Drama, Nonfiction, Literary Criticism, and Scholarship*. Hanover: UP of New England, 1999.

Vargas Llosa, Mario. "The Latin American Novel Today: An Introduction." *Books Abroad* 44.1 (1970): 7–12.

———. "Novela primitiva y novela de creación." *Revista de la Universidad de México* 23.10 (1969): 29–36.

Weber, Max. *The Protestant Ethic and the Spirit of Capitalism.* New York: Scribner's, 1958.

Williams, Bruce. "I Lost It at the Movies: Parodic Spectatorship in Héctor Babenco's *Kiss of the Spider Woman*." *Cinémas: Revue d'études cinématographiques* 10.1 (1999): 79–94.

Wyers Weber, Frances. "Manuel Puig at the Movies." *Hispanic Review* 49.2 (1981): 163–81.

Zalazar, Alejandro, and Rafael Freda. "Los homosexuales en la hoguera." *El porteño* 105 (1990): 31.

Zavala, Iris. *El bolero: Historia de un amor.* Madrid: Alianza, 1991.

INDEX

Modern Language Association of America
Approaches to Teaching World Literature
Joseph Gibaldi, series editor

Achebe's Things Fall Apart. Ed. Bernth Lindfors. 1991.

Arthurian Tradition. Ed. Maureen Fries and Jeanie Watson. 1992.

Atwood's The Handmaid's Tale *and Other Works*. Ed. Sharon R. Wilson, Thomas B. Friedman, and Shannon Hengen. 1996.

Austen's Emma. Ed. Marcia McClintock Folsom. 2004.

Austen's Pride and Prejudice. Ed. Marcia McClintock Folsom. 1993.

Balzac's Old Goriot. Ed. Michal Peled Ginsburg. 2000.

Baudelaire's Flowers of Evil. Ed. Laurence M. Porter. 2000.

Beckett's Waiting for Godot. Ed. June Schlueter and Enoch Brater. 1991.

Beowulf. Ed. Jess B. Bessinger, Jr., and Robert F. Yeager. 1984.

Blake's Songs of Innocence and of Experience. Ed. Robert F. Gleckner and Mark L. Greenberg. 1989.

Boccaccio's Decameron. Ed. James H. McGregor. 2000.

British Women Poets of the Romantic Period. Ed. Stephen C. Behrendt and Harriet Kramer Linkin. 1997.

Brontë's Jane Eyre. Ed. Diane Long Hoeveler and Beth Lau. 1993.

Emily Brontë's Wuthering Heights. Ed. Sue Lonoff and Terri A. Hasseler. 2006.

Byron's Poetry. Ed. Frederick W. Shilstone. 1991.

Camus's The Plague. Ed. Steven G. Kellman. 1985.

Cather's My Ántonia. Ed. Susan J. Rosowski. 1989.

Cervantes' Don Quixote. Ed. Richard Bjornson. 1984.

Chaucer's Canterbury Tales. Ed. Joseph Gibaldi. 1980.

Chaucer's Troilus and Criseyde *and the Shorter Poems*. Ed. Tison Pugh and Angela Jane Weisl. 2006.

Chopin's The Awakening. Ed. Bernard Koloski. 1988.

Coleridge's Poetry and Prose. Ed. Richard E. Matlak. 1991.

Collodi's Pinocchio *and Its Adaptations*. Ed. Michael Sherberg. 2006.

Conrad's "Heart of Darkness" and "The Secret Sharer." Ed. Hunt Hawkins and Brian W. Shaffer. 2002.

Dante's Divine Comedy. Ed. Carole Slade. 1982.

Defoe's Robinson Crusoe. Ed. Maximillian E. Novak and Carl Fisher. 2005.

DeLillo's White Noise. Ed. Tim Engles and John N. Duvall. 2006.

Dickens' David Copperfield. Ed. Richard J. Dunn. 1984.

Dickinson's Poetry. Ed. Robin Riley Fast and Christine Mack Gordon. 1989.

Narrative of the Life of Frederick Douglass. Ed. James C. Hall. 1999.

Early Modern Spanish Drama. Ed. Laura R. Bass and Margaret R. Greer. 2006

Eliot's Middlemarch. Ed. Kathleen Blake. 1990.

Eliot's Poetry and Plays. Ed. Jewel Spears Brooker. 1988.

Shorter Elizabethan Poetry. Ed. Patrick Cheney and Anne Lake Prescott. 2000.
Ellison's Invisible Man. Ed. Susan Resneck Parr and Pancho Savery. 1989.
English Renaissance Drama. Ed. Karen Bamford and Alexander Leggatt. 2002.
Works of Louise Erdrich. Ed. Gregg Sarris, Connie A. Jacobs, and
     James R. Giles. 2004.
Dramas of Euripides. Ed. Robin Mitchell-Boyask. 2002.
Faulkner's The Sound and the Fury. Ed. Stephen Hahn and Arthur F. Kinney. 1996.
Flaubert's Madame Bovary. Ed. Laurence M. Porter and Eugene F. Gray. 1995.
García Márquez's One Hundred Years of Solitude. Ed. María Elena de Valdés and
     Mario J. Valdés. 1990.
Gilman's "The Yellow Wall-Paper" and Herland. Ed. Denise D. Knight and
     Cynthia J. Davis. 2003.
Goethe's Faust. Ed. Douglas J. McMillan. 1987.
Gothic Fiction: The British and American Traditions. Ed. Diane Long Hoeveler
     and Tamar Heller. 2003.
Hebrew Bible as Literature in Translation. Ed. Barry N. Olshen and
     Yael S. Feldman. 1989.
Homer's Iliad *and* Odyssey. Ed. Kostas Myrsiades. 1987.
Ibsen's A Doll House. Ed. Yvonne Shafer. 1985.
Henry James's Daisy Miller *and* The Turn of the Screw. Ed. Kimberly C. Reed and
     Peter G. Beidler. 2005.
Works of Samuel Johnson. Ed. David R. Anderson and Gwin J. Kolb. 1993.
Joyce's Ulysses. Ed. Kathleen McCormick and Erwin R. Steinberg. 1993.
Works of Sor Juana Inés de la Cruz. Ed. Emilie L. Bergmann and Stacey Schlau.
     2007.
Kafka's Short Fiction. Ed. Richard T. Gray. 1995.
Keats's Poetry. Ed. Walter H. Evert and Jack W. Rhodes. 1991.
Kingston's The Woman Warrior. Ed. Shirley Geok-lin Lim. 1991.
Lafayette's The Princess of Clèves. Ed. Faith E. Beasley and
     Katharine Ann Jensen. 1998.
Works of D. H. Lawrence. Ed. M. Elizabeth Sargent and Garry Watson. 2001.
Lessing's The Golden Notebook. Ed. Carey Kaplan and Ellen Cronan Rose. 1989.
Mann's Death in Venice *and Other Short Fiction.* Ed. Jeffrey B. Berlin. 1992.
Marguerite de Navarre's Heptameron. Ed. Colette H. Winn. 2007.
Medieval English Drama. Ed. Richard K. Emmerson. 1990.
Melville's Moby-Dick. Ed. Martin Bickman. 1985.
Metaphysical Poets. Ed. Sidney Gottlieb. 1990.
Miller's Death of a Salesman. Ed. Matthew C. Roudané. 1995.
Milton's Paradise Lost. Ed. Galbraith M. Crump. 1986.
Milton's Shorter Poetry and Prose. Ed. Peter C. Herman. 2007.
Molière's Tartuffe *and Other Plays.* Ed. James F. Gaines and
     Michael S. Koppisch. 1995.
Momaday's The Way to Rainy Mountain. Ed. Kenneth M. Roemer. 1988.

Montaigne's Essays. Ed. Patrick Henry. 1994.

Novels of Toni Morrison. Ed. Nellie Y. McKay and Kathryn Earle. 1997.

Murasaki Shikibu's The Tale of Genji. Ed. Edward Kamens. 1993.

Pope's Poetry. Ed. Wallace Jackson and R. Paul Yoder. 1993.

Proust's Fiction and Criticism. Ed. Elyane Dezon-Jones and
   Inge Crosman Wimmers. 2003.

Puig's Kiss of the Spider Woman. Ed. Daniel Balderston and Francine Masiello.
   2007.

Novels of Samuel Richardson. Ed. Lisa Zunshine and Jocelyn Harris. 2006.

Rousseau's Confessions *and* Reveries of the Solitary Walker. Ed. John C. O'Neal
   and Ourida Mostefai. 2003.

Shakespeare's Hamlet. Ed. Bernice W. Kliman. 2001.

Shakespeare's King Lear. Ed. Robert H. Ray. 1986.

Shakespeare's Othello. Ed. Peter Erickson and Maurice Hunt. 2005.

Shakespeare's Romeo and Juliet. Ed. Maurice Hunt. 2000.

Shakespeare's The Tempest *and Other Late Romances*. Ed. Maurice Hunt. 1992.

Shelley's Frankenstein. Ed. Stephen C. Behrendt. 1990.

Shelley's Poetry. Ed. Spencer Hall. 1990.

Sir Gawain and the Green Knight. Ed. Miriam Youngerman Miller and
   Jane Chance. 1986.

Song of Roland. Ed. William W. Kibler and Leslie Zarker Morgan. 2006.

Spenser's Faerie Queene. Ed. David Lee Miller and Alexander Dunlop. 1994.

Stendhal's The Red and the Black. Ed. Dean de la Motte and Stirling Haig. 1999.

Sterne's Tristram Shandy. Ed. Melvyn New. 1989.

Stowe's Uncle Tom's Cabin. Ed. Elizabeth Ammons and Susan Belasco. 2000.

Swift's Gulliver's Travels. Ed. Edward J. Rielly. 1988.

Thoreau's Walden *and Other Works*. Ed. Richard J. Schneider. 1996.

Tolstoy's Anna Karenina. Ed. Liza Knapp and Amy Mandelker. 2003.

Vergil's Aeneid. Ed. William S. Anderson and Lorina N. Quartarone. 2002.

Voltaire's Candide. Ed. Renée Waldinger. 1987.

Whitman's Leaves of Grass. Ed. Donald D. Kummings. 1990.

Wiesel's Night. Ed. Alan Rosen. 2007.

Woolf's To the Lighthouse. Ed. Beth Rigel Daugherty and Mary Beth Pringle. 2001.

Wordsworth's Poetry. Ed. Spencer Hall, with Jonathan Ramsey. 1986.

Wright's Native Son. Ed. James A. Miller. 1997.